MW01120411

GENDER BASED VIOLENCE:

CAUSES AND REMEDIES

FAMILY ISSUES IN THE 21ST CENTURY

Additional books in this series can be found on Nova's website
under the Series tab.

Additional E-books in this series can be found on Nova's website
under the E-book tab.

SOCIAL ISSUES, JUSTICE AND STATUS

Additional books in this series can be found on Nova's website
under the Series tab.

Additional E-books in this series can be found on Nova's website
under the E-book tab.

GENDER BASED VIOLENCE:

CAUSES AND REMEDIES

JOHN SIMISTER

Nova Science Publishers, Inc.

New York

NOTICE TO THE READER

The Publisher has taken reasonable care in the preparation of this book, but makes no expressed or implied warranty of any kind and assumes no responsibility for any errors or omissions. No liability is assumed for incidental or consequential damages in connection with or arising out of information contained in this book. The Publisher shall not be liable for any special, consequential, or exemplary damages resulting, in whole or in part, from the readers' use of, or reliance upon, this material. Any parts of this book based on government reports are so indicated and copyright is claimed for those parts to the extent applicable to compilations of such works.

Independent verification should be sought for any data, advice or recommendations contained in this book. In addition, no responsibility is assumed by the publisher for any injury and/or damage to persons or property arising from any methods, products, instructions, ideas or otherwise contained in this publication.

This publication is designed to provide accurate and authoritative information with regard to the subject matter covered herein. It is sold with the clear understanding that the Publisher is not engaged in rendering legal or any other professional services. If legal or any other expert assistance is required, the services of a competent person should be sought. FROM A DECLARATION OF PARTICIPANTS JOINTLY ADOPTED BY A COMMITTEE OF THE AMERICAN BAR ASSOCIATION AND A COMMITTEE OF PUBLISHERS.

Additional color graphics may be available in the e-book version of this book.

LIBRARY OF CONGRESS CATALOGING-IN-PUBLICATION DATA

Gender based violence : causes and remedies / editor, John Simister.
    p. cm.
 Includes bibliographical references and index.
 ISBN 978-1-61942-786-0 (hbk.)
1. Wife abuse. 2. Women--Violence against. 3. Family violence. I. Simister, J. (John)
HV6626.G464 2011
362.82'92--dc23
                    2011053227

Published by Nova Science Publishers, Inc. ✝ *New York*

This book is dedicated to the campaigners, politicians, medical professionals, and researchers who work to prevent GBV: they are building a better world, where women will be less at risk from domestic violence. No woman should be abused.

CONTENTS

PREFACE

This book analyses domestic violence against women, inflicted by the woman's husband or cohabiting partner. The main focus is on physical violence and sexual and emotional violence is also dicussed. The term used to describe such violence is "Gender Based Violence" (GBV). GBV is a problem in every country; in the world as a whole, there may be over a billion women who have experienced domestic violence from their husband or male partner. For many women, such violence is a regular occurrence, and is seen as normal by many women and men. This book uses scientific data collected by household surveys, and from crime statistics; it investigates not only the prevalence of violence, but also attitudes to such violence – the extent to which a woman, and/or her partner, consider domestic violence against women to be acceptable or even appropriate in certain circumstances.

This book analyses domestic violence against women, inflicted by the woman's husband or cohabiting partner. The main focus is on physical violence, such as women being punched or kicked. There is also some data on sexual violence such as rape, and emotional violence such as public humiliation of a woman by her husband or partner.

This book has global coverage: it reports data on all countries for which data are available. The book analyses some of the causes of domestic violence, such as childhood socialization, alcohol, and extreme temperature; and examines possible solutions to the problem, such as education of males and females, and positive role-models. The book focuses on women in heterosexual relationships (it does not investigate violence in same-sex relationships). There is also some discussion of women who are violent to their male partner. This book summarizes research published in academic journals by the author, and by others, in the field of GBV.

Reading this book may make you want to change the world (if you don't already). Website www.saynotoviolence.org has ideas on how you can work with like-minded people, to improve the lives of a billion women.

Chapter 1

INTRODUCTION

"The experience of violence and the silent acceptance of violence by women undermines attempts to empower women and will continue to be a barrier to the achievement of demographic, health, and socioeconomic development goals"
(IIPS and ORC Macro, 2000: 79).

ABSTRACT

This chapter gives an overview of 'Gender Based Violence' (GBV). This chapter explains what the term GBV means. Even the name 'Gender Based Violence' is controversial, and writers who use it may be making a statement. Some of the debates about GBV are outlined.

INTRODUCTION

The term 'Gender-Based Violence' (GBV) is often used, to refer to domestic violence by a man against his female partner. Using the term GBV implies making two assumptions:

- that considering violence between spouses, more women than men are victims of domestic violence; and
- some men use violence to control their partner (Bott et al., 2005: 3).

Bhattacharya (2000: 18) translates an India proverb as "spices are controlled on the grinding wheel and wives are controlled by beating". Olmsted (2003: 84) wrote "Patriarchy is generally defined as a system where men dominate women, primarily through the enforcement of strict gender-role ideologies". Patriarchy is often considered relevant to GBV: if men use GBV to control their wife or partner, then GBV can be considered one of the main ways in which male power over women is maintained. If GBV can be reduced, this may lead to more equality, and to empowerment for women.

Not all domestic violence is GBV; other types of violence (such as a woman hitting her husband, parents hitting children, or violence in homosexual relationships) are not discussed in this book. Such problems are serious, and deserve further research in future.

OVER A BILLION WOMEN ARE EXPECTED TO EXPERIENCE GBV

Several writers have claimed at least a billion women are at risk of, or have already experienced, GBV (e.g. Women Win, 2011; Quicho, 2010). There is disagreement on what fraction of women have experienced GBV, partly because different definitions of GBV are used. Parish et al. (2004) examined 28 studies based on national samples, and found the median prevalence of such violence was 21%. UN (2006: 56) claim that about one-third of women worldwide experience GBV. The unweighted average of all surveys in the appendix of this book is 28.8% of women have ever experienced GBV (this refers to physical violence). At the time of writing, the world population is about 7 billion people, of which half are female: about 3.5 billion females. If we multiply 28.8% by 3.5 billion, we get an estimate of about 1.01 billion females have experienced, or will experience (if current prevalence rates remain), physical GBV. Note that some of these females are currently children.

If we were to expand this definition to include sexual as well as physical violence, and/or added emotional violence such as public humiliation of women by their husband, then this estimate would increase to far more than 1 billion. UN Women (2011) report that "up to 70 per cent of women experience physical or sexual violence from men in their lifetime – the majority by husbands, intimate partners or someone they know". The 70% prevalence rate suggests over two billion women are (or will be) victims of some kind of domestic violence.

There is no agreement about how we should define GBV. Estimates of GBV prevalence vary widely within and between countries, as explained in this book. In a few countries, I have not been able to obtain a reliable estimate of how many women are victims (chapter 4 has more details on data from different countries). I estimate that about a billion women who are alive today have experienced GBV; note, however, that this estimate (1 billion) is a rough estimate.

WHY GBV MATTERS

GBV is one of the biggest social problems on earth. The statistics in this book give an idea of how many women have experienced violence from their partner; it's not easy to give a simple figure for the number of victims, because it depends on the definition of violence used – for example, is it only actual violence, or should we also count how many women experience threats of violence? But it is clear from previous research (some of which is reported in this book) that GBV affects millions of women every year. For example, in a 2006 survey in Kenya, the respondents chose 'The lack of adequate laws to protect women against domestic violence and sexual abuse' as being the most serious problem facing Kenyan women (FIDA Kenya, 2006).

GBV causes direct physical harm to the victims (such as broken limbs, or even death in some cases).

In addition to direct harm from physical violence, GBV has indirect effects: "Women who experience domestic violence tend to have higher levels of psychological stress" (Ackerson and Subramanian, 2008: 1194). There are also long-term effects, such as depression, in the victims (Johnson and Ferraro, 2000: 957); GBV can increase the chance of a woman suffering from health problems such as chronic pain, physical disability, drug and alcohol abuse (Ellsberg and Heise, 2005).

Other members of the family (such as children) may be traumatized when they see their father hitting their mother. And GBV can give men power over household decisions, which sometimes lets them behave in ways which cause more harm: for example, some men may use violence to make their wife accept his excessive alcohol consumption – which can lead to alcoholism for the husband, and poverty for all household members (Gwagwa, 1998).

ARE MOST VICTIMS OF VIOLENCE FEMALE?

GBV is not the only term used to describe domestic violence: other popular terms include 'Intimate Partner Violence' (IPV) and 'Intimate Partner Terrorism'. There is general agreement that some women are violent to their husband/partner; this could be used to justify the term IPV: if some women and some men are violent, perhaps we might see domestic violence as a random event unrelated to patriarchy. However, there is a large body of evidence that in most domestic violence between husband and wife (or between cohabiting partners), women are much more likely than men to be victims. FIDA Kenya (2002: 952) claim "Domestic violence is gendered – hence numbers of the victims will reveal that it is disproportionately directed against women". More evidence is discussed in chapter 2 of this book. In my view, researchers and campaigners should use the term GBV rather than IPV, because GBV makes clear that a husband's power is related to his use (or threats of) violence.

OTHER TERMINOLOGY

In this book, 'partner' or 'husband' or 'wife' are all used to represent either a marital partner, or a partner in a cohabiting couple. Most of the household surveys used for this book do not distinguish between married couples and unmarried (cohabiting) couples. People in a polygamous marriage (common in some countries) are also included in surveys studied for this book. In this book, experience of GBV refers to 'ever' (i.e. since the start of the respondent's current marriage, if she is married; or since the start of the respondent's current marriage, if she is widowed or divorced). In some surveys (such as DHS), data are also available on the experience of GBV in the 12 months prior to the survey.

OVERVIEW OF THEORIES TO EXPLAIN GBV

Amirthalingam (2005: 695-6) claims we should think of theories of domestic violence on a spectrum, from individual (psychological) theories; through theories based on the family; to society-wide (sociological) theories. At one end of this spectrum, there are theories that focus on one individual person; an example is the claim that education reduces GBV risk (explored in chapter 7). Other causes of violence (at the individual person level) include personality disorders, predispositions to use violence, and childhood socialisation. Other such influences include alcohol consumption, and jealousy. Somewhere on this psychology-sociology spectrum, are theories based on the family. A dysfunctional family can produce conflict - for example, a husband and wife might disagree with each other on how to spend household income. At the other end of this spectrum of theories (psychology to sociology), there are approaches based on society: they investigate structural forces in a country, such as social class.

A somewhat different approach to Amirthalingam (2005) is the 'ecological model' reported in WHO/LSHTM (2010: 18-9), in which there are four types of explanations for GBV: Societal, Community, Relationship, and Individual. These explanations are 'nested' in WHO/LSHTM (2010: 18, Figure 1); a simplified diagram is shown in Figure 1 in this book.

In the 'ecological model' (as outlined in WHO/LSHTM, 2010: 19), the four types of explanation of GBV are "nested", as shown in Figure 1. Factors which determine an individual's behavior, such as the person's own experiences, affect the likelihood of GBV occurring; but this risk is also shaped by the relationship. For example, we could imagine an aggressive man, who might wish to use GBV, but this tendency could be reduced if his wife were also aggressive. This relationship context is also influenced by community factors: for example, a man's work colleagues might encourage or discourage him from using GBV against his wife. And finally, community factors are influenced by the 'societal' (i.e. national) culture, which includes laws against GBV.

The 'ecological model' is helpful, in giving a mental picture of the processes influencing whether or not GBV occurs in a particular household. But in practice, we don't usually have sufficient data to distinguish between the various levels. For example, is Mr. Smith violent because he was taught as a child that it is appropriate for men to control their wife, or because his friends encourage him to impose his authority on his wife? I am not aware of any survey which tells us the attitudes of a respondent's friends.

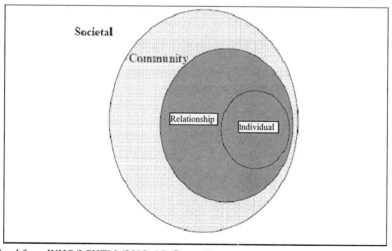

This is derived from WHO/LSHTM (2010: 18, figure 1).

Figure 1. The 'ecological model' explanation of GBV.

Delsol et al. (2003: 635) classify research into marital violence in two types: explaining violence in terms of psychological or socioeconomic variables was 'first generation' research – in contrast to 'second generation' research, which "take into account the heterogeneity among maritally violent men" – citing, as an example, a study which divides violent men into 15 types. Both 'family violence' and 'gender inequality' approaches can be seen as 'first generation' theories, in that they attempt to explain domestic violence (in general) by one theory. I would describe research in this book as 'second generation', in that I consider there to be several different factors which can cause violence (including, for example, alcohol as well as patriarchy).

This book does not investigate all possible explanations of GBV. For example, McKenry et al. (1995: 310) report that men who are violent are more likely to have a personality disorder such as impulsiveness, compulsiveness, or suspicion of other people.

SURVEY DATA USED IN THIS BOOK

This book uses data from 'Demographic and Health Survey' (DHS) surveys; they were previously known as the 'World Fertility Survey'. They are mainly funded by USAID (United States Agency for International Development), with additional support from other charities. In each country where DHS is carried out, the national government is also involved. Kishor and Johnson (2004) give an overview of some DHS surveys. Each DHS survey is a nationally-representative sample, containing thousands of respondents. In some DHS surveys, only women were interviewed; where men are included, there are usually fewer men than women in the sample. Women respondents in DHS surveys are usually aged 15 to 49, but men are sometimes interviewed up to a higher maximum age – this age range varies between countries. DHS are very impressive surveys, with large sample sizes and covering many topics. DHS data are provided free to researchers: the DHS website www.measuredhs.com has details. Not all DHS surveys include questions about GBV. In late 2010, I searched the DHS website to identify all DHS surveys with GBV data; I found 30 countries. I also found a few other countries where questions on attitudes to GBV were asked, but not whether or not the respondent had experienced GBV herself. For DHS surveys which ask respondents if they have had any *experience* of GBV, the GBV questions are usually only asked of women respondents (the only exception I know of is the 2004 DHS survey in Bangladesh, which asked male respondents about GBV in their household). Many DHS surveys ask the *attitudes* to GBV of women and men.

The second main data source for this book is 'Work, Attitudes and Spending' (WAS) surveys, carried out in ten countries so far. Each WAS survey interviewed approximately equal numbers of men and women respondents, of all adult ages: one adult was interviewed in each selected household. Website www.was-survey.org has more information. Occurrence of gender-based violence in most WAS surveys was identified by the questions 'Have you ever had an argument with your spouse?', then 'During these arguments have you been beaten by your partner?', and 'During these arguments, have you beaten your partner?' Hence violence against women is identified by female respondents who answered 'yes' to 'have you been beaten by your partner?' or by male respondents who answered 'yes' to 'have you beaten your partner?' The domestic violence question was only asked of married respondents (in this paper, 'married', 'spouse', 'husband', and 'wife' may include cohabiting couples or married people). More recent WAS surveys, such as the 2005/6 Egypt survey, asked similar questions to DHS surveys.

The third data source used in this book is the 'Multiple Indicator Cluster Study' (MICS), carried out by UNICEF. MICS surveys are large-scale, nationally-representative, questionnaire-based studies; so far, MICS surveys have been carried out in over 50 countries: mainly in poor countries. The term 'cluster' refers to the sampling method used – a location is chosen at random, and a cluster of interviews are then carried out at the same location (e.g. the same street); this is a standard technique, used in many surveys – including DHS, WAS, and WVS – to reduce transport costs for interviewers. The respondents are all adult men and women, aged 15 to 49. The UNICEF website www.unicef.org/statistics/index_24302.html has more details about MICS surveys. MICS tends to focus on child welfare such as nutrition. Some, but not all, of the MICS surveys include data on attitudes to GBV. As far as I know, no MICS surveys so far have asked respondents if they experienced GBV. I did not obtain access to MICS data in individual households, so all findings from MICS surveys reported in this book are the results of analysis by other researchers (including UNICEF).

The fourth main data source for this book is the 'World Values Survey' (WVS), a set of nationally-representative surveys of adults in about 50 countries, which began in 1981. The WVS surveys incorporate the 'European Values Survey' (EVS), and tend to be associated with rich countries; but some poor countries have been studied by WVS. The WVS website www.worldvaluessurvey.org has more details, and researchers can download data free of charge. I use data on attitudes to GBV and other attitude topics in WVS (2009), and additional attitude data from EVS downloaded from the WVS website. The main focus of WVS is political beliefs and values, but many WVS surveys include questions on attitudes to GBV. WVS and EVS questionnaires do not ask respondents if they have experienced GBV.

COMPLICATED CAUSES AND EFFECTS

WHO/LSHTM (2010: 7) describe a 'public health approach' to reducing the occurrence of domestic violence, in four steps:

1. defining the problem
2. investigating why the problem occurs
3. exploring ways to prevent the problem
4. disseminating information on the effectiveness of programs

The above four-step approach forms the structure of the WHO/LSHTM (2010) book. This book has a different structure. Like most previous research on domestic violence, this book suggests there are different causes of GBV, each of which could be solved in different ways. For example, there is evidence that alcohol is one factor leading to GBV (see chapter 12), but alcohol does not explain all GBV. This book tries to identify some of the major causes of GBV; and for each cause, it indicates some ways which have been put forward as possible ways to reduce the problem. I hope readers won't limit themselves to techniques which have been used before: activists may find new ways to reduce the risk of GBV in future.

As WHO/LSHTM (2010: 7) point out, we should not expect a simple explanation of why GBV occurs – we need insights from several academic disciplines such as medicine, epidemiology, sociology, psychology, criminology, education and economics. We could see GBV as the outcome of many causes – these causes interact with each other, at four levels of a nested hierarchy: individual; close relationship/family; community; and wider society (WHO/LSHTM, 2010: 7), as shown in Figure 1 in this book. Flake (2005: 367) claimed "Myriad factors combine to influence domestic violence". According to Fox et al. (2002: 794-5), domestic violence can be caused by stresses such as household poverty, male unemployment, and jobs which make men tired and irritable.

STRUCTURE OF THIS BOOK

This book defines some key terms, in chapter 2. Perhaps the most difficult term to define is 'Gender Based Violence': for example, should this include *threats* of violence? Should it include public humiliation, such as a man insulting his wife in public? There are many controversies in the subject of GBV, some of which are discussed in this book. Chapter 3 gives more details on the effects of GBV, including some of the medical problems which domestic violence causes – in the short-term, and in the long term.

Chapters 4 and 5 are about the geographical distribution of GBV: for example, which countries have the highest GBV prevalence rates? Chapter 4 focuses on the fraction of women in each country who have experienced GBV. Chapter 5 discusses attitudes to GBV, among men and women, in various countries. Chapter 6 discusses changes in the prevalence of GBV over time, and on changing attitudes to GBV.

The next set of chapters (7 to 14) focus on causes of GBV. Various possible causes of GBV are examined, starting with patriarchy in chapter 7; ethnic variations in cultures, in chapter 8; childhood socialisation in chapter 9; aggression by men who are physically strong against women who are less strong, in chapter 10; and female poverty in chapter 11. Chapters 7 to 10 might be described as sociological; chapter 11 has more of an economic focus.

The following three chapters discuss three possible causes of GBV which might be considered medical issues, rather than sociological or economic. Chapter 12 investigates the association between alcohol and GBV; in addition to medical issues (such as alcoholism), there are social and religious influences on alcohol consumption. Chapters 13 and 14 investigate the possible effects of stress hormones on GBV. Cortisol (studied in chapter 13) tends to be higher early in the morning.

Adrenaline and other stress hormones may be associated with extreme temperatures; chapter 14 investigates the possibility that this leads to more GBV in very hot countries, and also points out alternative hypotheses as to why hot countries may have higher rates of GBV prevalence, including culture. There are overlaps between ideas in the chapters of this book: for example, the childhood socialisation section (chapter 9) may explain how patriarchy (discussed in chapter 7) is passed from one generation to the next; and may also explain ethnic differences in GBV prevalence (discussed in chapter 8).

The last two chapters, 15 and 16, bring together some of the key ideas in the book. Chapter 15 argues that a global intervention is needed, to reduce the level of GBV in every country. Chapter 16 concludes with some suggestions for future research. The appendix contains some detailed statistics, which may be helpful for campaigners.

For data sources used in this book, there are more surveys which ask respondents about their attitudes to GBV, than surveys asking if GBV took place in those households. If there are many lines on a chart, it is difficult to distinguish one line from another. So most figures using data on *attitudes* to GBV are shown in colour; and the vertical axis is set with a maximum value of 100%. For figures which show the fraction of women who *experienced* GBV, the chart is shown in black and white, and the vertical axis is set to a maximum value of 76% (the highest value in any of the GBV prevalence charts in this book), except for Figures 4 and 5 (which have different units on the vertical axis).

CONCLUSION

GBV is one of the biggest social problems on earth, affecting a large fraction of adult women in every country. Researchers, campaigners, politicians, role models, and teachers can reduce this problem. There are national and international campaigns to reduce the incidence of GBV, such as the 'Say No: unite to end violence against women' campaign by 'UN Women' (formerly called UNIFEM) and the UN Secretary-General – see UN Women (2011) for details. Would public statements by role models be helpful, such as 'Live Aid' style concerts? Can counselling techniques such as 'Cognitive Behavioural Therapy' empower women and re-educate men? Are feminist 'consciousness-raising' groups effective? More research is needed, to identify effective means to reduce GBV.

This book brings together some of the previously published research on GBV, but there is too much to report it all in this book. There is also some new research in this book, in the form of charts and tables – mainly based on my analysis of DHS and WAS survey data.

Chapter 2

WHAT IS 'GENDER BASED VIOLENCE' (GBV)?

"Among women aged between 15 and 44, acts of violence cause more death and disability than cancer, malaria, traffic accidents and war combined. Perhaps the most pervasive human rights violation that we know today, violence against women devastates lives, fractures communities, and stalls development" (UN Women, 2011).

ABSTRACT

This chapter discusses some different views on what the term 'Gender Based Violence' means. It does not attempt to argue that any one definition of GBV is 'better' than any other definition: various different definitions have been put forward by previous writers, and there are advantages and disadvantages to each definition. Some controversial issues are discussed in this chapter, such as whether or not women are as violent as men.

INTRODUCTION

Academics often disagree about the meaning of 'domestic violence'. O'Leary (cited in Barnett, 2000: 344) suggests we could define such violence as "The presence of at least two acts of physical aggression within a year (or one severe act) and/or physical aggression that leads the partner to be fearful of the other or that results in injury requiring medical attention". DHS surveys (used widely in this book) give data on different types of violence, such as 'Twist your arm or pull your hair' and 'Try to choke you or burn you on purpose'. Ellsberg and Heise (2005: 90) list several definitions which have been used in previous publications, to decide whether or not domestic violence took place in a household:

- Any kind of physical, sexual, or emotional violence by anyone, at any time.
- One or more acts of physical violence by a partner at any time.
- Only 'severe' physical violence, or violence which was repeated a number of times.
- Only acts of partner violence occurring in the last year.
- Economic control, as well as physical, sexual, or emotional violence.

- Any behavior that women themselves call 'abusive' (this may include verbal aggression or humiliation, forced sex, or refusing to pay for household expenses).

Watts and Zimmerman (2002) claim "Research into violence against women is increasing, but there are no widely agreed definitions of the different forms of such violence that could be used to standardise research findings. Furthermore, context-specific variations in the willingness of respondents to disclose experiences of violence and differences in the populations in which the studies are done make cross-country and cross-study comparison difficult".

There is no definition of GBV which is accepted by all writers. Many kinds of violence are not reported in this book; perhaps future researchers will study more kinds of violence-related problems, such as threats or intimidation.

GBV, IPV, AND OTHER TERMS

Johnson (2005: 1127) claims there are three types of domestic violence between spouses:

'Intimate terrorism':	violence to control a partner;
'violent resistance':	violence reacting against intimate terrorism;
'Situational couple violence':	an effect of a specific series of conflicts.

In my view, Johnson's approach has not (yet) been adopted by most researchers studying domestic violence; so I do not use the above terminology for the rest of this book. The term 'Gender Based Violence' is used by many authors.

Several writers, when describing violence between husband and wife, use the term 'intimate partner violence' (Jewkes, 2002); other terms are also used, such as 'common couple violence'. This book uses the term 'Gender Based Violence' (GBV) to refer to domestic violence between married or cohabiting partners: to many writers, the term 'Gender-Based Violence' (GBV) seems appropriate, because some husbands use violence to control wives (Bott et al. 2005: 3). Many writers have argued that domestic violence is a way (some) men control their wife or cohabitee. For example, Jeffery, Jeffery and Lyon (1989: 30), in the context of India, report "in Dharmnagri and Jhakri, wife-beating was regularly mentioned, by women and men alike. Men regard it as their prerogative, an appropriate way to deal with insubordination, and an important buttress of a husband's rule."

To some writers, GBV is used only to refer to violence which occurs in the home. Other writers use the term differently, to include (for example) when boys studying at a school use violence or rape to control girls at the same school (Wilson, 2008: 4).

Another controversial issue in this field is the range of activities which would be included in GBV. Most or all writers would include physical violence as GBV, but other types of violence may or may not be considered to be GBV. Threats of violence are an example: this is clearly a problem for many women, but is it the *same* problem as being punched or kicked? Another type of behaviour which might be included is emotional abuse, such as a husband insulting his wife in public. Wilson (2008: 4) claims GBV might include schoolgirls being allotted domestic tasks, whereas schoolboys are not. The UN General Assembly in 1993 passed the 'Declaration on the Elimination of Violence against Women', which includes "violence perpetrated or condoned by the State, wherever it occurs" (UN General Assembly, 1994: Article 2b): this suggests a broad definition of GBV. This book focuses mainly on violence carried out by a husband against his wife (which, in my view, is the definition used by most writers who use the term GBV); but I do not claim this definition is any better than any other definition used in the literature on GBV.

ARE WOMEN AS VIOLENT AS MEN?

The term GBV implies that women are less violent than men – but this is controversial (Johnson and Ferraro, 2000): some writers claim women are as violent as men in intimate relationships, but such evidence is usually limited to rich countries such as USA (WHO/LSHTM, 2010: 9), and tends to refer to less severe forms of violence. Even in rich countries, women are more likely than men to die or suffer severe injuries from intimate partner and sexual violence, and women are more likely to be victims – according to statistics based on hospital and other medical reports (WHO/LSHTM, 2010: 9). For the world as a whole (i.e. in poor and rich countries), "the overwhelming burden of intimate partner and sexual violence is borne by women at the hands of men" (WHO/LSHTM, 2010: 9). FIDA Kenya (2002: 952) wrote "Domestic violence is gendered – hence numbers of the victims will reveal that it is disproportionately directed against women".

Umberson et al. (2003: 234-5) claim there are two theoretical frameworks for analyzing domestic violence: the 'family violence approach', which argues that stresses such as poverty make some people aggressive; and the 'gender inequality approach', which claims many men use domestic violence to force women to obey, and that such violence is based in gender inequality. Writers in the 'gender inequality approach' see violence in terms of gender, and we might expect such writers to use the term GBV; whereas writers using the 'family violence approach' might be expected to use a term like "intimate partner violence", in which domestic violence is not seen as essentially about gender inequality.

Social scientists who write about domestic violence have sophisticated and nuanced views; readers unfamiliar with these debates may find them confusing. At the risk of oversimplification, it may be helpful to divide writers (including academics, journalists, and others) into people who think men and women are about equally at risk of violence; and people who claim most victims are women, a view associated with feminism. Johnson (2005: 1126) wrote "Ever since Suzanne Steinmetz's 1977-1978 article on *"battered husbands"*, we have been hearing this lament – that the feminists are wrong, that women are as violent as men, that domestic violence is not about gender or patriarchy". The following two tables (Tables 1 and 2) will help us assess if we have been misled by a feminist conspiracy.

Empirical evidence from DHS surveys are reported in table 1. For this table, I treat a woman as being a victim if she said she had experienced any (one or more) of these types of physical violence: *"Did your husband (or partner)…*

slap you
push you, shake, or throw some-thing at you
punch you, with fist or something that could hurt
kick or drag you

try to strangle or burn you

attack you with a knife or gun

twist your arm or pull your hair?"

I assess the fraction of husbands who experienced violence from their wife by use of women's answers to the question "Have you ever hit, slapped, kicked, or done anything else to physically hurt your (last) husband when he was not already beating or physically hurting you?" (IIPS and Macro International, 2007: 129).

To simplify comparison of males and females (as regards the fraction who have been physically attacked by their spouse), table 1 only reports data from surveys for which that DHS survey asked about whether violence had been experienced by husband *and* by wife. Where there is more than one DHS survey in the same country with this information, Table 1 only reports findings for the latest survey. But the bottom row of table 1 is the average of all DHS surveys (weighted by the sample size in each survey).

Table 1. Fraction of men and women who experienced violence from their spouse

	year	Wife had experienced violence from her husband	Husband had experienced violence from his wife
Azerbaijan	2006	11 %	1 %
Cambodia	2005	11 %	6 %
Cameroon	2004	37 %	5 %
Colombia	2000	32 %	14 %
Dominican Republic	2007	16 %	12 %
Egypt	2005	30 %	1 %
Ghana	2008	19 %	7 %
Haiti	2005	11 %	3 %
India	2005	26 %	1 %
Kenya	2008	31 %	3 %
Liberia	2007	35 %	9 %
Malawi	2000	18 %	2 %
Mali	2006	2 %	0.5%
Moldova	2005	21 %	8 %
Nigeria	2008	16 %	2 %
Peru	2004	34 %	9 %
Philippines	2008	12 %	15 %
Rwanda	2005	24 %	1 %
Sao Tome	2008	27 %	10 %
Uganda	2006	45 %	7 %
Ukraine	2007	14 %	9 %
Zambia	2007	40 %	9 %
All DHS surveys (including surveys not shown above)		23 %	5 %

Source: DHS.

If we look at each row in Table 1 separately, we see a clear pattern that there are more female victims than male victims. In the 2006 DHS survey in Azerbaijan, for example, 11% of wives experienced GBV, compared with only 1% of husbands. There is one exception to this pattern, the Philippines survey in 2008 (where more victims were male than female: 12% of women, and 15% of men) – I do not know why the Philippines is different in this respect. But in general, Table 1 confirms the claims of many previous researchers (discussed earlier in this chapter) that most victims of violence between spouses are female. This confirms what might be called a 'feminist' view. Hence, the term GBV is appropriate: domestic violence is related to gender. Overall, about 23% of women respondents said they had been physically hit by their partner, and only 5% of women had hit their partner. Note, however, that many writers and campaigners who do not appear to be feminist object to violence against women; the term GBV is not specifically feminist.

Table 1 reports the opinions of women: would men agree or disagree that most victims of GBV are women? CDCP and ORC Macro (2003: 218) wrote "Although it may seem unlikely that men would report inflicting verbal and especially physical abuse against their partners, the data from Romania show in fact that this is not the case. Looking at verbal and physical abuse received by women and delivered by men, the perpetrated abuse reported by men was at least as high as the abuse reported by women. Lifetime and current prevalence of physical abuse was identical when we independently calculated it based on male reports and female reports". Hence, it may be possible to ask men as well as women about GBV. The data referred to above by CDCP and ORC Macro (2003) tells us about violence inflicted by men, and suffered by women; but as far as I am aware, no DHS survey has asked men if they have been beaten by their wife.

Most WAS surveys take a very different approach to DHS, as regards asking about GBV (except for WAS Egypt 2005/6, which uses a similar approach to DHS). A typical WAS survey questionnaire is WAS Cameroon, which asked male and female respondents these questions:

> Have you ever had an argument with your spouse?
> During these arguments, have you beaten your partner?
> During these arguments, have you been beaten by your partner?

For each of the above questions, respondents were asked to choose "*yes*", "*no*", or "*don't know*". Note that there are limitations to the WAS data, as discussed in the appendix: in particular, the India WAS survey only interviewed people in urban areas. Table 2 reports answers to the GBV questions asked in WAS surveys. The WAS Kenya 2004 survey produced ambiguous results.

In response to a question like the one shown above for WAS Cameroon, men said there were more male victims than female victims. However, the same survey also asked respondents the question "*Have you ever experienced any of the following yourself? [..] physical beating*".

This question produced responses indicating there are more female than male victims of domestic violence. This Kenya survey was complicated by the previous questions on the definition of GBV (see table 3 below). In view of the inconsistent results, WAS Kenya is excluded from Table 2.

Table 2. Male and female experience of domestic violence, by respondent's gender

	Male respondent		Female respondent	
	woman hit by husband	man hit by wife	woman hit by husband	man hit by wife
Cameroon 2009	28%	14%	25%	12%
Chad 2008	29%	18%	26%	19%
Egypt 2005			20%	7%
India 2007	8%	6%	7%	4%
Indonesia 2001-2	5%	7%	5%	9%
Nigeria 2005	8%	3%	9%	3%
Total	15%	9%	15%	8%

Source: WAS.

Table 2 allows us to compare the views of male respondents with those of female respondents. The bottom row of table 2 is the average of all WAS surveys except Kenya (weighted by the sample size in each survey). Female WAS respondents, shown on the right of table 2, can be compared with the (female) DHS respondents in table 1: according to women interviewed by WAS surveys, there are far more female victims (15%) than male victims (8%) of domestic violence. The pattern for male respondents is similar: the equivalent figures are that 15% of women were victims, compared with 9% of men. The question in WAS surveys is symmetrical, in the sense that men and women were asked the same questions; but the results are not symmetrical: in general, men and women both say there are far more women than men victims of domestic violence. This confirms the evidence from DHS surveys in table 1: domestic violence *is* related to gender.

Table 2 also indicates that in the WAS Indonesia survey, male and female respondents both said there are more male than female victims of violence; this may indicate a cultural pattern, because it seems similar to the DHS Philippines survey reported in table 1 (Indonesia and Philippines are both in southern Asia). But without more research, we cannot be sure that this isn't merely coincidence – for example, the WAS Indonesia sample is relatively small for samples analysed in this book (only 2,003 households: see appendix).

WHAT DO PEOPLE REGARD AS 'DOMESTIC VIOLENCE'?

In a survey in Kenya by FIDA (2002), over a fifth of respondents did not know the meaning of the term 'domestic violence;' and "the rest of the interviewees gave varied definitions with the majority describing it as fights, disagreements, mistreatment, harassment or negligence, physical abuse, psychological oppression or denial of human rights, and wife battering".

The WAS Kenya survey in 2004 included a set of questions asking what "domestic violence" means, shown in Table 3 (there is no equivalent set of questions in any DHS or MICS survey, as far as I know). Table 3 lists eight types of activity which might be called 'domestic violence.'

Table 3. Views on which actions are seen as types of 'domestic violence': Kenya

Do you consider this domestic violence?	Gender of respondent	
	Male	*female*
Chasing spouse from marital home	83%	92%
Physical beating	93%	95%
Verbal abuse	76%	84%
Deliberate denial of conjugal rights	68%	77%
Non-provision of financial support	62%	75%
Cold war	72%	81%
Humiliation in front of other people	71%	78%
Slap during argument	80%	88%

Source: WAS Kenya (949 men and 944 women).

These eight were suggested during planning of the WAS survey, by an employee of the survey firm SBO Ltd., when the questionnaire was being developed in English. The meaning of phrases such as 'verbal abuse' may have changed when the questionnaire was translated from English into other languages.

According to Table 3, there is a fairly high level of agreement among WAS respondents (male and female) that each of these eight activities is 'domestic violence'. This does not necessarily mean that researchers should include all eight forms of behavior when estimating GBV prevalence: for example, if some surveys in other countries only include some of these eight in their definition of 'domestic violence', it may be appropriate to only include some of them when studying WAS Kenya data. Table 3 indicates that 75% of women described "Non provision of financial support" as violence; many women in Kenya have no income of their own, so lack of financial support by husband could cause serious problems such as hunger – but this problem may be less serious in countries (such as UK) with a welfare state.

SHOULD RAPE BE INCLUDED AS GBV?

For many writers and researchers, rape by husband/partner is a form of violence. However, there are reasons to question including rape in GBV. One reason is motive: it seems likely that men rape women because men enjoy having sex; whereas GBV is generally thought to have a different aim – a man may use GBV to force his partner to obey him. An example is given in chapter 7, where it seems a man can sometimes persuade his wife to do most of the housework, even if she earns more than he does, by using violence.

Another aspect is what the respondent thinks, about whether or not rape is a form of 'domestic violence' (or a different problem). Table 4 reports evidence from DHS surveys, to assess this question. Table 4 compares answers to two questions: was the respondent raped by her husband or partner? And was she 'physically attacked' by her husband or partner? If respondents think of rape as a form of physical violence, then every woman who had been raped would say she had been physically attacked; but the 1990 Colombia DHS survey found that 32% of women who had been raped said they hadn't been physically attacked.

Table 4. Experience of physical violence and rape, in Colombia and Zambia

Survey	Respondent's answer to whether or not they had experienced physical violence from their husband or partner		Respondents' answer to the question "Has your husband ever done this to you? Physically force you to have sexual intercourse"	
			No	Yes
DHS Colombia 1990		no	76%	32%
		yes	24%	68%
	total		100%	100%
DHS Zambia 2001		no	56%	45%
		yes	44%	55%
	total		100%	100%

Source: DHS data.

It seems probable that many women answering 'yes' to domestic violence, on the right hand column of Table 4, experienced rape *as well as* other types of violence (e.g. kicked by their husband) – although I don't know a way to find out how many. Table 4 indicates that 32% of rape victims said they had *not* experienced physical violence. Of the rape victims who said they *had* experienced physical violence, an unknown number (perhaps all) of the victims were raped and also physically attacked; so it is plausible that when they said they experienced violence, they meant a type of attack other than rape, such as being punched. So the evidence in Table 4 implies that rape isn't seen (by many DHS Colombia respondents) as a type of physical violence, but as a separate problem.

Data from the DHS Zambia 2001 survey is also shown in Table 4, and it shows a similar but stronger pattern to Colombia data in the same Table. Apparently 45% of women who said they had been raped said they had not been physically attacked (in the right hand column of Table 4). That still leaves 55% of rape victims who said they had been physically attacked, but it is possible that many of these 55% experienced rape as well as other forms of violence.

I am not aware of any other surveys for which we could produce evidence of the type in Table 4, but I see no reason why Colombia and Zambia are unusual in this respect – hence, I think it likely that victims in other countries also see rape as different to physical violence. If rape victims don't consider rape to be a type of 'physical violence', then perhaps researchers and campaigners shouldn't, either. Hence, I exclude women who were raped but did not experience another type of physical violence from the definition of GBV.

This paper also excludes other forms of sexual violence from prevalence rates where possible (for some surveys, only a combined physical and sexual violence statistic is reported; some sources don't make their definition of GBV clear – in such cases, I include the reported statistic on violence as an estimate of GBV). Rape is an extremely serious problem, and must be addressed urgently by national governments, charitable organizations, and campaigners; but rape is not the main focus of this book.

Table 5 shows data on various types of abuse of women. DHS surveys ask various questions about abuse of women by their partner, including what they describe as 'emotional violence'.

Table 5. Fraction of women reporting various forms of non-physical GBV

Country	year	Has your husband ever done this to you?				
		force you to have sexual inter-course	Sex abuse, e.g. force you to touch his private parts	Insult you	Humiliate you in front of other people	Threaten you or someone close, with harm
Cambodia	2005	38%	0.3%	14%	11%	10%
Uganda	2006	30%	16%	42%	23%	20%
Congo D R	2007	27%	13%		31%	29%
Bangladesh	2007	17%				
Zambia	2007	15%	9%	17%	17%	10%
Cameroon	2004	14%	3%		21%	21%
Bolivia	2003	14%				
Rwanda	2005	13%	6%		12%	6%
Malawi	2000	13%	4%		11%	4%
Kenya	2008	13%	4%	21%	17%	15%
Tanzania	2010	12%	7%	29%	13%	8%
Colombia	2005	11%		27%		
Zimbabwe	2005	11%	11%	25%	10%	10%
Peru	2004	10%	5%		25%	13%
Haiti	2005	9%	6%	13%	11%	6%
Liberia	2007	9%	6%	31%	25%	11%
Jordan	2007	8%			15%	13%
India	2005	8%	4%	8%	11%	5%
Philippines	2008	7%	2%	11%	7%	6%
Nicaragua	1997	6%	4%		17%	11%
Sao Tome	2008	6%	4%	21%	20%	15%
Ghana	2008	6%	3%	29%	17%	9%
Egypt	2005	6%			17%	6%
Dominican R	2007	5%	3%	23%	14%	8%
Moldova	2005	4%	2%	16%	17%	10%
Nigeria	2008	4%	2%	17%	14%	6%
Azerbaijan	2006	3%	1%	4%	7%	2%
Ukraine	2007	2%	1%	17%	16%	7%
South Africa	1998		0.4%			

Source: DHS.

For comparability, Table 5 uses only DHS surveys. In some countries, more than one DHS survey asked respondents about abuse of women by husbands; in such cases, Table 5 only reports data from the most recent DHS survey.

Table 5 provides evidence on various types of abuse. Rows in Table 5 are sorted in descending order by the rape column; this indicates that countries with the highest prevalence of rape tend to be in Africa (near the top of table 5). Where there are gaps in table 5, it indicates that a question was not asked in that country (these gaps are not zero).

Each type of behaviour in Table 5 is harmful; but many people would not call them "violence". For example, public humiliation of a wife by her husband may harm women's mental health, so it is a problem which should be addressed by governments and campaigners – but many people would consider humiliation a separate problem from physical violence. Most statistical data studied in this book do not include 'emotional violence' (such as threats or public humiliation by the husband) as physical violence. Hence, where possible, I exclude data on emotional violence from tables and figures and maps in this book. There is general agreement among researchers that sexual and emotional violence are serious problems; but such forms of abuse are not my main topic – this book focuses mainly on physical violence.

CONCLUSION

In my opinion, there is little chance of finding a definition of GBV which everyone would agree with. For research purposes, it is useful to adopt a definition which is used by many different surveys, so we can compare different countries; this approach will be used in the rest of this book.

It would be reasonable to classify rape within marriage as a form of GBV. No evidence in this book proves that rape should not be included in GBV statistics, and nothing in this book should be taken as a criticism of writers who include rape as a form of GBV. However, this book does not include rape or other types of forced sexual activity as a form of GBV (except for the relatively small fraction of published research studies in Table 40, where I cannot distinguish between rape and other forms of violence). If I had included rape victims with other types of violence in this book, the risk of violence against women would be even higher than the estimates of GBV prevalence shown in the following chapters.

Table 5 indicates that sexual violence such as rape, and 'emotional violence', are both global problems. I hope campaigners and governments will do all they can to prevent rape and emotional violence, as well as GBV. The rest of this book will focus on physical violence, such as women being pushed or stabbed by their husband or partner.

Chapter 3

GBV HARMS WOMEN AND CHILDREN

"Wives who are beaten usually face a consequent loss of control over household decisions and thus suffer in the allocation of resources within the family. Family resources may be transferred away from the wife and her children to other members of the household. More importantly, the husband and wife are not able to construct a strong marital bond; which is reflected in the extent to which the husband cares for the welfare of his wife and children. Regardless of the mechanism, when a wife is hit not only does she suffer but her children are also adversely affected" (Rao, 1998: 8).

ABSTRACT

This chapter assesses how much GBV is a threat to women's health, and to the well-being of other household members. It considers various types of harm experienced by the victims of GBV – there may be direct effects, such as cuts and scars; and indirect effects, such as mental health problems among women who have been beaten frequently. This chapter also considers the effects of GBV on other household members, especially children of the victim: for example, children may be less well-fed as a result of GBV, because violent men are more able to control household spending (and may prefer to spend money on alcohol rather than food, for example).

INTRODUCTION

Astbury (2006) discusses various types of harm which women experience due to GBV, including physical, mental, reproductive, and psychosomatic disorders. Previous research has found evidence that GBV leads to physical injuries and mental ill-health, which in turn cause further problems such as sick leave from work (WHO/ LSHTM, 2010: 5-6).

Domestic violence is associated with various types of physical and psychological harm to victims; GBV adversely impacts women's health, including gynaecologic morbidity and attempted suicide (Ackerson and Subramanian, 2008: 1194; Ward et al., 2005: 122).

Although not central to this book, it is important to note that children can be harmed by observing GBV in their family. There is evidence (discussed in chapter 9) that if a girl saw her mother beaten by her husband/partner, she is more likely to be a victim of violence herself when she grows up. Children (boys and girls) could also be traumatised by witnessing GBV in their own home (Ward et al., 2005: 122).

GBV Leads to Medical and other Problems

A study in Victoria, Australia estimated that among women age 18–44, GBV was associated with 7% of the overall burden of disease. Such violence was a larger risk factor than others such as high blood pressure, tobacco use, and obesity (cited in WHO/LSHTM, 2010: 5).

Murders of women, and suicides, are associated with GBV (Astbury, 2006: 51). Studies from Australia, Canada, Israel, South Africa and USA suggest between 40% and 70% of women who have been murdered were killed by their husband or boyfriend (Ward et al., 2005: 122). A 1998 study in USA found 37% of all violence-related visits to a medical 'emergency room' by women were due to GBV (Ward et al., 2005: 121). Other consequences of GBV include reproductive health problems: gynaecological disorders such as pelvic inflammatory disease, chronic pelvic pain, and urinary tract infections (Astbury, 2006: 52).

GBV also has indirect effects. WHO/LSHTM (2010: 5) report evidence that if a child grows up in a household where GBV occurs, that child is more likely to have behavioural problems such as truancy and crime. Experiencing GBV as a child can lead to emotional and behavioural problems in later life (Ward et al., 2005: 122).

Women face various other types of disadvantage in addition to violence, such as male control of decision-making in households. Such problems are often made worse by GBV, because male violence against women can increase a man's power, and decrease a woman's power.

Survey Evidence: Harm Experienced by Women

This section uses data from DHS surveys, to assess three types of harm which women respondents reported as part of DHS surveys. I attempted to obtain data from all DHS surveys released at the time of writing (2011); more DHS surveys are being carried out on a regular basis, so future researchers will be able to shed more light on evidence in this book.

In a few countries, DHS have carried out more than one survey which included questions on GBV (e.g. Haiti surveys in the year 2000, and the more recent 2005 survey in Haiti); in such cases, I generally use the most recent available data. Where the most recent survey did not include all three effects of GBV (e.g. Bolivia 2008), I report findings from the latest survey as well as a previous survey in the same country. For Haiti and Kenya, Table 6 reports data from two surveys in the same country because the latest survey did not include all of these three measures of harm. Gaps in Table 6 (such as the fraction needing medical help in Azerbaijan) indicate missing data, not zero. I round each percentage in Table 6 to the nearest whole number, except where a number is below 1%. Table 6 reports evidence on the severity of GBV to victims. There is a lot of variation from one country to another, perhaps because of cultural expectations on what types of behaviour are seen as 'acceptable' (regarding the extent to which men can use violence against women).

Table 6. Bruising, injury and need to visit medical facility due to GBV, by country

country	Year	respondent bruised by GBV	respondent injured or wounded by GBV	respondent needed medical help from GBV
Azerbaijan	2006	4 %	2 %	
Bolivia	2003	26 %	6 %	
Cambodia	2005	5 %	1 %	1 %
Cameroon	2004	9 %	6 %	4 %
Colombia	2005	15 %	4 %	5 %
Dominican R	2007	6 %	3 %	3 %
Egypt	2005	10 %	3 %	2 %
Ghana	2008	6 %	4 %	
Haiti	2005	4 %	3 %	
Haiti	2000	3 %	2 %	2 %
Honduras	2005	0.4%	0.1 %	0.1 %
India	2005	9 %	3 %	0.03%
Jordan	2007	5 %	1 %	2 %
Kenya	2003	10 %	3 %	5 %
Kenya	2008	9 %	5 %	
Liberia	2007	9 %	7 %	
Malawi	2000	5 %	1 %	1 %
Mali	2006	0.1%	0.04%	0.1 %
Moldova	2005	11 %	5 %	
Nicaragua	1997	11 %	2 %	2 %
Nigeria	2008	4 %	2 %	
Peru	2004	21 %	5 %	5 %
Philippines	2008	4 %	2 %	
Rwanda	2005	6 %	4 %	2 %
Sao Tome	2008	10 %	8 %	
South Africa	1998			2 %
Uganda	2006	16 %	10 %	
Ukraine	2007	8 %	2 %	
Zambia	2007	9 %	4 %	
Zimbabwe	2005	10 %	4 %	

Source: DHS (latest survey, if there is more than one DHS survey in the country).

A key lesson from Table 6 is that GBV often causes physical harm to women: this applies to every country for which I have obtained data. Table 6 suggests GBV is more harmful in some countries than in others: for example, a small fraction of GBV victims in Honduras and Mali reported physical injury or other medical problems. There may be a connection between this pattern and the fact that Mali and Honduras also seem different to most countries, in other tables in this book (such as Tables 1, 30, and 34). Honduras and Mali have surprisingly low

GBV prevalence, if the survey findings are to be trusted. I cannot explain why Mali or Honduras seem different in this respect – more research could be helpful.

Some writers divide GBV into 'more severe' versus or 'less severe' forms: a slap may seem less harmful than a punch, for example. But referring to the 'Conflict Tactic Scales' (CTS), Schröttle et al. (2006: 26) argued "Studies using the CTS frequently define severity as if it were inherent in the concrete act. This is empirically not well founded. Sometimes acts that seem to be quite minor can cause severe injuries: *"pushing someone angrily"* for example could be an act that is not important and severe at all, or it could be an act that may cause very severe harm, e.g. when a person is pushed to the ground or down the stairs [..] in numerous cases acts that seemed minor in themselves actually had caused physical injuries". It is not clear how to divide GBV into 'more severe' and 'less severe'; rather than invest more time in this debate, it may be appropriate to assert that any GBV is unacceptable, so we can direct our efforts to reducing the risk of GBV (of any type) happening in future.

The 2008 DHS Bolivia survey provides a different type of evidence. Women respondents who had experienced GBV in the last 12 months were asked 'As a result of assaults (by your partner), are you constantly fearful of your partner?' 73% of the respondents who answered this question said yes. The same Bolivian survey asked 'As a result of assaults (by your partner), do you feel anxious and depressed?' Among the women who answered the question, 69% said they have felt anxious and depressed as a result of GBV. I don't know of any other survey (apart from DHS Bolivia 2008) which asked either of these questions.

GBV can continue for years. In India, for example, a study by CSR (2005: 4) found that victims who filed a complaint of GBV to the police had suffered physical and/or mental abuse for at least three years. Some DHS surveys provide evidence on the number of times GBV happened to the respondent; evidence on frequency of violence is not analysed in this book, but future researchers might use such data to gain more understanding of the causes and effects of GBV.

WOMEN'S ACCESS TO HEALTHCARE

For many women in India, access to healthcare is limited by her husband's control (Bhattacharyya, 2000). In the 2005 India DHS survey, women were asked who decides if she can obtain health care; a large fraction (about 39%) of respondents said the decision is made by their husband (as opposed to the respondent herself, jointly, or others).

The 2005 DHS survey in India also asked women 'Are you usually allowed to go to the local health center?' 48% of the respondents said they can only go if accompanied by another adult, and 5% of women respondents said they cannot go outside the house without their husband's permission. Perhaps a man might prevent his wife from attending a health facility because he does not wish his violence to be discovered – if so, it makes it more difficult for researchers to assess how often GBV occurs. To the victim, a more important effect of a husband preventing his wife from seeking medical attention is that medical professionals cannot then provide the medical help which the GBV victim needs. It seems inevitable that denying women access to healthcare will worsen the harm caused by a husband's violence. Women should be able to access healthcare when they need it.

Respondents in several surveys were asked if getting permission to visit a health facility was a problem. For example, the 1999 DHS Zimbabwe survey asked "When you are sick and want to get medical advice or treatment, is each of the following a big problem, a small problem, or no problem for you? [..] Getting permission to go" (CSO and Macro International, 2000: WE23). Among women respondents, 3% said getting permission was a 'Big problem'. I interpret this question to be about women getting permission from their husband or partner: most women respondents are married in this Zimbabwe survey (and in DHS and WAS surveys in general), but in some cases it may refer to women seeking permission from another household member such as her father. DHS surveys in other countries asked a similar question; the proportion of women who said getting permission was a 'Big problem' was 3% in the 1999 Dominican Republic survey; 5% in the 2005 India survey; 8% in the 2001 Benin survey; 9% in the 2003 Nigeria survey; 13% in the 2003 Madagascar survey; 17% in the 2001 Nepal survey; and 70% in the 2004 Bangladesh survey. I do not know why so many Bangladeshi women found getting permission to access healthcare a big problem; perhaps Bangladesh's culture is central to this. A related question was asked in other DHS surveys, but with a different question wording – this book does not investigate all available DHS data, but future researchers may find DHS data very helpful.

CONTROL OVER HOUSEHOLD SPENDING

In many countries, a worryingly large fraction of children are undernourished (Millman and DeRose, 1998: 137). Chapter 11 of this book investigates the possibility, reported by previous researchers, that undernutrition is more common in households which have experienced GBV.

Rao (1998: 20-1) claims that mainstream economic analysis (based on bargaining between household members) is incompatible with GBV: "Clearly everyone in a violent household would be better off with the same allocation and without the violence. Why then does violence exist? No theoretical model of intra-household behavior, that I am aware of, allows for inefficient equilibria". But Rao implies GBV is carried out at least partly so the husband can control household spending. Chapter 11 examines the extent to which women control spending in households, focussing on food; it offers evidence that in many households, children go hungry even though the household has sufficient income to buy enough food.

CONCLUSION

GBV can increase a husband's control of household decisions. Perhaps the main motive for violent men to use GBV is to force his wife or partner to accept his preferences. Where a husband controls household spending, he may decide to allocate spending to his own preferences – including, for example, spending on alcoholic drink for himself. This may lead to harmful consequences for other members of his household, such as there not being enough money left for their food. Child undernutrition causes long-term medical and psychological damage (Raynor and Rudolf, 2000: 365). Much of the hunger in the world is associated with low household incomes, where the family cannot afford to buy enough food; but there is some risk of some hunger in relatively well-off households, because the husband misspends money on luxuries such as cars.

This chapter reports evidence that many women need medical attention as a result of GBV. This is clearly a cause for major concern. But even more worryingly, there is evidence that many women are prevented from seeking healthcare when they need it, because in many households, a husband decides whether or not his wife can go to a medical facility.

We need to be careful not to assume all men are identical: not all men are violent, and not all men misspend money. But there is a considerable amount of evidence that some children go hungry because too small a share of household income is assigned for buying food; and GBV appears to be part of the process by which such misspending occurs.

Chapter 4

PREVALENCE OF GBV WORLDWIDE

"In spite of the provisions of the IPC [Indian Penal Code], the police, being a part of the value system which condones wife beating, would not register a complaint against a husband for assaulting the wife even when it had resulted in serious injury which was punishable u/s 324 or 326, i.e. causing grievous hurt with or without weapons. It is generally assumed that a man has a right to beat his wife/ward. At the same time, a wife who actually mustered enough courage to approach a police station would be viewed as brazen and deviant. The police would counsel the woman about her duty to please and obey her husband, and send her back without even registering a complaint" (Kosambi, 1993: 42).

ABSTRACT

GBV is a major problem in many countries (Martin et al., 2002). This chapter reports information from numerous sources on GBV prevalence. Warnings are given about inconsistencies between surveys, such as definitions of GBV. This chapter includes a map based on all GBV prevalence data I am aware of, subject to some constraints (I use these constraints with the aim of improving comparability of data between sources). This chapter gives reasons why it may be helpful for future household surveys to adopt definitions used by previous researchers, so GBV data can be compared between countries and over time.

INTRODUCTION

This chapter aims to give a global picture of how frequently GBV occurs, comparing different countries. There are several problems with this task:

- Different survey organisations select different types of respondent – for example, some interview only pregnant women.
- In some surveys, married and cohabiting respondents are combined (perhaps the risk of GBV for married women is different to the risk for cohabiting women).

- Different surveys interview women with different age ranges: for example, most DHS surveys interview women age 15 to 49 years of age, whereas WAS surveys also include respondents over the age of 49.
- Some surveys ask respondents if they have ever experienced GBV; other surveys ask respondents their experience of GBV since the respondent married (which may exclude GBV which occurred in a relationship before the respondent's current marriage).
- There are many definitions of GBV: e.g. some surveys include sexual violence, others only ask about physical violence.
- Some questionnaires give a specific definition of violence (e.g. DHS: 'Have you experienced this? Slap during argument'); in other surveys, the questions are less precise, leaving the definition of violence to respondents.
- Questions are asked in different languages; it seems impossible to know how much translating a question into another language affects the results.
- This book uses household survey data from different years; as explained in chapter 6, it seems probable that the risk of GBV varies between years.

Despite complications such as the above list, several writers have compiled data on GBV prevalence rates from different sources (usually household surveys). For example, Ellsberg and Heise (2005: 13-5), and Alhabib et al. (2010), summarise GBV prevalence rates in many countries. Previous writers warn readers of the risks of comparing data from such different sources, and this chapter brings some problems to the attention of readers. I think it reasonable to use data in this chapter to compare different countries, but there is a risk that we may have a distorted impression of how the risk of GBV varies across the globe.

Each year, many women are killed by domestic violence (Kapoor, 2000: 6). So, to properly measure the size of the global GBV problem, we could analyse crime statistics such as NCRB (2009) on how many women are murdered during an episode of domestic violence; and then use survey data such as DHS and WAS, to assess how many women (who have not been murdered) experienced GBV.

DIFFICULTIES IN ESTIMATING GBV PREVALENCE

According to Watts and Zimmerman (2002: 1233), "The most accurate data on the prevalence of intimate partner violence comes from cross-sectional population surveys". Similarly, WHO/LSHTM (2010: 12) wrote "Owing to the small proportion of cases recorded in routinely collected statistics from victim care facilities and the police, both victimization and perpetration are most accurately measured through population based surveys". Coomaraswamy (2000: 11) wrote "Most police, prosecutors, magistrates, judges and doctors adhere to traditional values that support the family as an institution and the dominance of the male party within it. It is therefore necessary to train law enforcers and medical and legal professionals who come in contact with those experiencing violence to understand gender violence, to appreciate the trauma of those suffering and to take proper evidence for criminal proceedings".

Household surveys have many advantages over published crime statistics: for example, it may be difficult to compare crime statistics in UK and India, because the definitions (what is called a crime in each country) in Indian law is different to the UK law. But Rosenberg (2006: vi) warns of the dangers of using household surveys to compare domestic violence prevalence rates in different countries: different surveys use different methodologies, different question wording, and different target populations (such as the range of ages of respondents). To make data as comparable as possible, I rely heavily on DHS surveys as the main data source for this book: most DHS surveys use a common methodology – but early DHS surveys use a different approach, as explained below. For this chapter, I also use a much wider range of data sources, to produce the most comprehensive picture I can.

DATA AND METHODS

In this book, I include data on GBV risk from a household survey if the source is quantitative (rather than qualitative), and if the survey attempted to interview a sample representative of women in general (or of married/cohabiting women). To reduce bias, I ignore data sources based on samples which we might expect to be associated with violence, such as a survey in hospital 'Emergency Room'. I include all survey results I found, which satisfy these limitations. The methods used in this book might be considered a scientific approach to the analysis of GBV. I consider it vital to supplement quantitative analysis (as used in this book) with qualitative analysis (as used in Gwagwa, 1998, for example): there are advantages and disadvantages of each approach. Qualitative methods can be especially helpful in understanding motives of people – for example, why do (some) men use GBV?

For this book, national surveys are ideal; but this paper also includes surveys limited to a region, city, urban residents, or other sub-population – as explained in the appendix to this book. This book does not claim to report a complete list of survey results relevant to GBV: there may be many other surveys which estimate GBV prevalence rates which I haven't seen. Finding relevant research findings is difficult: for example, many reports on DHS surveys (on the ORC Macro website) are not available in English. More surveys are being produced all the time.

SURVEYS AND CRIME STATISTICS MAY UNDERSTATE RISKS OF GBV

GBV prevalence rates are thought to be under-reported in many (or even all) sources, because of the sensitivity of the subject (Watts and Zimmerman, 2002; McMillan, 2007: 20). Previous research (e.g. Ellsberg and Heise, 2005: 90) shows that prevalence rates (such as those reported in this book) are underestimated: data from household surveys such as DHS and WAS, and crime statistics relevant to domestic violence, are all prone to underestimation. Jejeebhoy and Cook (1997: sI10) state "women are liable to under-report actual experiences of violence". CBS et al. (2004) wrote "There is a culture of silence surrounding gender-based violence, which makes collection of data on this sensitive topic particularly challenging. Even women who want to speak about their experiences of domestic violence may find it difficult because of feelings of shame or fear". Rao described meeting two respondents who had been interviewed in a household survey: "Despite the fact that both these women were assaulted in our presence, neither said that they had ever been physically abused by their husbands in response to the survey questions. In fact, only 4 women out of 21 women interviewed in Halli admitted to being beaten. Why? One indication is given by the fact that 88% of women in Halli said that if they were beaten by their husband they would accept it quietly as opposed to about 50% in the other two villages. Another is that 3 of the 4 women beaten were assaulted severely enough to require medical attention. All of this points to the possibility that beating is acceptable behavior in Halli and only the most severely beaten women considered their problem worthy of a "yes" response to the question" (Rao, 1998: 15-6). Table 7 reports the fraction of 'severe' GBV victims (i.e. a woman who was strangled, burned, threatened with a knife or gun, or attacked with a knife or gun) who reported the domestic violence to the police.

Table 7. Fraction of women experiencing 'severe' GBV who reported GBV

Country	Year	fraction who told the police about having experienced violence
Azerbaijan	2006	5 %
Bangladesh	2007	0.4%
Bolivia	2003	3 %
Cambodia	2005	4 %
Cameroon	2004	1 %
Colombia	2005	12 %
Dominican Rep	2002	18 %
Ghana	2008	2 %
Haiti	2005	2 %
India	2005	1 %
Jordan	2007	1 %
Kenya	2008	3 %
Malawi	2000	1 %
Moldova	2005	26 %
Nicaragua	1997	20 %
Nigeria	2008	1 %
Philippines	2008	3 %
Rwanda	2005	8 %
Sao Tome	2008	11 %
Tanzania	2010	6 %
Uganda	2006	3 %
Ukraine	2007	27 %
Zambia	2007	5 %
Zimbabwe	2005	5 %

Source: DHS.

This table includes all DHS surveys which ask the question on this topic (if more than one DHS survey was carried out which asked about telling the police, only the most recent survey in that country is reported in Table 7). Numbers in Table 7 are rounded to the nearest whole percentage, except where the percentage is below 1%. Table 7 indicates that the fraction of victims who reported the problem to the police varied dramatically – varying from 0.4% in Bangladesh to 27% in Ukraine. This suggests that crime statistics may greatly underestimate the problem of GBV – a topic discussed in the next section.

COMPARISON BETWEEN CRIME STATISTICS AND SURVEY DATA

The fraction of respondents reporting GBV to the police (in Table 7) may seem surprisingly low to some readers, but previous research has also found very few victims report GBV to the police (e.g. Kishor and Johnson, 2004; McMillan, 2007: 20). This implies the fraction of women who are shown as victims in crime statistics is also much lower than the true value. To test this, consider a case study of India. The Indian government has a crime called 'Cruelty by husband or other relatives'; my research (not reported here) on DHS India data indicates that most domestic violence against women is perpetrated by husbands (as opposed to other relatives). The 2005 prevalence rate of 'Cruelty by husband or other relatives', according to NCRB (2006: 249), is 5.3 per 100,000 people; this is much lower than the GBV prevalence rate in DHS and WAS surveys. This section investigates such crimes in India.

To have a realistic chance of a successful criminal prosecution against a husband, a GBV victim may need to visit a medical facility, to prove she has been harmed; and to make a complaint to the police. In many cases, the GBV victim did not visit a medical centre (as discussed in chapter 3). The 2005 DHS India survey asked women if they were allowed to go a local health centre on their own, and only 53% said they were – almost half of the women could only go with another adult, or couldn't go at all without their husband's permission. My analysis of DHS India 2005 data shows the following levels of risk for female respondents (in each case, out of 100,000 women interviewed):

- 23,289 women experienced physical violence;
- 7,812 women visited a medical facility, due to violence from their husband;
- 4,053 women complained to the police about violence from their husband;
- 666 women visited a medical facility and complained to the police, due to GBV.

To compare the above figures with NCRB data, I assume only some of the 4,053 cases led to convictions. No male victims could obtain a conviction for domestic violence under IPC code 498a ('cruelty by husbands and other family members'); so the rate falls by half from 4,053 per 100,000 (female) respondents to 2,027 cases per 100,000 adults. In DHS India 2005, 61.4% of people in the households studied were age 18 or above; assuming no children under 18 reported such violence, this suggests 2,027*(61.4/100) = 1,244 per 100,000 people would report GBV to the police in India.

CSR (2005: 4) studied a sample of legal cases filed under IPC 498a, and found that only 2% of those cases led to conviction. If 2% of the 1,244 cases per 100,000 people reported to the police (based on the DHS 2005 India survey), this suggests about 25 convictions per 100,000 people; this is much higher than the NCRB figure of 5.3 convictions per 100,000 people. The difference between 25 and 5.3 may be because the police only pursue a small fraction of cases. Kosambi (1993: 42) reports that police in India often make it difficult for a woman who has experienced GBV to register a complaint against her husband. Of the women who complained to the police, only a fraction lead to a formal complaint by the police against the husband: "when a victim of domestic violence seeks help from any of the agencies, be it family, friends, NGOs, or lawyers, before registering a complaint, at each stage she is asked to reconcile the matter or to put up with the situation. Reconciliation in 498A cases takes place at every stage including the police station, Crime Against Women Cells and courts" (CSR, 2005: 4).

For the small fraction of 'cruelty' (GBV) cases which reach the courts in India, "The trial process is quite lengthy [..] In the cases tracked, the normal trial period was between five to ten years" (CSR, 2005: 4-5). Presumably such delays are another reason why many women who suffer GBV do not contact the police, or abandon the case before a conviction is obtained.

Few of the Indian men accused of 'cruelty' are convicted; this does _not_ mean that these men are innocent. CSR (2005: 5) report, from the cases they studied in detail, that "The cases where the accused were convicted had been filed under Section 498A along with section 304B and 302, which are applicable after the death of the victim. There were no convictions in any of the cases registered only under Section 498A. [..] there is not a single case where the accused has been convicted only under Section 498A. The accused have been acquitted (11 cases) by the court where the prosecutor failed to provide evidentiary proof of cruelty, mainly mental, inflicted on the victim as provided under Section 498A IPC. It is difficult to prove cruelty when the victim is still alive. This makes conviction only on the basis of Section 498A, difficult. Only in cases where Section 498A is used along with other Sections is the conviction rate high." It appears that in India, if a woman suffers GBV, justice will only be achieved if she is murdered. Even then, it seems likely that many men murder their wife and escape punishment – in India, and elsewhere. It is vital that governments and police forces worldwide do more to achieve an appropriate response to GBV.

WHY DON'T MORE GBV VICTIMS COMPLAIN TO THE POLICE?

The previous section suggests some reasons why most women who experience GBV (in India, at least) do not complain to the police about it. Some DHS surveys (not including India) asked women respondents who experienced GBV (but did not tell the police about it) why the victim did not seek justice. Table 8 reports female respondents who had experienced GBV at the time of interview, but chose not to report the incident(s) to the police or other authorities. The question wording differs slightly between countries, so it is not clear how to interpret differences between the countries. If more than one DHS survey in a country asked the same question, I only report the most recent survey.

Table 8 investigates why the respondent who experienced GBV did not report it to the authorities.

Table 8. Main reason for not seeking help about experiencing GBV, by country (%)

	Cambodia 2005	Cameroon 2004	Colombia 1990	Egypt 2005	Haiti 2000	Malawi 2000	Peru 2004	Rwanda 2005	Dominican R 2007
don't know who to go to	10	7	3	5	7	10	13	5	13
no use	16	50	14	7	51	30	35	50	34
part of life / not important / can handle herself	5	19	33	60	9	25	4	13	9
thinks he will change	0	0	7	0	0	0	0	0	0
afraid of divorce / being poor	2	1	6	4	0	5	8	3	3
afraid of further beating	8	5	16	4	13	5	2	7	10
afraid to get him in trouble	2	3	0	6	3	2	11	1	7
don't want to disgrace family	0	8	0	2	0	14	17	6	0
embarrassed	46	4	0	12	17	7	7	12	14
other reason / don't recall	11	4	21	1	0	2	3	3	10
Total	100	100	100	100	100	100	100	100	100

Source: DHS.

For six of these nine countries surveyed, the most common reason given was 'no use', implying that the respondent thought there was no point in making a complaint. Some GBV victims gave other reasons, such as being afraid of further beatings from their husband if they were to complain. In other countries such as UK, the police are unwilling to get involved in what they consider a 'domestic dispute' (McMillan, 2007: 20).

ESTIMATING GBV PREVALENCE FROM HOUSEHOLD SURVEY DATA

The Indian case study (earlier in this chapter) indicates that GBV prevalence rates in crime statistics are much lower than the true prevalence rate. Survey data such as DHS is widely thought to be more accurate than crime data, when assessing GBV prevalence (e.g. Watts and Zimmerman, 2002: 1233; WHO/LSHTM, 2010: 12).

Most DHS surveys use a modified version of the 'Conflict Tactics Scale' (CBS et al., 2004); the WAS Egypt 2005-6 survey used similar methods, but other WAS surveys used a different type of question.

In most WAS surveys, a female respondent's experience of GBV is measured by the question "Have you been a victim of domestic violence?" (yes or no); for men, the question is "Have you ever used domestic violence against your partner?" (yes or no). Hence, WAS surveys (apart from WAS Egypt) are very different to most DHS surveys. This makes comparison between WAS and DHS surveys difficult. Similar problems arise with other surveys.

GBV PREVALENCE RATES BY COUNTRY

Table 9 reports data from DHS surveys, but other surveys have asked similar questions (see appendix for more data sources of GBV prevalence). In each country where more than one DHS survey has been carried out, Table 9 only reports data from the most recent survey. There are some gaps in Table 9, which indicate that a question was not asked in that survey (no prevalence rate is zero, among the countries for which I have found data).

Table 9. Fraction of women respondents experiencing GBV from their husband

Country	Year	Has your husband ever done this to you?					
		Slap you	Push you, shake, or throw some-thing at you	Punch you, with fist or something that could hurt	Kick or drag you	Try to strangle or burn you	Threaten or attack you with a knife or gun
Bangladesh	2007	48%	31%	17%	16%	6%	2%
Congo D R	2007	44%	31%	20%	13%	8%	4%
Zambia	2007	42%	12%	14%	13%	4%	
Uganda	2006	40%	25%	20%	22%	7%	7%
Bolivia	2003	37%	43%	10%		7%	
India	2005	35%	14%	11%	12%	2%	1%
Liberia	2007	33%	17%	10%	17%	5%	
Cameroon	2004	33%	20%	17%	10%	3%	2%
Kenya	2008	32%	19%	12%	15%	3%	
Tanzania	2010	31%	15%	16%	11%	3%	
Colombia	2005	29%	34%	9%	13%	5%	8%
Egypt	2005	28%	25%	13%	6%	1%	1%
Rwanda	2005	27%	17%	15%	8%	2%	2%
Zimbabwe	2005	26%	12%	12%		8%	4%
Moldova	2005	20%	19%	11%	6%	3%	3%
Ghana	2008	17%	9%	5%	8%	1%	2%
Nigeria	2008	16%	5%	4%	6%	1%	1%
Malawi	2000	16%	7%	8%	6%	2%	1%
Jordan	2007	13%	15%	9%	6%	1%	1%
Cambodia	2000	12%	11%	6%	6%	1%	4%
Nicaragua	1997	11%	14%	13%	6%	5%	6%
Dominican R	2007	11%	12%	8%	3%	3%	3%
Azerbaijan	2006	10%	8%	3%	3%	1%	1%
Haiti	2005	10%	9%	6%	4%	2%	2%
Ukraine	2007	8%	11%	5%	3%	1%	0.5%
Philippines	2008	7%	7%	4%	3%	2%	2%

Source: DHS.

Table 9 shows large differences between prevalence rates for each type of GBV, between countries. Table 9 is based on DHS data; the questions are intended to allow comparison between countries - but there are small differences in question wording, as discussed in chapter 5, so variations in question wording may explain some of the variation in GBV prevalence rates between countries.

Rows in Table 9 are sorted in order, by the 'Slap during argument' column: countries in which the largest fraction of women were slapped (Bangladesh, Congo Democratic Republic, Zambia, etc.) are at the top of the table. This helps us to assess if the countries where most 'slap during argument' occur are the same countries where most 'pushing, shaking, or throwing something' takes place: the pattern is not entirely clear, but there is a tendency for countries near the top of Table 9 to have high rates of each type of violence (compared to countries near the bottom of Table 9). Some countries are more violent than others, as regards GBV.

Figure 2 indicates a complicated geographical variation in GBV prevalence. There are gaps in the map, where I have been unable to find any estimate of GBV in a country; and there may be doubts on whether or not the different data sources used are really comparable with each other. But I feel there is one pattern in figure 2 which stands out: that Africa (south of the Sahara) and the Middle East generally have high GBV prevalence rates.

There is also a cluster of countries on the Western side of South America with high GBV prevalence. I do not know why this pattern occurs; but other chapters in this book may shed light on the issue – including, for example, chapter 14 on the effect of stressful temperatures. Cultural factors, investigated in chapters 7 and 8, may offer an alternative explanation. More research is needed.

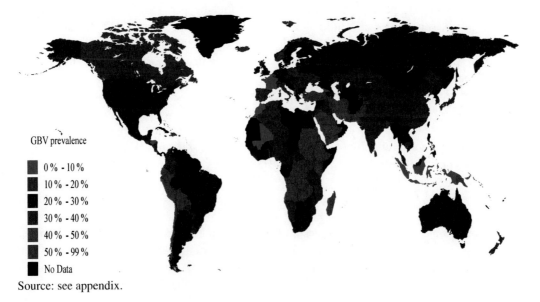

GBV prevalence

- 0 % - 10 %
- 10 % - 20 %
- 20 % - 30 %
- 30 % - 40 %
- 40 % - 50 %
- 50 % - 99 %
- No Data

Source: see appendix.

Figure 2. GBV prevalence by country.

CONCLUSION

There are many reasons why the reader might dispute the evidence reported in this chapter. Some writers (from a qualitative research background) argue that household surveys – based on a questionnaire – can never explore the subtleties of a topic such as GBV: in-depth interviewing is required, perhaps taking several hours. Quantitative data, of the kind discussed in this book, is seen by some people as shallow and superficial (in contrast to the more nuanced and sophisticated insights of qualitative research). It's possible to argue that scientists can never test a new drug properly, because they can't accurately control for all influences on blood pressure; hence, we cannot know for certain if the new drug works. But if doctors did not use scientific methods to test new medicines, would we ever have treatments to help patients who have high blood pressure (for example)? A philosopher once concluded he couldn't tell if he was a human or a butterfly (Möller, 1999); such debates won't stop social scientists from doing research, or stop campaigners and activists from bringing justice for women.

There are many different definitions of GBV, and different writers disagree about which definition should be adopted. It can be claimed that different surveys use different question wording, so we cannot compare results from (for example) DHS surveys with WAS surveys. It could be argued that even if every survey began with the same question wording, translation of that question into different languages will distort the question so much that we cannot compare the resulting prevalence rates. In my opinion, such criticisms should be taken seriously: researchers in future could try to adopt a common questionnaire for collecting data – one way to achieve this is for one agency to carry out a survey in every country in the world; alternatively, perhaps different agencies could be persuaded to adopt a common methodology. But there seems little agreement on the best way to study GBV; and even if there were agreement, it might be difficult to impose this method on agencies which carry out surveys. And translation from one language to another may distort results, no matter how careful the investigating agency is.

There are reasons to criticise social surveys, as regards their sampling techniques. For example, if we obtain data on one city, is this 'typical' of the whole country? If we rely on data from women age 15 to 49, can we assume this represents the views of women of all ages? If some women refuse to be interviewed, does this cast doubt on how representative the data are? For large-scale surveys such as DHS, investigators go to great lengths to ensure their samples are representative of the population; issues such as design effects, oversampling, and weighting are discussed in reports such as CBS, MOH, and ORC Macro (2004).

Some people might claim the process of interviewing (on the topic of GBV) is unethical. If an interviewer asks a woman about GBV, her husband might later discover this, and beat his wife as a punishment. Survey researchers are aware of such dangers, and attempt to safeguard the safety of respondents; but such risks can never be entirely eliminated (for example, if a husband returns home while an interview is taking place).

Another type of problem with survey data is that we don't know if people tell the truth. For example, if a woman has been beaten by her husband/partner, she might feel ashamed and not want to admit it to a stranger (i.e. the interviewer). Other reasons for mistrusting the data are if a woman is afraid of her husband finding out what she said to the interviewer. There are also other possible distortions, such as the interviewer mishearing the response, or a typist mistyping the answer. Social scientists who use survey data are aware of such problems, and presumably do all they can to minimise such errors.

For readers not put off by arguments in the preceding few paragraphs, this chapter has presented a method of combining data from different sources, to produce a single estimate of GBV in each country – shown in the appendix to this book. This chapter has also created a map based on the same data, which attempts to give a global picture of GBV prevalence. In my view, this map is a helpful guide to campaigners: it gives an indication of where GBV prevalence rates are the highest, and hence where most resources should be concentrated. I hope 'UN Women' (formerly called UNIFEM) and other agencies will find this map helpful. However, we should consider the findings in this book as provisional, and subject to revision as more data becomes available.

As explained in this chapter, data sources used in this book are all likely to underestimate GBV prevalence; but there seems no way to assess how much higher the true prevalence rates are (than the estimates reported in publications such as this book).

Chapter 5

ATTITUDES TO ACCEPTABILITY OF GBV

"The fight to end violence against women is both historic and universal. Historic, because gender inequality, which lies at the root of this violence, has been embedded in human history for centuries and the movement to end it challenges history, custom, and most critically, the status quo. Universal, because no society is an exception to the fact that violence against women is perpetrated through social and cultural norms that reinforce male power structures. The struggle is nothing less than a demand for full human rights to be unconditionally extended to all people everywhere" (Ward et al., 2005: 225).

ABSTRACT

This chapter attempts to assess how attitudes to GBV differ between countries. Data from different sources are reported and compared. Findings from many household surveys are shown and discussed, including a table to compare findings from DHS, MICS, and WAS surveys (which appear to be comparable with each other), and then combined with WVS data (which uses a very different method).

INTRODUCTION

This chapter investigates attitudes to GBV: in particular, to what extent do people consider GBV is acceptable behaviour by men? Are there differences between countries? This chapter is based on attitude questions, in household surveys such as DHS and WAS.

It has been claimed that women who have experienced GBV, or men who have carried out GBV, are more likely to say GBV is acceptable: evidence for this has been found for women in Haiti, South Africa, Jordan, and Zambia (Hindin et al., 2008: 23); and for men in Bangladesh, Bolivia, Kenya, Malawi, Moldova, Rwanda, and Zimbabwe (Hindin et al., 2008: 33). Hindin et al. (2008: 23) point out that it is difficult to assess whether acceptance of GBV is a cause, or an effect, of having had first-hand experience of GBV.

Perhaps women become victims because they are prepared to accept GBV in order to stay married – in many countries (such as Saudi Arabia), there are few opportunities for women to earn their own incomes.

ATTITUDES TO GBV ARE RELATED TO THE RISK OF GBV

Hindin et al. (2008: 27) studied DHS data from several countries, and report that in most of the countries studied, there is a significant correlation between a woman experiencing violence, and her attitudes towards violence. In Bolivia, Dominican Republic, Kenya, Malawi, Moldova, Zambia and Zimbabwe, women who said GBV was justified in at least one of the situations in the questionnaire (burning food, arguing with her husband, going out without telling him, etc.) were more likely to have experienced GBV. Hindin et al. (2008: 27) comment that it's unclear if acceptance of GBV is a cause or an effect of experiencing GBV (perhaps women who experienced GBV are more likely to describe it as normal; or perhaps women who think GBV is normal are more likely to say they experienced it). Hindin et al. (2008: 31) also investigated *male* attitudes to GBV, and found prevalence of GBV is associated with male acceptance of GBV, in Bangladesh, Bolivia, Kenya, Malawi, Moldova, Rwanda, and Zimbabwe.

Delsol et al. (2003: p.637) claim husbands' aggression is associated with attitudes condoning such violence; Rao (1997) studied a southern India community, and found the risk of wife abuse more common where such behaviour is seen as 'legitimate' by the community.

DIFFERENCES IN QUESTION WORDING

To assess attitudes to GBV, consider Egypt as a case study. The 1995 DHS Egypt survey asked women the following question:

> "Sometimes a wife can do things which annoy or anger her husband. Please tell me if a husband justified in beating his wife for each of the following situations:
> When she burns the food?
> When she neglects the children?
> When she answers him back?
> When she talks to other men?
> When she wastes his money?
> When she refuses him sex?" (El-Zanaty et al., 1996: 345).

The equivalent question in the 2005 DHS Egypt survey was phrased slightly differently to the above (1999) version. Here is the question wording used in 2005:

> "Sometimes a husband is annoyed or angered by things that his wife does. In your opinion, is a husband justified in hitting or beating his wife in the following situations:
> If she goes out without telling him?
> If she neglects the children?
> If she argues with him?
> If she refuses to have sex with him?
> If she burns the food?" (El-Zanaty and Way, 2006: 347).

The two versions of the question are a little different: for example, the 1995 questionnaire asked about "beating", whereas the 2005 question asked about "hitting or beating". In countries other than Egypt, some DHS surveys include the term "hitting or beating"; other

DHS surveys use "hit" only; and other DHS surveys use "beat" only. Yount et al. (2011: 879) use regression analysis on 67 DHS surveys in 48 countries, and found this difference in question wording between 'hit or beat' and 'hit' and 'beat' appears to cause statistically significant differences in the fraction of respondents who said 'yes'. Similarly, changing the preamble to this question also appeared to influence the fraction of women respondents saying 'yes' to the question. In addition, translation into local languages may influence responses. Some readers may be tempted to dismiss such debates, wondering if such a small change in question wording is important. Because the DHS surveys have large samples, it is possible for analysis of the type Yount et al. (2011) to produce statistically significant differences, even if the percentage of people who agree with the statement is fairly similar if different versions of the questionnaire were used.

The above differences between wording in the 1995 and 2005 DHS Egypt surveys are not dramatic. It can be argued that the differences between question wordings are small enough to be ignored, so we can compare these two surveys (for example, to assess if attitudes in Egypt changed between 1995 and 2005). But other surveys use completely different questions. To show this, table 10 reports findings from three household surveys in Kenya, as another case study.

Table 10. Attitudes to GBV by gender of respondent, in three Kenya surveys

	men	women
DHS 2003: "Sometimes a husband is annoyed or angered by things that his wife does. In your opinion, is a husband justified in hitting or beating his wife in the following situations:		
If she goes out without telling him?	39%	41%
If she neglects the children?	52%	55%
If she argues with him?	45%	47%
If she refuses to have sex with him?	28%	31%
If she burns the food?"	14%	16%
WAS 2004: Agreement with the statement: 'There are situations when it is justified for a man to beat his wife'	48%	26%
Afrobarometer 2003: Agreement with the statement: 'A married man has a right to beat his wife and children if they misbehave"	35%	28%

Source: DHS (11,395 cases); WAS (3091 cases); Afrobarometer (2391 cases).

Table 10 reports evidence on acceptance of GBV, using three Kenyan surveys. Because the question wording differs between surveys, we cannot directly compare the findings from these three (DHS, WAS, and Afrobarometer) surveys. Readers might wonder 'which is the correct answer?' But many social scientists (especially those using a postmodernist approach – as many anthropologists do, for example) would deny that any of the prevalence rates in Table 10 is objectively "correct". It can be argued that any percentage in Table 10 could be chosen, and reported as the fraction of Kenyans who consider GBV acceptable; and there are millions of other ways in which such a question could be asked – each of which would produce a different percentage of respondents who said they condoned GBV.

There are many advantages in using a standardized questionnaire: this should allow us to assess if attitudes differ between countries, or over time. But there are other considerations: perhaps we can gain a deeper understanding of (attitudes to) GBV by asking a wider range of questions.

TRANSLATION OF QUESTION WORDING

DHS surveys are intended to produce data which can be compared between countries. Even if a question wording were designed in one language (presumably English, because DHS is mainly funded by USAID), translating this question from English to other languages may introduce other forms of distortion.

I do not speak languages used in these surveys (apart from English), so I cannot assess how well the translations from English to languages such as Kikuyu. Similar problems apply to other surveys carried out in many countries, such as WVS, MICS, and WAS.

If translation has a significant effect on answers to questions about GBV, this will reduce the reliability with which we can compare GBV prevalence rates; it may also affect comparisons between different ethnic groups in the same country. Perhaps readers should consider the possibility that translation may affect data reported in this book; there seems no way to assess how important it is (for example, qualitative techniques such as in-depth interviews and focus groups may also be affected by translation).

DATA TO COMPARE ATTITUDES IN DIFFERENT COUNTRIES

DHS, MICS, and WAS surveys provide data on attitudes to GBV between countries which seems comparable.

As an example of this type of question, the 2005 DHS survey in Egypt asked women: "Sometimes a wife can do things which annoy or anger her husband. Please tell me if a husband justified in beating his wife for each of the following situations:" "When she burns the food?" and other scenarios (El-Zanaty et al., 1996: 345). I report data from the latest available survey in table 11 in each country; there are some gaps in the table, because the list of questions sometimes varies from one survey to another (a gap indicates missing data, not zero). For some surveys, the fieldwork took place in more than one year (such as Peru DHS 2004-8); in such cases, the 'year' column in table 11 indicates the first year in which fieldwork took place.

As well as variations between countries, there are often variations within one country. GBV prevalence varies between different geographical parts of India (Simister, 2011a); this may be due to cultural differences between regions – for example, Dutt and Noble (1982) describe cultural differences within India. Another type of variation within a country is by ethnic group, such as Kenya (Simister, 2010).

Table 11. Attitudes to GBV in different situations, by country

Country	Source	Year	Percentage of women who say a husband is justified in beating his wife, if she ...				
			Argue with him	Burn the food	Goes out without telling him	Neglects the children	Refuse sex with him
Albania	MICS	2005	9	3	17	20	9
Algeria	MICS	2006	31	25	56	54	43
Armenia	DHS	2005	16	2	11	20	4
Azerbaijan	DHS	2006	35	13	47	39	17
Bangladesh	DHS	2007	22	8	18	16	9
Belize	MICS	2006	4	2	3	9	3
Benin	DHS	2006	36	21	39	39	19
Bolivia	DHS	2008	5	3	6	12	2
Bosnia/ Herzegovina	MICS	2006	1	1	1	4	2
Burkina Faso	MICS	2006	55	23	48	48	41
Cameroon	DHS	2004	26	18	33	45	20
Chad	WAS	2008	18	14	39	43	16
Congo	DHS	2005			51	49	36
Congo Dem R	DHS	2007	49	29	55	57	42
Côte d'Ivoire	MICS	2006	42	34	42	50	30
Dominican Rep	DHS	2007	1	2	2	4	1
Egypt	DHS	2008	18	10	35	33	25
Eritrea	DHS	2002	45	29	52	51	48
Ethiopia	DHS	2005	52	50	58	59	39
Gambia	MICS	2005	37	16	57	53	62
Georgia	MICS	2005	2	1	2	6	1
Cambodia	DHS	2005	27	12	37	49	13
Ghana	DHS	2008	22	10	24	29	15
Guinea	DHS	2005	62	40	77	74	67
Guinea Bissau	MICS	2006	37	12	25	27	28
Guyana	MICS	2006	6	5	7	13	5
Haiti	DHS	2005	9	10	23	23	9
Honduras	DHS	2005	7	7	7	13	4
India	DHS	2005	28	18	28	36	13
Indonesia	DHS	2002	7	5	23	25	8
Iraq	MICS	2006	36	20	47	43	34
Jamaica	MICS	2005	1	1	1	5	1
Jordan	DHS	2007	21	9	41	47	

Table 11. (Continued)

Country	Source	Year	Percentage of women who say a husband is justified in beating his wife, if she …				
			Argue with him	Burn the food	Goes out without telling him	Neglects the children	Refuse sex with him
Kazakhstan	MICS	2006	4	2	3	7	2
Kenya	DHS	2008	30	13	31	40	24
Kyrgyzstan	MICS	2006	26	11	21	22	10
Laos	MICS	2006	36	45	60	64	45
Lesotho	DHS	2004	38	14	26	38	22
Liberia	DHS	2007	43	15	42	44	21
Macedonia	MICS	2005	11	5	12	16	7
Madagascar	DHS	2008	6	8	20	29	10
Malawi	DHS	2000	16	15	16	21	17
Mali	DHS	2006	49	22	59	51	56
Moldova	DHS	2005	5	4	7	17	3
Mongolia	MICS	2005	11	3	5	12	6
Morocco	DHS	2003	53	25	52	51	46
Mozambique	DHS	2003	32	22	35	37	33
Namibia	DHS	2006	18	14	22	29	13
Nepal	DHS	2006	8	3	9	21	3
Nicaragua	DHS	2001	6	6	8	13	4
Niger	DHS	2006	47	43	56	51	58
Nigeria	DHS	2008	29	18	35	33	28
Peru	DHS	2004	1	1	2	4	1
Philippines	DHS	2008	3	2	6	13	2
Rwanda	DHS	2005	7	10	26	41	14
Sao Tome	DHS	2008	8	7	12	13	6
Senegal	DHS	2005	53	25	54	52	50
Serbia	MICS	2005	2	1	2	6	1
Sierra Leone	DHS	2008	55	25	51	38	39
Somalia	MICS	2006	52	29	53	56	64
Suriname	MICS	2006	2	1	3	10	1
Swaziland	DHS	2006	18	3	10	11	4
Tajikistan	MICS	2005	68	44	62	61	48
Tanzania	DHS	2010	34	15	34	36	28
Togo	MICS	2006	22	28	35	41	19

Country	Source	Year	Percentage of women who say a husband is justified in beating his wife, if she ...				
			Argue with him	Burn the food	Goes out without telling him	Neglects the children	Refuse sex with him
Trinidad/Tobago	MICS	2006	1	1	1	7	1
Turkey	DHS	2003	29	6		23	17
Turkmenistan	DHS	2000	34	22	40	44	21
Uganda	DHS	2006	41	25	53	57	32
Ukraine	DHS	2007	1	0.2	1	3	1
Uzbekistan	DHS	2002	49	27	61	58	24
Vietnam	MICS	2006	37	18	39	57	18
Zambia	DHS	2007	43	33	43	44	38
Zimbabwe	DHS	2005	27	13	34	32	25

Source: DHS (author's analysis; Statcompiler website for some countries), WAS and MICS.

The 'burns the food' column in Table 11 is used to create figure 3 below, which gives a visual picture of geographical variation in attitudes. Table 11 is helpful to put this map in context: we can see that the fraction of women who say GBV is acceptable varies, depending on the scenario: for example, in Zimbabwe, 13% of women say GBV is acceptable if she burns food – this is used to create the figure 3; but a much larger fraction of Zimbabwean women (34%) say GBV is acceptable if a wife goes out without telling her husband. If the 'goes out without telling him' column of table 11 were used in the map (instead of the 'burns the food' column), then we would see very different shading on the map. But if we adjust the method of shading figure 3 (as shown in the legend at the bottom left corner of the map: e.g. replace '0% to 10%' by '0% - 20%' and recreate the map), a similar overall geographical pattern would result: for example, Ukraine has much lower acceptance of GBV than Zimbabwe, whichever numerical column we use.

In table 12, the DHS/MICS data column is the percentage of women who say a husband is justified in beating his wife 'if she burns the food'. The WVS figures are an index from zero (husband's violence is never justifiable) to 100 (husband's violence is always justifiable). Table 12 lists all countries for which I have such attitude data for WVS and for DHS and MICS (a country is excluded from Table 12 if I have attitude data only from WVS, or only data from DHS/MICS). Sample sizes for WVS surveys in table 12 are shown in table 13.

We can see a large difference between WVS and DHS/MICS, for many countries (e.g. Ethiopia) – I am unable to explain why there are such large differences, or which survey is more reliable. Other countries are fairly similar in different columns of Table 12 (such as India: 21 and 18). The overall average of these two columns is similar: 15.2 out of 100 for WVS, and 14.6% for DHS/MICS. Because these two averages are similar, I combine WVS data with DHS/MICS data in the map below (Figure 3) – while accepting that it would be better to use one data source for every country, if that were possible. Because the sample sizes in DHS and MICS data are much larger than WVS samples, I use DHS or MICS where possible; I also include a similar question from the WAS survey in Chad. I only use WVS data if none of the surveys asking the question about burning food (DHS, MICS, and WAS) provide data for this attitude question. In practice, DHS and MICS and WAS data are available for poorer countries, and WVS mainly for richer countries.

Table 12. Comparison of women respondents' views on GBV in WVS, DHS and MICS

Country	WVS		DHS / MICS	
	Index of accepting GBV	year	fraction who say GBV is acceptable if wife burns food	survey
Burkina Faso	23	2007	23 %	MICS 2006
Ethiopia	6	2007	50 %	DHS 2005
Ghana	14	2007	10 %	DHS 2008
India	21	2006	18 %	DHS 2005-6
Indonesia	3	2006	5 %	DHS 2002
Jordan	3	2007	9 %	DHS 2007
Mali	39	2007	22 %	DHS 2006
Moldova	9	2006	4 %	DHS 2005
Morocco	9	2007	25 %	DHS 2003
Rwanda	14	2007	10 %	DHS 2005
Serbia	42	2006	1 %	MICS 2005-6
Trinidad and Tobago	8	2006	1 %	MICS 2006
Turkey	4	2007	6 %	DHS 2003
Ukraine	10	2006	0.2 %	DHS 2007
Vietnam	6	2006	18 %	MICS 2006
Zambia	33	2007	33 %	DHS 2007
average	15.2		14.6 %	

Source: WVS, DHS, and MICS (author's analysis).

Table 13. Index of acceptance of GBV, by country and gender

Country	Men's attitude to a man beating his wife		Women's attitude to a man beating his wife	
	Index	sample size	Index	sample size
Andorra	3	503	1	498
Argentina	2	452	2	524
Australia	5	621	3	771
Brazil	7	620	5	871
Bulgaria	11	440	6	525
Burkina Faso	35	745	23	717
Canada	2	891	2	1250
Chile	4	446	4	546
China	9	878	7	1019
Colombia	4	1507	2	1511
Cyprus	10	508	6	537
Ethiopia	7	766	6	724
Finland	4	486	2	525

Country	Men's attitude to a man beating his wife		Women's attitude to a man beating his wife	
	Index	sample size	Index	sample size
France	4	480	2	520
Georgia	2	689	1	785
Germany	8	1817	5	1814
Ghana	18	763	14	745
Great Britain	4	499	3	521
India	26	1036	21	717
Indonesia	5	1043	3	953
Iran	10	1317	7	1314
Italy	3	500	1	500
Japan	8	473	7	593
Jordan	9	593	3	605
Malaysia	25	599	21	602
Mali	46	699	39	653
Mexico	11	747	11	763
Moldova	12	487	9	538
Morocco	20	591	9	600
Netherlands	3	510	2	527
Norway	3	512	2	506
Poland	4	504	1	485
Romania	10	774	5	928
Russian Federation	9	909	4	1064
Rwanda	18	742	14	761
Serbia	43	550	42	558
Slovenia	7	464	5	539
South Africa	17	1481	14	1480
South Korea	10	597	6	602
Spain	6	587	5	594
Sweden	2	500	2	498
Switzerland	4	555	4	680
Taiwan	9	620	5	606
Thailand	18	749	16	777
Trinidad and Tobago	10	449	8	552
Turkey	7	673	4	667
Ukraine	12	319	10	636
United States	6	597	3	589
Uruguay	8	440	9	553
Vietnam	7	760	6	725
Zambia	41	740	33	720

Source: WVS (author's analysis).

Table 13 allows us to compare male and female attitudes to GBV, in different countries. There is a tendency that in a country where many men consider GBV acceptable, many women also consider GBV acceptable. Considering the last two countries, for example, only a small fraction of people in Vietnam consider GBV acceptable (the average of the index is 7 among male respondents, 6 among female respondents); whereas acceptance of GBV is much more common in Zambia (the index averages 41 among men, and 33 among women). This pattern in table 13 suggests that the variation in the index is not random; figure 3 below helps to visualise the data.

Figure 3 is intended to give a global picture of how attitudes to GBV vary, by displaying data from DHS, MICS, WAS and WVS surveys – as shown above in Tables 11, 12, and 13. To make the map as complete as possible, each sample is limited to women respondents (several surveys only interviewed women, or only asked GBV questions of women). Most of the data used to generate Figure 3 are from questions such as "Sometimes a wife can do things which annoy or anger her husband. Please tell me if a husband justified in beating his wife for each of the following situations: 'When she burns the food?' " (this version is from the 1995 DHS Egypt survey: El-Zanaty et al., 1996: 345). For countries without such data from DHS or MICS or WAS, I use the WVS index of acceptance of GBV (as shown in Tables 13). There are still some countries which are blank in Figure 3, due to lack of suitable data; I expect future surveys to help us fill in some of these gaps.

Figure 3 indicates a pattern, that the highest fractions of women who say that GBV is acceptable are in Africa (the highest prevalence rates are shown in red, in figure 3). Other areas where GBV is accepted by women include parts of south Asia, such as India (shown in dark blue on figure 3).

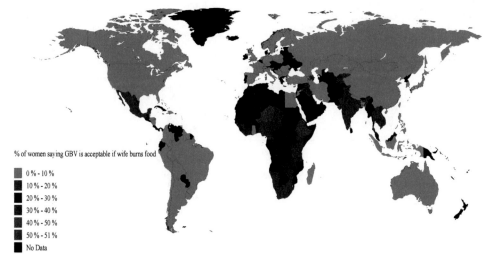

Source: DHS, MICS, WAS and WVS; female respondents only.

Figure 3. Acceptance of GBV among women respondents, by country.

CONCLUSION

This chapter reports attitude data from various surveys, in the form of tables. The chapter then combined data from various sources to produce a global map – Figure 3 – showing the fraction of women who considered GBV acceptable in a particular circumstance (from DHS, MICS, and WAS surveys); or (for countries where no comparable attitude data is available from DHS, MICS, or WAS), a different type of attitude question, from WVS surveys. Many readers may feel it is inappropriate to combine data from different sources, into one map. I accept that there are dangers with producing such a map: the apparent geographical variations on the map may not be genuine differences in attitudes between countries, but be due to the different question wordings used in different surveys. It would be possible to reduce some of this risk, by removing WVS survey data from the information I used to generate this map; but that change may not be enough to satisfy all readers – it is possible to argue that differences in question wording between DHS surveys mean we should not compare findings from one DHS survey with findings from another DHS survey. There are no guarantees as to the accuracy of the apparent patterns in figure 3, and I leave it to the reader to decide the extent to which the map can be trusted.

As a justification for the use of maps in this book, it can be argued that figure 3 is useful because it helps us to identify apparent geographical patterns in attitudes; any apparent difference between (groups of) countries can be investigated using data tables in this chapter. For example, figure 3 appears to show a fairly clear pattern: the highest levels of acceptance of GBV are in some African countries. This is not a simple distinction between Africa and the rest of the world – for example, some African countries have a fairly small fraction of women who accept GBV. But this 'Africa is different' pattern can be confirmed by studying data in Table 11; or by using data in Table 13.

Chapter 6

TRENDS IN GBV PREVALENCE, AND IN ATTITUDES TO GBV

[In India] "Until recently, domestic violence was not regarded as a crime, and women victims had no legal redress except through divorce proceedings. It is only recently that amendments to the Indian Penal Code (IPC) and Criminal Procedure Code (CrPC) made the requisite provisions, but these were mainly applied in cases treated as dowry deaths"
(Kosambi, 1993: 3).

ABSTRACT

The previous chapter attempted to give a snapshot of which parts of the world have the highest GBV. But what about changes over time? This chapter attempts to assess if GBV prevalence rates are falling, or rising, over time. There is no reason to assume every country has the same type of change, so perhaps each country should be considered separately. This chapter can't report evidence on trends, for most countries discussed in chapter 4 – in many countries, I only have data from one survey; and in other countries, I feel the methods adopted by different research organisations are incompatible. Hence, I rely on a handful of countries, where there has been more than one survey which use methods I consider 'similar'. If other researchers produce alternative results, by using different methods, it would be possible to assess how sensitive the findings are to different approaches.

INTRODUCTION

This chapter attempts to assess if there are trends in GBV prevalence, or in attitudes to GBV. This requires evidence for different years in the same country; I have only found suitable data for a fairly small number of countries. This chapter mainly considers India and Egypt, to assess changes in attitudes to, and prevalence of, GBV. I chose these two countries because I found more data available than for other countries. These two countries are useful case studies; but there seems no way to assess if these countries are typical of the world as a whole. There are reasons to doubt that the household surveys analysed in this chapter are typical of countries in general. For example, an organisation such as ORC Macro (which carries out DHS surveys) may decide to interview in a country if they suspect violence against women is high, or increasing. Nevertheless, for countries in which more than one survey has been carried out (and which asked the same question in more than one year), it is possible to use such surveys to assess if there are changes in GBV prevalence or attitudes to GBV in that country. This chapter reports some such evidence, but more research is needed.

Another approach used for this chapter is crime statistics. In the previous chapter, crime statistics were of little help to compare different countries, because the definition of GBV varies between countries. In this chapter, it offers the potential for annual data on GBV prevalence, for a few countries. Unfortunately, there seems no way to tell if the crime statistics in this chapter are representative of the world as a whole.

TRENDS IN GBV PREVALENCE OVER TIME IN UK

For the UK, the British government produce annual data on GBV prevalence, using the 'British Crime Survey'. I extract data for several years – from Povey et al. (2008), and similar reports for earlier years on the same website. In Figure 4, we can refer to domestic violence against women as GBV; for male victims, GBV is not an appropriate term (GBV implies men hitting women, rather than women hitting men). Figure 4 suggests UK GBV prevalence rose from 1981 to 1993, but since 1993 has generally declined; and a similar pattern applied to violence against men. I am not aware of explanations of why there was an increasing risk of violence from 1981 to 1993, or of why there was a declining trend since then.

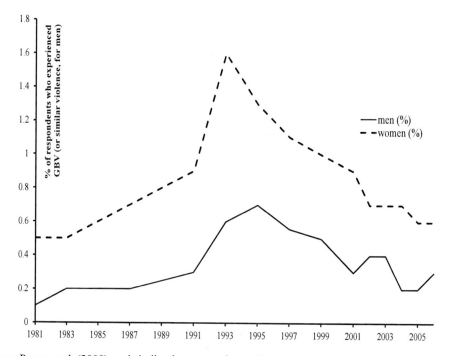

Source: Povey et al. (2008), and similar documents for earlier years on the same website.

Figure 4. UK prevalence of violence against men and women.

TRENDS IN INDIA REGARDING GBV

This section examines long-term trends in Indian society, regarding domestic violence between husband and wife, and attitudes to such violence. It analyses crime data, and uses data from several Indian household surveys: WAS surveys (1992 to 2007); 'World Values Survey' (1990, 1995, 2001 and 2006); and DHS surveys (1992-3, 1998-2000, and 2005). Several trends are apparent – some changes suggest that Indian women are becoming more liberated; but others imply worsening conditions for Indian women, such as more violence against women.

If GBV prevalence is increasing in India, then this increase in violence may be temporary, as India is in transition to a more modern society: there is evidence that some GBV is a male response to increasingly "modern" attitudes among Indian women. Describing India, Khanna and Varghese (1978: 41) wrote "A significant change in the division of labour is apparent among the urban middle class. More women are going out to work. They earn part of the family income". Such changes in behaviour affect attitudes: Khanna and Varghese (1978: 46; 39) claimed "A woman is no longer content with domestic chores alone, functioning mechanically as the caretaker of the house"; and "some working women become bossy and authoritative because they earn as much as their husbands do". If Indian women are becoming empowered, there may be problems of adjustment. Mathur (1996: 48) wrote, "According to the theory of patriarchal control, husbands develop standards of gratification for completely dominating their wives and children. When this domination is threatened they feel deprived, suffer psychic distress and in their uncontrollable rage they beat their wives for domestic domination."

This section reports empirical evidence of changes in India, in the last few years. It begins by investigating GBV, using summary data on crime statistics and analysis of household surveys.

Figure 5 focuses on two types of crime against women: 'Cruelty by husband or relatives' (which includes GBV, but also some violence against women by other household members); and 'dowry deaths'. Figure 5 indicates increasing prevalence of cruelty against women from 1995 (the first year such data are reported) to 2009: this prevalence rate increased dramatically in recent decades (as explained in chapter 4, it is almost certain that the prevalence of GBV is much higher than that suggested by Figure 5). Data from two DHS surveys indicates an increase in GBV from about 9% in 1998, to about 16% in 2005. This increase seems broadly consistent with the increase in crimes against women, shown by the trend in 'Cruelty by husbands' in Figure 5.

This section considers the possibility that Indian society and culture are changing. Table 14 considers changing attitudes to GBV (and divorce) since 1992. Table 14 reports the percentage of respondents who replied 'yes' to the question 'Is being violent sufficient reason for divorce?' Table 14 indicates a dramatic change in attitudes to divorce since 1992. Among men, the proportion who say a woman should not stay married to a violent spouse rose steadily from 33% in 1992, to 78% in 2007; a similar pattern can be seen among women respondents in Table 3, rising from 35% to 75%. Table 14 refers to just 2 cities; but my analysis of other 11 cities in WAS surveys shows similar trends since 1997. This suggests that Indian women now feel less pressure to stay in a violent marriage, compared to women in previous decades. There has been a small decline in the acceptance of GBV among DHS women respondents, from 22% in 1999 to 18% in 2006.

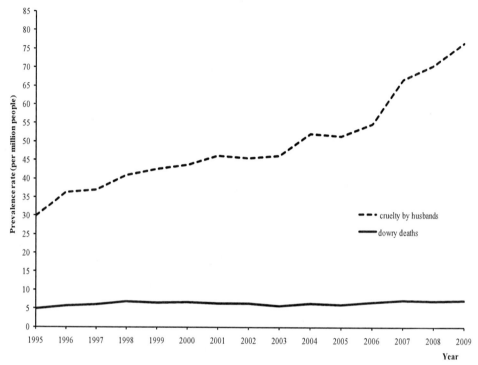

Source: calculated from NCRB (2001), and more recent editions of 'Crime in India'.

Figure 5. Prevalence of GBV and dowry deaths, in India.

Table 14. Changing attitudes to divorce and GBV in India, by year

	Gender of respondent	1992	1997	2002	2007
Percentage of respondents who agree that 'Domestic violence is sufficient for divorce'	Male	33%	59%	62%	78%
	Female	35%	53%	62%	75%

Source: WAS (Bombay and Madras only).

It is often claimed that adjusting to 'modern' values is associated with a period of increased violence. For example, Khanna and Varghese (1978: 99) wrote "The independent outlook fostered by better education, improved status and greater opportunities brings about a change in women, and leads to conflicts with family members".

An increase in GBV prevalence may be because women reject traditional ideas that men have about relationships; "Such conflict is likely to increase as their freedom increases" (Mittal, 2008). Perhaps the increased prevalence of violence against women is temporary – a sign of India becoming a modern, relatively affluent, country; but this trend has lasted for decades already, and there is no sign of a reduction in GBV prevalence rates so far.

ARE ATTITUDES TO GBV CHANGING IN EGYPT?

Table 15 reports findings from five surveys in Egypt which asked similar questions: DHS surveys in 1995, 2005, 2008, and WAS survey in 2005/6.

The WAS Egypt question on attitude to GBV was based on the DHS question wording; each of the two WAS samples (2005 and 2006) were designed to be nationally representative of Egypt, but note that the sample sizes (shown in Table 15) of the WAS surveys are much smaller than the DHS surveys; and WAS samples were located in fewer governorates than were the DHS surveys.

In Table 15, there are huge differences between the fractions of women respondents who agree with the statement. The question wording in DHS Egypt 2008 is identical to that in DHS Egypt 2005 (El-Zanaty and Way, 2006: 347, and equivalent questionnaire for 2008 on the DHS website), and identical to the WAS 2005/6 questionnaire (on the WAS website), so the question wording cannot be the only explanation of the different fraction of women saying 'yes' to this question. The 1995 questionnaire is slightly different to the later surveys, so this might partly explain why the 1995 findings are different to later surveys.

To some extent, the differences between rows in table 15 may reflect changes in Egyptian society between 1995 and 2008; but if a strong trend explains changes in Egyptian women's attitudes to GBV, we would expect the WAS survey in 2005 to have very similar findings to DHS 2005.

Table 16 investigates two of the five surveys in Table 12 – both referring to 2005. In Table 16, each survey is divided into regions; it is conventional to divide Egypt into 'upper Egypt' (the southern area), and 'lower Egypt' (near the Mediterranean).

Table 15. Fraction of women who consider GBV acceptable, in five surveys

Survey	Fraction of women who agree with the statement "it's justified for a man to hit his wife ..."					Sample size
	...if she argues with him	...if she burns the food	...if she goes out without telling him	...if she neglects the children	...if she refuses to have sex with him	
DHS Egypt 1995	74 %			56 %	78 %	20,647
DHS Egypt 2005	39 %	20 %	43 %	42 %	36 %	26,257
DHS Egypt 2008	18 %	10 %	35 %	33 %	25 %	21,858
WAS Egypt 2005	9 %	14 %	28 %	25 %	20 %	1,119
WAS Egypt 2006	4 %	5 %	20 %	32 %	15 %	1,437

Source: DHS and WAS (female respondents only).

In DHS and WAS surveys, respondents in the 'urban governorates' are in Cairo, Alexandria, Port Said or Suez (these could be grouped in 'lower Egypt'). The 'frontier governorates' are in desert regions, where few Egyptians live – no WAS respondents were sampled there, hence the gap in Table 16; this may partly explain why the fraction agreeing with the statement in WAS Egypt 2005 differs from DHS Egypt 2005. Having divided the sample into different regions, WAS Egypt 2005 looks more similar to DHS Egypt 2005.

The number of years the respondent spent in education (in Table 16) may at least partly explain the differences between rows in Table 16. Previous research in many countries has shown a tendency for better-educated respondents to be less likely to consider GBV acceptable – this topic is discussed in more detail in chapter 7.

Table 16. Fraction of women who consider GBV acceptable, in Egypt

	Average number of years in education (DHS 2005)	Percentage of women who agreed with statement 'it's justified for a man to hit his wife … if she burns the food'	
		DHS 2005	WAS 2005
urban governorates	9	10 %	8 %
lower Egypt	7	19 %	4 %
frontier governorates	7	11 %	
upper Egypt	5	26 %	27 %

Source: DHS and WAS (women respondents only).

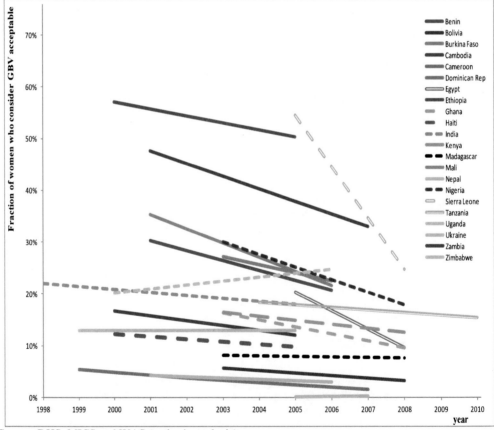

Source: DHS, MICS and WAS (author's analysis).

Figure 6. Changes in women's attitudes to GBV, by country.

CHANGES IN ATTITUDES TO GBV: ALL AVAILABLE COUNTRIES

This section considers whether the fraction of respondents who consider GBV acceptable has changed over time, for a wider range of countries than just Egypt and India discussed above; it uses household survey findings. However, it is only possible to assess a change over time in countries where we have survey estimates from more than one year.

Figure 6 shows a fairly clear downward trend, for almost every country where I have been able to assess changes over time (i.e. in countries where there has been a survey on this subject in more than one year). The only exception, where there is a rising trend in GBV, is Uganda (which rose from 20% in DHS 2000, to 25% in DHS 2006); I do not know why Uganda shows this worrying pattern.

The reduction in GBV prevalence for the other countries is encouraging; but this reduction in acceptance of GBV seems inconsistent with the upward trend in GBV prevalence discussed in India (earlier in this chapter). I am not able to explain this inconsistency, but it may be related to the number of people who are prepared to report domestic violence in India – a topic discussed in Chapter 4.

CONCLUSION

This chapter has attempted to see if GBV prevalence rates are changing over time. It appears that they are, in every country studied in this chapter (except Uganda). The main cases studies in this chapter are India and Egypt, but data from a number of other countries are used in figure 6. There appear to be two trends: an increase in the fraction of women who experience GBV, at least in India; and a reduction in acceptance of GBV, in many countries. More research is needed into which countries have rising rates of GBV, and why.

Ellsberg et al. (2001) wrote "younger women, on the whole, seem to be less tolerant of partner violence and more willing than women of their mothers' generation to end a relationship as soon as it becomes violent."

Chapter 7

GBV AND PATRIARCHY

"to preserve the family's and the girl's honor, marriages took place at around age twelve,
or the onset of puberty, without the girl's consent and often without her knowledge. One 34
year old woman from Fufore, Mairama, the mother of eight children, describes her marriage: I
was married at the age of thirteen, and I have no idea how the marriage came about. My
parents just arranged everything and I never laid eyes on my husband before the marriage. We
are related through the grandparents. I really felt that I was too young to be married, but I had
no choice but to obey my parents. I knew that if I went back home, I'd be beaten. Mariama,
like many women, objects to having had no say in the choice of her marriage partner nor of
the time of her marriage. Yet she could not dispute her family's decision. Many other women,
even those marrying at present, report similar predicaments, but admit that under all
circumstances they must obey their guardians. Mariama, like many girls of her age and
younger was also deprived of the choice to attend school" (VerEecke, 1989: 62).

ABSTRACT

This chapter investigates two hypotheses: the first is about GBV and patriarchy; and the
second hypothesis is about whether GBV is related to housework. This chapter also
investigates education, which is strongly correlated with the risk of GBV taking place. These
three themes are inter-related: for example, more education may reduce a person's likelihood
of having patriarchal attitudes.

Patriarchy is a pattern of inequality against women, and it is a global phenomenon. GBV
is also a worldwide problem. However, some countries seem more patriarchal than others: in
Saudi Arabia for example, a woman cannot drive a car, or appear in public without being
veiled. GBV prevalence rates also vary from one country to another. This chapter examines
the hypothesis that GBV is related to patriarchy.

Some writers have claimed men don't do as much housework as we would expect, if a
woman earns more than her partner. The term 'gender deviance neutralization' is sometimes
used, to describe such behaviour: in a household in which the wife earns more than her
husband, both husband and wife feel uncomfortable about being 'gender deviant' (breaking
from conventional behaviour). In such households, men do less housework than expected, and
women do more housework than expected. This chapter uses WAS data to investigate this

hypothesis. There appears to be a link, of some sort, between 'gender deviance neutralization' and GBV. This may be an example of patriarchal attitudes.

This chapter suggests an effective remedy to deal with patriarchy is education. Previous research, and new evidence shown in this chapter, provide evidence that a respondent's attitudes to GBV are strongly related to his or her education level.

INTRODUCTION

The aim of this chapter is to assess the claim that GBV is a result of patriarchy, as has been claimed by several writers (e.g. Bird et al., 2007: 120). To some people, such a claim (if true) might seem depressing: GBV would then seem part of a huge system, rather than being an isolated problem. However, we could see this more positively: if GBV is a result of culture, then it can be changed – whereas if it were related to human biology or to religion, it would seem more difficult to change. Bird et al. (2007: 113) claim "the hegemonic cultural model of masculinity that generates GBV against women is deeply ideological but not unchangeable".

Jejeebhoy and Cook (1997: sI11) wrote "not only is wife-beating seen as a normal part of womanhood but also women are acutely aware of their limited options, and that socio-economic factors provide them few alternatives to the life of violence". Johnson and Ferraro (2000) claimed that GBV is mainly caused by men using violence to control "their women" – a control to which many men feel they are entitled, and which is supported by patriarchal culture. This chapter also considers whether GBV is related to 'gender deviance', which may be associated with patriarchy.

This chapter argues that an effective remedy for GBV is education. Empirical evidence in this chapter suggests education can explain much, but not all, of the variation in GBV risk in the countries analysed in this book.

PREVIOUS LITERATURE ON 'PATRIARCHY'

Patriarchy is a global problem. The term 'patriarchy' originally meant rule by a patriarch, i.e. a dominant person (usually assumed to be male); this suggests a single male controls his family – for example, a father might control his wife, sons, and daughters; hence, many males might seem relatively powerless in such a family. In recent decades, social scientists have used the term patriarchy in a different sense, which emphasises the control of men in general over women in general – for example, some writers might include the control which a male factory owner has over his employees as patriarchal, particularly if he uses his power to carry out sexual harassment of female employees.

In current mainstream social science analysis (especially sociology), the term 'gender' is associated with patriarchy. Gender is used to emphasise that many aspects of inequality between men and women are not due to biology, but due to social (and perhaps cultural) influences. There is general agreement among academics, for example, that women are paid less than men for the same job; for many writers, such pay differences cannot be explained by biological differences between men and women – we need to understand the attitudes of employers and employees towards gender roles.

Regarding GBV, gender is a useful way to understand why many men are violent. WHO/LSHTM (2010: 6) wrote "the gender perspective emphasizes patriarchy, power relations and hierarchical constructions of masculinity and femininity as a predominant and pervasive driver of the problem. These are predicated on control of women and result in structural gender inequality". Hence, GBV is not an isolated topic, but exists as one element of a network of interacting forces. It is not coincidence that most presidents are male, or that most corporations and trade unions are dominated by men.

Burazeri et al. (2005) claimed GBV is closely associated with ideas of male superiority over women. These appear in different ways in different countries, but violence is usually used to create and enforce gender hierarchy and punish transgressions; to resolve relationship conflict; and to seek resolution of crisis of masculinity by providing a sense of powerfulness for the male perpetrator of GBV.

One aspect of patriarchy (according to many authors) is GBV. In India, for example, Satish Kumar, Gupta and Abraham (2002: 12) claimed domestic violence "is prevalent and [a] largely accepted part of family life in India". And such violence is part of a wide range of gender inequalities. Zimmer-Tamakoshi (2009: 573) wrote "violence against women has long been accepted in many Papua New Guinean societies as a legitimate means of controlling women and expressing or affecting men's relations with other men".

Flake (2005: 366), studying Peru, claimed that women who *control* decision-making responsibilities in the family are more likely to be abused than are women who *share* decision-making jointly with their partners; "These findings suggest that when women challenge the patriarchal power structure, their likelihood of being abused increases".

The following section tests the hypothesis that GBV is related to patriarchy. One of the biggest problems in such a test is that writers disagree on what 'patriarchy' means; a related problem is how to measure patriarchal attitudes.

EDUCATION OF FEMALES REDUCES THE RISK OF GBV

There is widespread agreement that, in general, a woman is less likely to be a victim of domestic violence if she is more educated. Previous research has produced a lot of evidence that the risk of GBV is reduced by education (Bott et al., 2005: 5; Hindin et al., 2008: 22; Jejeebhoy and Cook, 1997: sI11; Jewkes, 2002: 1425; Martin et al., 2002: 569). Kishor and Johnson (2004: 31) wrote "the more education a woman has, the less likely she is to report having ever experienced violence".

An "extensive body of evidence exists with respect to household-level determinants of domestic violence [..] One of the most consistently reported relationships has been an inverse association between the wife's educational level and reported violence" (Koenig et al, 2003: 272). Hindin et al. (2008: 26) found women's education tends to reduce the risk of GBV in Bangladesh, Bolivia, the Dominican Republic, Kenya, Moldova, Rwanda, and Zimbabwe. There is also evidence that acceptance of GBV tends to decline with increasing education, in Papua New Guinea (Zimmer-Tamakoshi, 2009: 573).

Regarding the link between education and the respondent's experience of GBV, previous research has produced complicated findings. Many researchers found a consistent trend, in which the more educated a woman is, the lower her risk of GBV (this is called a 'monotonic' relationship). This has been found in Bangladesh (Koenig et al., 2003: 280); Cambodia, India, and Nicaragua (Kishor and Johnson, 2004: 28); India (Simister and Makowiec, 2008; Simister, 2011b); Uttar Pradesh and Tamil Nadu, India (Jejeebhoy and Cook 1997: sI11); Karnataka, India (Rao, 1998); Kenya (Simister, 2010); Nigeria (Oyediran and Isiugo-Abanihe, 2005); and in Moldova, Romania, Russia and Ukraine (CDCP and ORC Macro, 2003: 216).

On the other hand, some other research gave different findings – a woman's education seems to have little or no effect on GBV prevalence, until a threshold: above this, education lowers her GBV risk. Research by the Gujarat Institute of Development Studies, and by the International Clinical Epidemiology Network (INCLEN), found education of females only reduces violence if women have "relatively high levels of education" (Burton, 2000: 14). In Bangladesh, Bates et al. (2004: 197) found a woman's education cut her GBV risk, but only if she had six or more years of education. In Colombia, the risk of GBV is almost unaffected by primary education, but is lower if she has education above primary school level (Kishor and Johnson, 2004: 28).

Other research found a third pattern: an inverted U-shape, in which a few years of education of a girl seems to *raise* her risk of GBV (when she is married), up to a threshold education level; but more education above this level *lowers* her risk of GBV. Regression results for Uttar Pradesh (India) in Koenig et al. (2006: 135) imply GBV risk for women with 1 to 6 years of education is more than the risk for women with no education, or the risk for women with over 6 years' education. Bott et al. (2005: 31) report an inverted U-shape in which women with least or most education have less GBV risk than women with some education, in USA and in South Africa. In Jordan, regression results by Clark et al. (2008: 128) imply GBV risk is highest for women with secondary education, compared to 'primary school or less' or 'higher' education. Some studies find women with primary education are at most risk: Dominican Republic, Egypt, Peru and Zambia (Kishor and Johnson, 2004: 28); Egypt (Akmatov et al., 2008: Table 3). Flake (2005: 365) found GBV prevalence in Peru rose from no education to incomplete secondary education, and then fell if the female respondent had completed secondary education or post-secondary education (in regression which controlled for numerous other factors).

So, some researchers found a 'monotonic' pattern between education and the risk of GBV, but other researchers did not. It isn't clear if this inconsistency is because of the methods used, or because different countries have different behaviour patterns. Evidence in this chapter may shed some light on this issue.

EDUCATION OF MALES REDUCES THE RISK OF GBV

The education of males seems to help reduce the risk of GBV. Visaria (1999: 12) wrote "Reported violence declined with the increasing education of both men and women". Ackerson et al. (2008) found for India that men's and women's education were independently associated with reducing GBV prevalence, for 'ever experienced GBV', and for 'experienced GBV in the past 12 months'. An Indian man is less likely to consider domestic violence acceptable if he is educated (Martin et al, 2002: 569). Hassan et al. (2000) found a less-educated woman married to a less-educated husband to be three times more at risk of physical violence than a highly-educated couple.

The education of men influences their behaviour towards women. Heaton et al. (2005: 288) wrote "The relationship between men's education and women's autonomy is complex. [..] As a husband's education increases, he adopts egalitarian views and sees the importance of spousal communication and joint decision-making. However, the opposite effect of men's education is also apparent in the literature. As a man gains higher educational status, it reinforces his gender role as the dominator and provider, thus suppressing his wife's voice and autonomy".

EDUCATING FEMALES BUT NOT MALES MIGHT CAUSE GBV

A woman's education sometimes increases her risk of experiencing GBV, if she is more educated than her husband (Kishor and Johnson, 2004: 36; Kodoth and Eapen, 2005: 3283). Similarly, regression analysis by Flake (2005: 365) indicates that the risk of GBV in Peru tends to be higher if a woman had more education than her husband. It is not clear why her education can increase her risk – perhaps a highly-educated woman is not prepared to be controlled by her husband, if he is less educated than herself.

Previous research has found that women with more education than their spouses were more likely to report 'ever experienced violence' and 'experienced recent violence', in India (Ackerson et al., 2008); Peru (Flake, 2005); and in China and Kenya (Hindin et al., 2008: 22). This indicates an important lesson for organisations such as the United Nations: while a focus on educating girls is clearly essential, it would be a mistake to ignore education of boys. It is vital that *both* boys *and* girls are educated, to prevent GBV in future.

WHY IS GBV RISK RELATED TO EDUCATION?

If education is related to GBV, what is the connection? If education level is so important for GBV risk, we might wish to consider some possible mechanisms. Education has complicated effects on women. Flake (2005: 356) wrote "Women with education are typically more autonomous; therefore, they possess the resources necessary to better recognize and terminate a potentially abusive relationship". Education can empower women, and help women to use information and other resources (Callaway, 1984; Jewkes, 2002: 1425). Heaton et al. (2005: 287) wrote "Education systems expose women to nontraditional role models and modern ideas that foster individualism and independence. Education also leads to greater human capital and potential for better employment". Zimmer-Tamakoshi (2009: 574) wrote about Papua New Guinea, "Women with more education have potentially greater opportunities to live life differently than their mothers' generation". Jewkes (2002: 1425) stated "Education confers social empowerment via social networks, self confidence, and an ability to use information and resources available in society". Hadi (2005: 187) found a woman is less likely to experience violence if she is more educated; "the learning process in school might have increased their spousal communication and, thus, raised their capacity to protect themselves from violence".

Rao (1998: 20-1) argues that GBV is an inefficient form of behaviour, because the benefit (if any) to the husband is much smaller than the harm to the wife. Perhaps educated people will generally be able to find better ways to solve household disputes. For example, if a man came home drunk from a bar, he might be violent to his wife in response to a situation which a neutral observer would consider trivial, such as a meal not being cooked quickly enough (in the husband's opinion). The resulting GBV would be very painful to the wife, but of little benefit to the husband. Perhaps education helps both partners to resolve disagreements without violence – for example, by improving their social skills, empathy, or self-control.

So far, this chapter has discussed experience of GBV; the remainder of this chapter now turns to attitudes to GBV, rather than experience of it – attempting to shed light on whether attitudes to GBV are related to education. An Indian man is less likely to consider domestic violence acceptable if he is more educated (Martin et al., 2002: 569; Simister and Makowiec, 2008). Acceptance of GBV is related to education in Kenya (Simister, 2010). My research (not reported in this book, but to be published in a journal article) indicates a fairly high correlation between attitude to GBV, and whether or not the respondent has experienced GBV herself (in DHS surveys, experience of GBV is only asked of women; whereas attitudes to GBV are asked of women and men).

Data for Figures 7 to 18 in this chapter are from DHS surveys, listed in Table 16: this table indicates the sample size in each survey, and the year(s) when fieldwork was carried out. The samples are divided by gender, to clarify sample sizes. For many DHS surveys, no men were interviewed (for this question, at least).

Some WAS surveys could also be used for this type of research, but WAS surveys generally have much smaller sample-sizes than do DHS surveys; and WAS surveys are generally less detailed than DHS surveys, as regards the education level of the respondent. My research (not reported here) indicates that for topics in this chapter, WAS surveys generally provide similar findings to DHS surveys, in countries where both sources provide relevant data.

This chapter uses graphs to investigate the possibility of education affecting attitudes to GBV. In this chapter, the vertical axis of each graph shows attitude of respondents to GBV in a particular circumstance, i.e. if a wife argues with her husband; I set the upper limit of the vertical axis on each graph to 100%, to make it easier to compare different figures. The horizontal axis shows how well-educated the respondent is, measured by the number of years she or he spent in education. Rather than report all countries in one graph, I divide the data into six geographical regions: these regions were chosen by me, so that not too many countries are included in any one graph. In each region, I present a figure for male respondents, and a separate figure for female respondents.

DHS report the exact number of years' education each respondent received; but I found that if I used this information, the graphs were too complicated to interpret, being full of vertical 'spikes' – due to the small sample at each number of years (because few respondents have exactly 9 years of education, for example). To simplify the appearance of figures in this chapter, I group the respondent's education into four categories: '0 to 5 years' (including respondents who have never been to school); '6 to 10 years'; '11 to 15 years'; and 'over 15 years'. I think it is typical, in most countries, for education to start when a child is 5 years old:

I ignore pre-school education, on the grounds that this is often supervised play rather than an attempt to teach children; but this assumption is debateable – for example, some kindergartens claim they can give children a good start in life, by teaching useful skills. If education does start at age 5, then we'd expect a respondent with over 15 years' education to leave education when they are at least 21 years old – hence, I expect most people in the 'over 15 years' category to be graduates, or (in a few cases) postgraduates.

Table 17. Sample sizes for 'it is justified for a man to hit his wife, if she argues'

Country	year	men	women
Armenia	2005	1345	6143
Azerbaijan	2006	2311	7798
Bangladesh	2007	3760	10964
Benin	2006	5225	17340
Bolivia	2003	6132	17644
Burkina Faso	2003	3424	12096
Cambodia	2005		3978
Cameroon	2004		10365
Congo Democratic Republic	2007		9423
Dominican Republic	2007	27658	27102
Egypt	2008		16426
Ethiopia	2005	5907	13832
Ghana	2008	4536	4866
Guinea	2005		7617
Haiti	2000	3020	9829
Honduras	2005		19635
India	2005	73293	121910
Indonesia	2002	8210	28824
Jordan	2007		10770
Kenya	2008	3383	8209
Lesotho	2004	2732	6997
Liberia	2007	5719	6708
Madagascar	2008	8477	17064
Malawi	2000	6288	24465
Mali	2001	3275	12508
Moldova	2005	2351	7137
Morocco	2003		16711
Mozambique	2003	2639	12398
Namibia	2006	3763	9419
Nepal	2006	4396	10777
Nicaragua	2001		9780
Niger	2006		8986
Nigeria	2008	15019	32144
Peru	2004-8		35255
Philippines	2008		13415
Rwanda	2005	4740	10978

Table 17. (Continued)

Country	*year*	men	women
Sao Tome and Principe	*2008*	2146	2451
Senegal	*2005*		14302
Sierra Leone	*2008*	3169	6963
Swaziland	*2006*	4094	4881
Tanzania	*2004*	2467	10168
Turkey	*2003*		7905
Uganda	*2006*	2491	8311
Ukraine	*2007*	3025	6663
Zambia	*2007*	6447	6977
Zimbabwe	*2005*	6921	8819

Source: DHS.

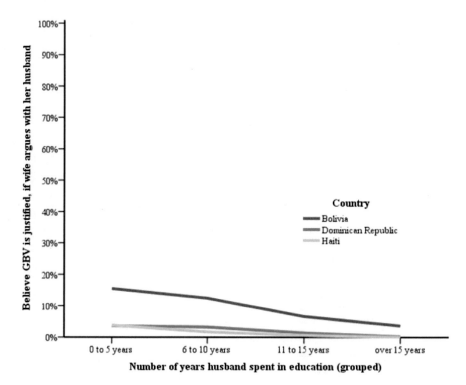

Source: DHS.

Figure 7. Attitude to GBV in Latin America: male respondents.

Figure 7 shows information on three Latin American countries: Bolivia, Dominican Republic, and Haiti. The effects of education can be seen clearly in the downward slope of each line in Figure 7: a man is less likely to accept GBV if he is more educated. Figure 7 may be affected by variables related to education: for example, educated households are less likely to be poor, because educated people tend to get better-paid jobs. We cannot be sure that education is the cause, and attitude the effect: for example, it is possible that people from middle-class families have more education, and middle-class values include modern attitudes to GBV. Nevertheless, Figure 7 is consistent with the view (discussed in the literature review to this chapter) that education is associated with less acceptance of GBV.

Another feature of Figure 7 is that the three lines are not at the same height: the Bolivia line is above the other two lines. This tells us that education is not the only influence on attitudes to GBV; but it is not obvious why Bolivia is different to the other two countries.

Figure 8 is based on women respondents, whereas Figure 7 used data on male respondents. There are six countries in Figure 8, compared with only three countries in Figure 7: this is because the DHS surveys in Honduras (2005-6) and Peru (2004-8) only interviewed women; the Nicaragua (1997-8) survey did interview a sample of men, but did not ask these men their attitudes to GBV.

Figure 8 (like Figure 7) shows downward sloping lines; this suggests that more education (of female respondents) is associated with less acceptance of GBV by these women. Like Figure 7, we see more acceptance of GBV in Bolivia than in Dominican Republic; but Haiti is similar to Bolivia in Figure 8 (unlike Figure 7). It is not clear why such differences exist between respondents in different countries, but local culture may be relevant.

Figure 9 uses data on male respondents in Asia. There are four countries in Figure 9, each of which shows a clear downward trend as we go from left to right (this pattern is less clear for Indonesia, where the line looks almost horizontal). This indicates that in each of these four countries, more-educated men are less likely (compared to less-educated men) to approve of a man hitting his wife.

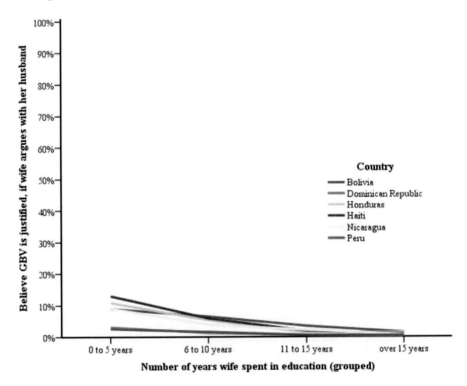

Source: DHS.

Figure 8. Attitude to GBV in Latin America: female respondents.

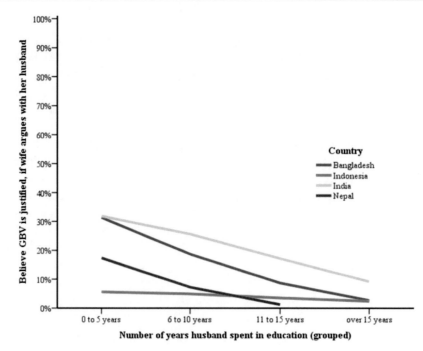

Source: DHS.

Figure 9. Attitude to GBV in Asia: male respondents.

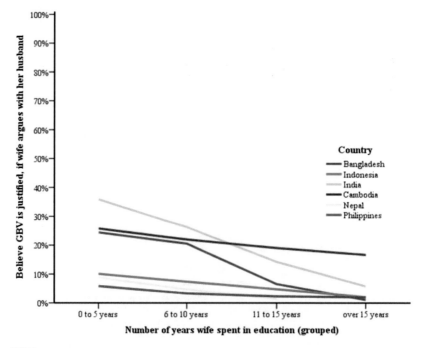

Source: DHS.

Figure 10. Attitude to GBV in Asia: female respondents.

It is also clear that if we control for education, there is more GBV in India than the other three countries in Figure 9. I have not attempted to investigate whether education systems differ between countries, but this may be a helpful subject for future research.

Figure 10 uses data on women respondents, in six Asian countries. There are more lines in Figure 10 than in Figure 9, because in Cambodia and the Philippines, DHS surveys interviewed only women – not men.

Like the three previous Figures, we see clear downward sloping lines in Figure 10; in all six countries, educating females tends to reduce the chance that they will consider GBV acceptable (in the case of a woman arguing with her husband, at least). This pattern is less clear in Cambodia than in the other countries in Figure 10: the line for Cambodia is almost horizontal. As in Figures 7 to 8, there are noticeable differences between countries: the lowest fraction of women accepting GBV are in the Philippines, with Nepal and Indonesia also having a low percentage of women accepting GBV. Figure 11 shows attitudes to GBV in four Middle Eastern and European countries, by education. There is a clear downward slope in each line, indicating a man is less likely to consider GBV acceptable if he is more educated. There is also a striking difference between countries in Figure 11: Azerbaijan and Armenia both have a very high fraction of men accepting GBV. I cannot explain why there are such large differences between countries, but future research may explain this. In Azerbaijan, even men with over 15 years' education (most of whom are graduates or postgraduates, presumably) are likely to accept GBV if a woman argues with her husband.

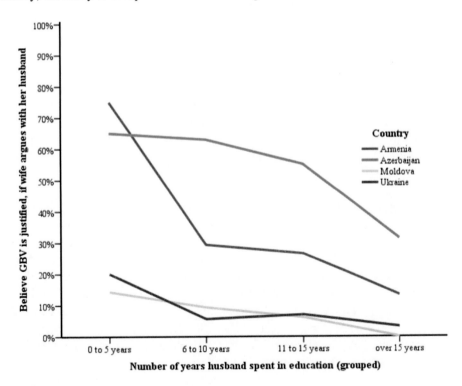

Source: DHS.

Figure 11. Attitude to GBV in Middle East/Europe: male respondents.

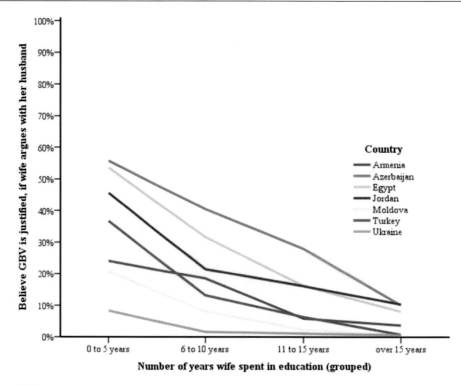

Source: DHS

Figure 12. Attitude to GBV in Middle East/Europe: female respondents.

Figure 12, like Figure 11, is based on countries in the Middle East and Europe; but Figure 12 uses data on women respondents. Note, also, that Figure 12 has data for more countries (the DHS surveys in Egypt, Jordan, and Turkey did not interview men, so they are not included in Figure 11). In both Figures 11 and 12, Azerbaijan stands out as having very high acceptance of GBV. In Figure 12 (like Figure 11), respondents in Ukraine are unlikely to say GBV is acceptable, in the case where a wife argues with her husband.

All seven lines in Figure 12 slope down, indicating that education appears to reduce the chance of a respondent finding GBV acceptable. Figure 12 is perhaps the most persuasive Figure in this chapter, as regards the apparent effect of education: for example, the chance of a woman in Azerbaijan accepting GBV falls from 56% (if she has zero to five years' education), to 11% (if she spent over fifteen years in education). The remaining figures in this chapter use data on Africa. DHS surveys have been carried out on many African countries; if they were all placed on the same Figure, it would be difficult to make sense of the many lines. So for the remaining Figures in this chapter, I divide Africa into three regions, which I call western Africa; mid Africa; and southern Africa (this division of Africa into regions could be done in many other ways – future researchers may choose different geographical regions). Figure 13 uses data on seven countries in what I call 'western Africa'. There is a general tendency for the line to fall as we go from left to right, in each country; this suggests education reduces the chance of a man considering GBV to be acceptable (but as for all Figures in this chapter, other factors such as social class may also be influencing acceptance of GBV).

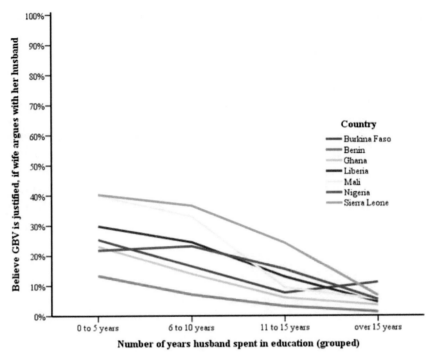

Source: DHS.

Figure 13. Attitude to GBV in western Africa: male respondents.

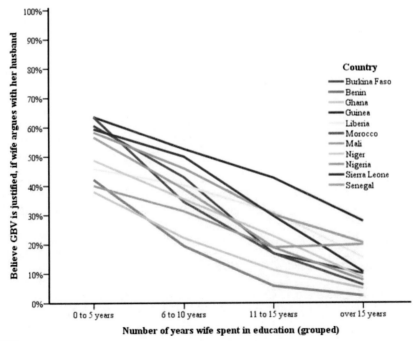

Source: DHS.

Figure 14. Attitude to GBV in western Africa: female respondents.

There is an increase in acceptance of GBV for Burkina Faso, as we go from '11 to 15 years' to 'over 15 years'; I consider this to be a "spurious" result (the result of random variation in a small sample), because only 36 men in the Burkina Faso sample had over fifteen years' education.

Figure 14 is the equivalent for women respondents, of Figure 13. Figure 14 has data on more countries than Figure 13, because some DHS surveys did not interview men. There is, again, a tendency for women in 'western Africa' to be less likely to accept GBV if they are more educated (i.e. women on the right-hand-side of Figure 13): this is clear because the lines in Figure 14 are generally downward-sloping. And like the previous Figures in this chapter, there are clear differences between countries as regards acceptance of GBV. Women in Benin are the least likely to accept GBV, if we control for education; at the other extreme, women in Guinea, Sierra Leone and Mali are the most likely to accept GBV (in the scenario where a wife argues with her husband).

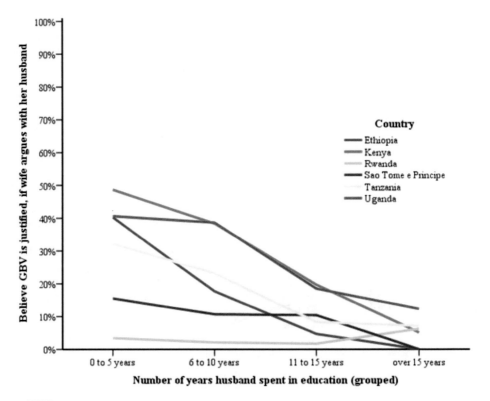

Source: DHS.

Figure 15. Attitude to GBV in mid Africa: male respondents.

Figure 15 uses data on male respondents, in six countries in the region I call 'mid Africa'. For these six countries, there is a tendency for more education to reduce their chance of accepting GBV (as shown by the downward-sloping lines in Figure 15). As in previous Figures in this chapter, there are large differences between countries as regards general acceptance of GBV: for example, Rwanda has a low fraction of men accepting GBV (except for men with over 15 years' education: but only 32 men in Rwanda had spent over 15 years in education, so this apparent increase in acceptance of GBV is unreliable, and is probably due to random variation in a small sample).

Figure 16 (for female respondents) is based on data on respondents living in the same countries as Figure 15 (for male respondents); but there are eight countries included in Figure 16, compared to only six countries in Figure 15, because there were no interviews with male respondents in Congo Democratic Republic or in Cameroon. Most lines in Figure 16, as in previous Figures in this chapter, show a downward trend as we go from left to right; this suggests educating girls and women tends to reduce their acceptance of GBV. Sao Tome and Principe (near the bottom of Figure 16) seems to be an exception, in that there is more acceptance of GBV in the 'over 15 years' category than for other education levels; but only six respondents in Sao Tome and Principe had over 15 years' education, so I think this apparent increase is probably "spurious" (i.e. random variation, due to a small sample).

Figure 17 shows attitudes to GBV among men in eight countries, in the region I call 'southern Africa'. There is a general tendency for acceptance of GBV to decline as we go from left to right (shown by the downward slopes of lines in Figure 17); hence, education of boys/men seems to make a difference to attitudes regarding GBV. As in other figures in this chapter, there are clear differences between countries as regards men's acceptance of GBV (in the case where a wife argues with her husband): there is less acceptance of GBV in Madagascar and Malawi than in the other six countries in Figure 17. This might be a result of the local culture in those two countries.

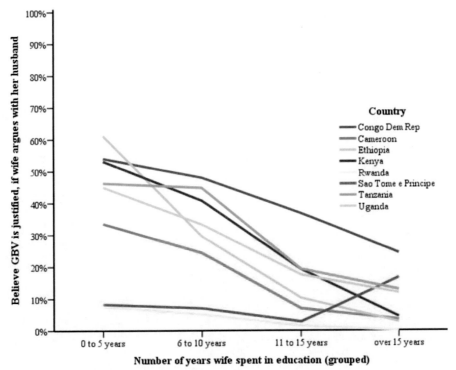

Source: DHS.

Figure 16. Attitude to GBV in mid Africa: female respondents.

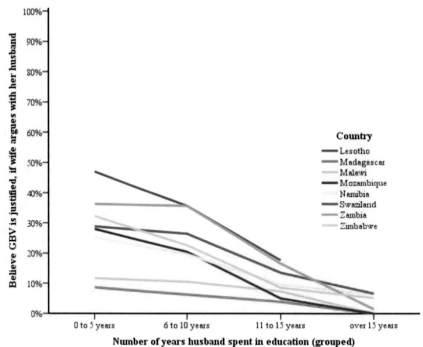

Source: DHS.

Figure 17. Attitude to GBV in southern Africa: male respondents.

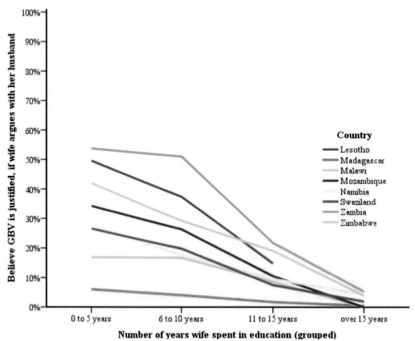

Source: DHS.

Figure 18. Attitude to GBV in southern Africa: female respondents.

Figure 18 is the female-respondent equivalent of Figure 17. Like Figure 17, we see a clear downward trend in all eight of these southern African countries; this implies that education reduces acceptance of GBV. As for other Figures in this chapter, there are clear differences between countries – which cannot be explained by education level of the respondent. Madagascar shows less acceptance of GBV (a finding which also applies to men, in Figure 17). Perhaps ethnicity (examined in the following chapter) at least partly explains such differences between countries.

If education is a fundamental influence on GBV, it may be helpful to consider how this might affect GBV prevalence globally. This is explored in Figure 19, which is mainly based on data from United Nations Statistics Agency (2011). For countries where this source does not provide data on education levels, I supplement it with data from WVS or DHS data – if both WVS and DHS data are available for a country which isn't in United Nations Statistics Agency (2011), I calculated the average of DHS and WVS education levels. In each country, the education level in Figure 19 is the average for men and women, measured by the average number of years in education for the population.

Figure 19 shows the distribution of education around the world: the countries with the lowest average education levels (shown in brown) are mainly in Africa and the Indian subcontinent. If education tends to reduce GBV risk, as evidence in this chapter shows, we would expect the highest rates of GBV prevalence to occur in Africa. We can assess this by comparing Figure 19 with GBV prevalence rates in Figure 2 (in chapter 4). Both maps show Africa and India standing out as being different to most of the rest of the world: Africa and India tend to have low education levels, and high GBV prevalence. However, more careful analysis indicates that the pattern is not as simple as 'Africa and India' versus 'the rest of the world', in either of these two maps (Figures 2 and 19).

Some previous researchers have found a 'monotonic' link (a clear trend in which more education is associated with less GBV risk); but others did not. Acceptance of Gender-Based Violence seems to be associated with low education levels, according to Figures in this chapter. It is clear, though, that education is not the only influence on attitudes to GBV: for example, the heights of each line varied between countries, in Figures 7 to 18.

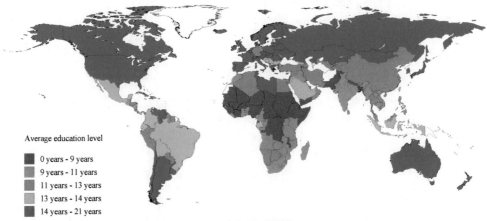

Source: United Nations Statistics Agency (2011), DHS, WVS.

Figure 19. Average education level (number of years in education), by country.

Figures in this chapter show a downward trend, in which acceptance of GBV tends to fall as education level (of the respondent) increases. How should we interpret this pattern? This chapter reports evidence that education reduces acceptance of GBV. As is common in social sciences, we can never be sure of "cause and effect" in the Figures shown in this chapter. For example, it is possible that richer families can afford to keep their children in education longer, and that richer families have middle-class values which consider GBV unacceptable (if so, education and attitudes would both be effects of a different cause, namely social class). It would be difficult to prove or disprove such a viewpoint: for example, there is much disagreement about what social class is, and how we should measure it.

Any reader who disagrees with my interpretation of Figures in this chapter can download data from surveys such as DHS, and do their own research. In my view, the obvious explanation of Figures in this chapter is that education is the 'cause', because schoolchildren and students learn skills and knowledge; and attitude to GBV is the 'effect'.

The evidence on attitudes to wife's obedience to her husband is puzzling. Almost all respondents in WAS surveys agree that 'a wife should always obey her husband', whatever their education level. Clearly, education is not the only influence on attitudes; for example, religious beliefs may also be important.

This chapter does not provide evidence on *how* education helps reduce the risk of GBV. Perhaps it is by changing values; or it may increase a woman's options to leave a violent partner, by increasing her wage rate or by improving her chance of finding a paid job.

Evidence in this chapter suggests campaigners can be confident that improving access to education will reduce domestic violence. However, it will take decades for school education to reduce GBV prevalence in the adult population; hence, education of adults is also needed.

GENDER ROLES

The rest of this chapter combines data from WVS, WAS, and DHS, to assess if there is a link between GBV and attitudes to gender roles. It would be possible to report the GBV prevalence in almost every country, and attitudes to gender roles in many countries, in a table; but there would be a risk of missing the overall pattern, because the resulting table would be very big (due to the large amount of countries). Another approach is to use a map, but WVS data may look unclear on a map because there would be too much missing data on the map (WVS cover an impressive number of countries; but there are few WVS surveys in African countries, for example).

For the questions used to create Table 16, only two columns have data on North America and Oceania ('If a woman earns more than her husband, it's almost certain to cause problems' for men and women); to avoid gaps in the table, North America and Oceania are merged with Europe in Table 16. The definition of 'East Asia' is China, Indonesia, Japan, South Korea, Philippines, Russia and Taiwan. Note that none of the main surveys studied in this book (DHS, WAS, MICS, and WVS) include many Pacific countries.

The providers of DHS surveys, ORC Macro, group some types of violence together as 'severe violence' (variable D107, in most DHS surveys which include GBV data). A female respondent is considered to have experienced severe violence (from her husband or cohabiting partner) if she says she has been strangled, burned, threatened with a knife or gun, or attacked with a knife or gun. This information is in the right-hand column of table 16.

Table 16 is sorted into order by the wife's education level, in the column on the right hand edge of Table 16; the more developed regions (Europe, North America, Oceania, and Asia East) have a much lower prevalence of severe violence than do the poorer regions (Asia west, Africa, and Latin America). Perhaps education is central to the differences between rows in Table 16.

Table 16 indicates that the highest risk of GBV are in west Asia, Africa, and Latin America; and that these regions appear most traditional – as regards attitudes to GBV, and attitudes to women earning more than men. This suggests a link between GBV, the two columns on the right; and patriarchal attitudes, the four numeric columns at about the middle of table 16. The attitudes of men (first and third numeric columns from the left) and of women (second and fourth numeric columns from the left) tend to increase as we go down the table: for example, only 2% of Asia East men think burning food is sufficient justification for GBV; whereas 11% of African men think burning food justifies GBV.

To examine a possible link between GBV and attitudes to women's behaviour, Table 17 reports evidence that GBV is related to attitudes to women's obedience. Table 17 uses WAS data for three countries (the question on obedience is not included in DHS surveys).

Table 17 indicates there is a link between two attitude questions: considering GBV acceptable if a wife argues with her husband, and attitude to a wife obeying her husband. Considering respondents in Cameroon, among those who agree that a wife should obey her husband, 17% felt GBV acceptable for arguing; only about half as many (8%) of Cameroonians accept GBV, if they disagree with the obedience statement. Similarly in Chad and Egypt: if the respondent thinks a wife should obey her husband, then the respondent is more likely to think GBV is acceptable (if she argues with him).

Table 16. Patriarchal attitudes and GBV risk, by geographical region

Survey: *respondent's gender:* Region:	% agree with 'if a woman earns more than her husband, it's almost certain to cause problems' WVS / WAS		% agree with 'is a husband justified in beating his wife if she burns the food' WVS / WAS		Wife has been beaten by her spouse DHS	Wife suffered severe violence from her spouse DHS	Years the wife spent in education DHS
	male	*female*	*male*	*female*	*female*	*female*	
Europe, N America, Oceania	39	41	1	2	18	10	13
Asia east	45	41	2	4	12	11	8
Latin America	51	55	3	4	27	21	7
Asia west	64	50	10	17	21	17	5
Africa	71	60	11	23	23	20	5
World	52	49	9	16	23	19	5

Source: WVS, DHS and WAS.

Table 17. Connection between attitude to GBV, and attitude to obedience

Survey	Respondent's agreement with the statement: 'A wife should always obey her husband'	Fraction who say GBV is justified if she argues with her husband	Number of cases
Cameroon 2009	Agree	17%	2922
	neither agree/disagree	5%	97
	Disagree	8%	448
Chad 2008	Agree	22%	2294
	neither agree/disagree	10%	52
	Disagree	9%	157
Egypt 2005-6	Agree	9%	4768
	neither agree/disagree	6%	109
	Disagree	6%	86

Source: WAS (men and women combined).

I expect most readers (being highly educated) will share my view that there is no justification for GBV; many writers find it appalling that so many women and men consider it acceptable for a man to hit his wife. To some observers, it may seem even worse that 'arguing with her husband' is seen as sufficient cause for GBV, because it suggests women are expected to obey their husband. In the right-hand column of Table 17, the number of cases indicates that in these three countries, almost all respondents agree that a wife should always obey her husband. As far as I am aware, such questions are not asked in developed countries: for example, this question was asked in some WVS surveys in Africa and Asia west - but not included in WVS surveys carried out in Europe, north America, or Oceania.

In summary, evidence in this chapter is consistent with the hypothesis that GBV is related to patriarchal attitudes. In particular, the risk of a female respondent experiencing GBV seems to be related to whether or not she says she thinks GBV is acceptable; but it is unclear about which is cause, and which is effect. There also appears to be a link between attitudes to GBV, and attitudes to other gender issues such as women obeying their husband.

REMEDY FOR PATRIARCHAL ATTITUDES: EDUCATION

In previous publications discussed earlier in this chapter, it was argued that education is a way of reducing GBV. Another possibility is that a woman can be protected from GBV if she earns sufficient income to support herself. However, among some publications discussed in this chapter, there has been a claim that many men feel uncomfortable about their wife being the main earner in the household: in such households, men often feel 'gender deviant', and this can lead to GBV. Hence, women's earnings may increase, rather than reduce, her risk of GBV. The following figures are intended to help us assess the most effective ways to prevent GBV associated with patriarchy: education, or women's earnings.

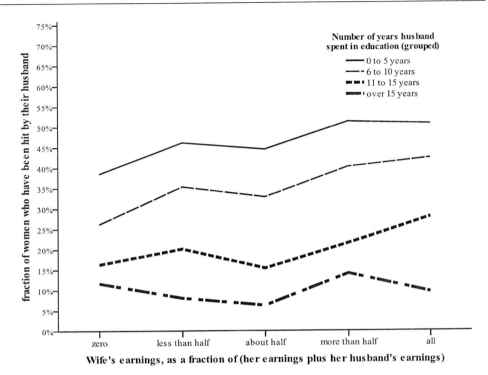

Source: DHS India 2005 (women respondents).

Figure 20. GBV and gender deviance neutralization, by education: India.

Figure 20 is an attempt to assess if education could solve the problem of GBV associated with 'gender deviance neutralization'. In my view, education does seem to solve the problem: if we compare the four lines in Figure 20, we see the line where the husband is more educated is near the bottom of the figure, indicating that more-educated husbands are less likely to be violent.

And encouragingly, this line is relatively flat: we do not see a large increase on the right hand side, where the wife earns more than half (or all) of the couple's joint income. Hence, education seems to reduce GBV in general (across the whole spectrum, from wife earns nothing on the left to wife earns all on the right). If (some) GBV is caused by gender deviance neutralization, then it appears to do so among the least-educated men (0 to 5 years' education): about 39% of such men committed GBV if their wife earned nothing, but about 51% of least-educated men carried out GBV if the wife was the main or only earner.

If education reduces the risk of GBV, what about women's earnings: do they protect women from GBV? Figure 20 suggests the opposite: the risk of GBV tends to increase, not to fall, as we go from left to right. We should be aware that the horizontal axis of Figure 20 is women's relative earnings, as opposed to her earnings expressed in (for example) Rupees per hour; but if we were to choose a way to reduce GBV, it seems that education is far more likely than women's employment to reduce the risk of a woman being beaten. The remainder of this chapter will ignore women's earnings as an influence on GBV risk, and focus on education.

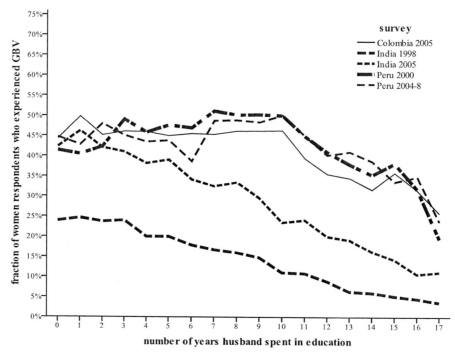

Source: DHS.

Figure 21. GBV risk by husband's education level, in the 5 largest DHS samples.

To assess whether or not education can reduce GBV, I show one figure combining the five largest DHS samples which include a (female) respondent's experience of GBV. I use DHS rather than WAS surveys, because DHS have much bigger sample sizes, and because WAS surveys use a much less detailed measure of education than DHS. I limit Figure 21 to only five surveys partly because they are among the clearest patterns for this type of figure (at least partly because of the large samples), and because putting more than five lines on this figure would make it less easy to interpret.

Figure 21 indicates a fairly clear tendency for education (of husbands) to reduce the risk of GBV (by wives). The right hand side of Figure 21 show households with the more educated husbands, and they tend to have less risk of GBV for the female respondents in those households. The pattern is not always linear: it appears that for the three south American surveys (in Colombia and Peru), the risk of GBV only starts to fall if the respondent's husband spent over ten years in education (this type of pattern has been referred to as a 'threshold' level of education, in some previous research: see the literature review of this chapter). Figure 21 suggests that for India, at least, educating men is an effective way to reduce the impact of this cause of GBV.

CONCLUSION

There seems widespread agreement among researchers that there is a strong link between education and the risk of GBV: there tends to be much lower risk of GBV among highly-educated people. But previous research is inconsistent: some studies find that a few years in school has little or no effect on a woman's risk of being hit by her husband. The link between education and violence may vary between countries. In countries studied in this chapter, there is clear evidence that education reduces the likelihood of respondents considering violence acceptable.

It appears that education of boys and men, and the education of girls and women, are generally beneficial in reducing the risk of GBV. Another consideration is that a woman's education may be less helpful, or could even be harmful regarding the risk of GBV, if she is more educated than her husband or partner.

Education seems to be related to patriarchy: traditional attitudes are less common among highly-educated respondents (according to surveys, such as WAS). If patriarchy is the problem which causes GBV, then education may be the best remedy. For education to reduce GBV in future, we need to ensure both male and female pupils stay at school, and (if possible) college or university, as long as possible. However, it would take decades for this remedy to work (when children now at school leave education, and become adults); it is very important to provide education for adults of all ages.

Chapter 8

EFFECTS OF FEMALE SECLUSION AND NOMADIC PASTORALISM ON GBV RISK

"Among the Yoruba of southwest Nigeria, husbands are referred to as 'olowo ori mi' (the one who owns me) by their wives. Among the Igbos of south east Nigeria, until a husband pays the bride price on his wife, the children whom the woman gives birth to belong to her father. The reason underlying this practice, it seems, is that the husband is yet to acquire the ownership of the 'machine for producing children'; the transfer of ownership is affected through the payment of the bride price" Ogunjuyigbe et al. (2005: 220).

ABSTRACT

This chapter investigates ethnic differences in attitudes to GBV. In particular, it studies a possible link between GBV and 'nomadic pastoralism', a type of extensive farming in which cattle are taken long distances in terms of pasture. Nomadic pastoralism is common in many parts of the world, including Africa; West Asia; and South America (Tangka et al., 2000: 9). If there is a link between GBV and nomadic pastoralism, it might be because of the nature of such farming (such as the need for physical strength of people who do cattle herding); or because of a common culture among the ethnic groups which spread through Africa and elsewhere in search of their livelihood. Other topics discussed in this chapter include female seclusion, and Islam.

INTRODUCTION

The main topic in this chapter is the possibility that GBV, and attitudes to GBV, may vary systematically between ethnic groups. Simister (2010) reported evidence that attitudes to GBV differ between ethnic groups in Kenya. If ethnic groups really are different in their GBV risk, it is not obvious *why* these ethnic groups differ; but evidence reported in this chapter suggests that female seclusion and nomadic cattle farming may explain much of the apparent difference in GBV prevalence between ethnic groups.

There are differences in GBV risks in different countries, as shown by the varying heights of lines in figure 21 (in chapter 7). Perhaps such differences in GBV prevalence can be explained by differences between ethnic groups.

CULTURAL DIFFERENCES REGARDING GBV

Amirthalingam (2005: 698-9) debates whether some cultures are more prone than other cultures, to have high rates of domestic violence. GBV prevalence rates appear to vary between ethnic groups: for example, in the USA, the 1995-6 'National violence against women' survey suggested a GBV prevalence rate of 13% among women from Asia/Pacific Islander backgrounds, compared with 26% for African Americans, and 31% for native Americans in Alaska (Johnson and Ferraro, 2000: 953). Simister (2010) found ethnic groups in Kenya differ greatly in their attitudes, regarding the acceptability of GBV.

There has been much debate about whether Islam has affected women's autonomy. For example, VerEecke (1989: 53) wrote "Among Africanists, some attention has also been paid to Muslim African women [..] Although many of these women's extra-domestic activities have been curtailed by Islam and by men who adhere literally to Islam's tenets and behavioural prescriptions, these studies emphasize how women can be highly active, especially in the economic domain. These activities are viewed as derived from traditional, pre-Islamic African social forms that have continued to operate within the confines of Islam." This suggests Islam harms women's interests, but Islam's impact has been limited by traditional African cultures. Comments by Callaway (1984: 436) seem consistent with this view: "The social position and ambiguous circumstances of Hausa women today are partly a consequence of the interplay between Islamic injunctions and indigenous Hausa culture which pre-dated Islam". But Callaway (1984: 436) also suggests that Islam has improved the position of Hausa women.

VerEecke (1989: 58-9) wrote about Fulani tribe (also known as Fulbe), "Islamic ideology and culture radically altered the world view and behavior of Fulbe women. Islam is highly prescriptive about nearly all aspects of life, penetrating into economic, political, and social domains. Thus, among Islamic societies from the Middle East to the West African Sudan, there are marked cultural and behavioral similarities. One of the many uniform aspects of Islamic culture is prescriptions for the position of women in relation to men. The Islamic view of women, which derives primarily from the Qur'an, has become elaborated as follows: men are socially and morally superior to women and can thus legitimately dominate them. [..] It is, therefore, the duty of men to provide for, guide, and exact obedience from women. If that fails, they can admonish or beat them." Callaway (1984: 436) quotes section 4:34 of the Koran: "Men have authority over women because Allah has made the one superior to the others, and because they spend their wealth to maintain them. Good women are obedient. [..] As for those from whom you fear disobedience, admonish them and send them to beds apart and beat them". This suggests Muslim men are generally more violent towards women than non-Muslims; but WAS Nigeria 2005 data rejects this suggestion: 6% of Muslim women had been beaten, compared with 12% of Christian women (the sample of respondents interviewed included 1,020 Christians and 1,259 Muslims). Further evidence on this topic is included later in this chapter, in the Nigeria case study.

It is sometimes claimed that Islam is harmful to women's interests in other ways, apart from GBV, such as women's paid employment. This is a complicated topic, according to Olmsted (2003: 83): "While a commonly held belief is that low labor force participation rates are somehow linked to Islam, some scholars have disputed this claim. A number of Islamic countries, particularly outside the Middle East, do not have low female participation rates".

Nadia Hijab and Ivy Papps argue that the role of religion as an influence on women's employment has been overstated (cited in Olmsted, 2003: 83). According to Callaway (1984: 444), many Nigerian Muslim women don't want 'liberation' in the Western sense – "Women believe the only rights they are entitled to are defined in the Koran or *Sharia*" (Callaway, 1984: 445).

FEMALE SECLUSION

'Female seclusion', or 'purdah', is where a woman does not leave her home, except with her husband – or, in some versions, accompanied by her children. Seclusion occurs in northern India, and in parts of northern Africa such as the north of Nigeria: for example, "Over 95 per cent of the married women in Kano City live in purdah" (Callaway, 1984: 431). Islam is often considered to be the cause of female seclusion: for example, many Muslim women in Northern Nigeria practice female seclusion (Lewis Wall, 1998; Callaway, 1984; Entwistle and Coles, 1990: 275-6); "Islamic beliefs concerning the proper rôle and behaviour of women emphasise that seclusion is the appropriate living arrangement for married women" (Callaway, 1984: 431). A proverb from northern Nigeria says "a good Muslim woman crosses the threshold of her husband's house twice; when she is brought in as a bride, and when she is carried out as a corpse" (Werthmann, 2002: 127).

VerEecke (1989: 59) wrote "In North Africa and the Mediterranean Arab world, this system centers around the themes as embodied in the concepts honor (sharaf in Arabic, daraja in Fulfulde), and shame ('ird in Arabic and semteende in Fulfulde). The concept of honor has been so prominent in these societies that it has been considered a dominant cultural theme or symbol (Meeker 1976). A family's honor is contingent upon honorable, respectable, and emulatable behavior: men in terms of their prestige or influence and women in their modesty and sense of shame. The honor of families is not a given but depends on the moral and virtuous behavior of its members. Any shameful act by a male member, such as adultery, verbal insult, or incest reduces the honor of a family. But even more devastating to a family's reputation are a woman's shameful acts, such as losing her virginity, exposing parts of her body, overt public display, and of course any illicit sexual act. One Islamic means of preventing this is to require women to be in full or partial seclusion (purdah)."

Female seclusion may be a tradition which started before Islam began (Callaway, 1984: 436). Purdah is more common among Muslims in northern Nigeria than among Muslims in southern Nigeria (Entwisle and Coles, 1990: 275); in most countries, Muslims do not practice female seclusion. Some writers claim some aspects of life we associate with Islam are actually part of Arabic culture (rather than religion), being transferred to areas such as north India and north Africa by the Mughal empire – perhaps this could include female seclusion. In Africa, some ethnic groups practise female seclusion, while others do not. Kritz and Makinwa-Adebusoye (1999: 421) study five ethnic groups in Nigeria, and find two ethnic groups in the north (Hausa and Kanuri) have a "clearly articulated set of norms regarding appropriate behaviors for women and those norms dictate that women should not participate in public life", which is very different to the three ethnic groups they study in southern Nigeria (Yoruba, Igbo, and Ijaw).

Jejeebhoy (1995: 45) claims that female seclusion limits women's autonomy. Many writers, such as Mason (1986: 296-7), consider segregated women to be victims of patriarchy; "those in purdah appear to be withdrawn, obedient, and deferent. Typically, their eyes are downcast, their smiles are rare, and their words are few" (Callaway, 1984: 431). Female seclusion limits women's income-earning activities in northern Nigeria; whereas local cultures in some southern Nigerian regions encourage women to earn substantial income (Entwistle and Coles, 1990: 275-6).

However, some writers have a less negative view of seclusion. Secluded women in northern Nigeria earn money by processing crops grown by their husband (Kabeer, 1994: 120). Some writers see advantages to women being in seclusion. According to Werthmann (2002: 119), female seclusion may "provide a means of protecting female spaces in which women pursue autonomous activities". Kintz (1986) claims a segregated woman tends to have higher social status than non-segregated woman. Some women may prefer not to leave home, to indicate that they have servants for tasks such as shopping. When a Fulani woman's husband entertains guests, "she chooses to show just a little of herself so that it escapes none of her guests' attention that she disappears immediately" (Kintz, 1986: 13). "A high-status Fulani woman will sometimes say, with visible satisfaction, 'I never go out of my courtyard'" (Kintz, 1989: 13).

The following section considers one possible explanation of why female seclusion is practised more by some ethnic groups than by others: nomadic farming.

NOMADIC PASTORALISM

Nomadic cattle farming, also called 'transhumance', refers to farming where cattle are transferred between different grazing areas, in different seasons: this sometimes involves taking livestock over long distances, for a period of weeks or months. It is practised in several parts of the world, for different reasons – including rainfall, and temperature. In south Nigeria, in the rainy season, Tsetse flies bite cattle and cause trypanosomiasis; many farmers take cattle from north to south Nigeria only when lack of tsetse-flies cuts the risk of trypanosomiasis (Fasona and Omojola, 2005: 14; Kalu, Oboegbulem and Uzoukwu, 2001). In such families, husbands and sons take cattle to places with good grazing; wives and daughters stay in north or east Nigeria (Kintz, 1989: 14). A man practising transhumance may fear his wife will be sexually active when he is away seeking pasture for cattle, and insist on female seclusion to prevent her being unfaithful (Callaway, 1984: 439; Werthmann, 2002: 121). Hence, nomadic pastoralism may explain female seclusion.

In contrast, rather than suggesting seclusion is an effect of nomadic pastoralism, VerEecke (1989: 54-5) implies seclusion is *less* common among nomads than among settled people, in the Fulani tribe in Adamawa: "nomadic women enjoy a considerable amount of social and economic freedom while their sedentary counterparts are, partially or fully, in *purdah* (seclusion)" (VerEecke, 1989: 54-5). However, VerEecke (1989: 56) warns that nomadic Fulani women are "dependent upon their husbands. These women's esteem is indeed quite negligible in comparison with their husband's. Men obtain honor (ndottaku) through age, honesty, knowledge, ownership of cows, and generosity, while women share their husbands status and honor. Women, for their part, get the virtue ndewaku from their domestic competence and servitude and essentially from their womanliness. They must gain self-satisfaction, reward, and dignity (ned'd'aaku) from their subservience (dewal) and obedience (nedi) to their husbands, for this is their primary role in the Fulbe community. Indeed, the word for woman debbo (pl. rewVe) derives from the root rew (follow, serve)".

Hodgson (1999: 41-2) argued that among East African pastoralists, including Masai, men's control of cattle gives them control over women in their household; but Masai women are not secluded (Hodgson, 1999: 47-9; Tangka et al., 2000: 14). If there is more control of women by men in some ethnic groups, it may be due to nomadic cattle farming rather than because of seclusion. Cohen and Vandello (1998: 570) wrote "Anthropologists note that herdsmen the world over tend to be quite vigilant against threats and encroachments because they are in a very precarious situation – that is, their livelihood can be rustled away from them instantly. Thus, to deter potential predators they adopt a tough, *"don't mess with me"* stance". Lott and Hart (1977) argue that in cattle-herding tribes such as the Fulani, dominance and aggression are essential to control cattle; and this affects behaviour towards other humans: Fulani males are socialised (from the age of 6) to be aggressive. Among the Masai tribe, "Cattle herding is seen to be too strenuous for girls" (Tangka et al., 2000: 15). Lott and Hart (1977: 175-6) claim that Fulani and other tribes such as Masai must be aggressive, because in a cattle herd, a dominant animal forces other animals to be subservient – and a Fulani herdsman needs to dominate the entire herd. "If a herdsman has the sort of personality needed to display sufficient aggression to maintain his position as dominant over all cattle in his herd, we might expect that his interactions with people would also involve assertive and aggressive behavior" (Lott and Hart, 1977: 177). In some locations, such as the Gabra tribe on the border of Kenya and Somalia, and the Tuareg tribe in Mali and Niger, pastoralists are at risk of attack from other groups of people (Rasmussen, 2009: 170). In societies where keeping cattle is the main source of food and income, this control over the family's livelihood may lead to male dominance of women; this might cause more men to use GBV (because male power is seen as normal); or may reduce GBV prevalence (if a man controls his wife because only he has access to income, he may not need to use GBV to have power over his wife).

Myres (1941) claimed that nomadic pastoralist tribes spread south from Egypt along the Nile, into east Africa, then along the Equatorial Highland into the Congo forest, and on as far as South Africa. Myres claimed that there are cultural similarities between a number of ethnic groups practising cattle farming – each tribe is "socially not very different in essentials from cattle-herders in Sudan and along the southern Sahara margin" (Myres, 1941: 27). This culture (including female seclusion) has also spread to former nomadic tribes who have now become settled. Myres (1941: 38) wrote "the custom of the desert intervened once more to create that fatal seclusion which has done more than anything else to keep society stagnant and futile all round the great Old World grasslands"; then, "the effects upon society may be foreseen; that attitude of men towards women which treats them as intrinsically weak, defenceless, and dependent upon the physical services of men" (Myres, 1941: 40). GBV prevalence, and attitudes to GBV, may be affected by such patterns of thought.

The above evidence indicates that nomadic pastoralism is associated with male control of cattle, which may give men power over women. However, it can be argued that there is no physical reason why women cannot be herders, because some women do herd cattle – in Somalia, for example (Tangka et al., 2000: 15). Many nomadic cattle-herders in Africa take a rifle or machine-gun to protect themselves and their herd from cattle thieves; but women can also use such weapons. This argument suggests the reason most cattle-herding is done by men is cultural, rather than biological.

Another argument relating patriarchy to cattle farming is the view that societies which are based on foraging tend to use matrilineal descent (property is inherited by a woman's family: e.g. when a man dies, his property is passed to his sister's sons); whereas pastoralist societies tend to be patrilineal (property is inherited to a man's family, e.g. the man's own sons). In this view, inheritance in each society is determined by local resources (e.g. can crops provide adequate food for a family, or is extensive faming with nomadic pastoralism the only way for a family to survive?). Aberle said "the cow is the enemy of matriliny" (cited in Holden et al., 2003: 100). Widespread use of matrilineal descent in some societies could be explained by the fact that in some societies, a man cannot be confident that his wife's children are genetically his offspring (because she may have been unfaithful to him); but other possible explanations have been put forward, such as 'daughter-biased investment', such as grandmothers investing in their granddaughters (Holden et al. 2003: 102).

In summary, the situation of women in some countries may be affected by female seclusion, or by nomadic cattle farming, or both; if men practise transhumance, they may insist their wife remain secluded, to avoid her being unfaithful. As a result, GBV prevalence may vary between ethnic groups in the same country.

THREE CASE STUDIES

This rest of this chapter chooses three countries, to investigate some of the factors which appear to be related to GBV. For these cases studies (Cameroon, Nigeria, and India), there are figures and tables which show differences within the country. Rather than give details of every country, this chapter looks in detail at three countries which seem to offer useful lessons about investigating GBV. For example, much of this chapter focuses on ethnic differences within a country, and uses respondent's language to determine ethnicity. Studying a country like Egypt would be less helpful, because almost everyone in Egypt speaks Arabic; there may be different ethnic groups within Egypt, but we cannot use language to distinguish one ethnic group from another.

Analysis of ethnicity is complicated by inter-related factors. For example, we could consider the word "Jew" to refer to a religious group; or to a cultural group (e.g. eating Kosher food); or to a racial group (because in many cases, a person is considered a Jew if and only if s/he has a Jewish mother); or to a 'tribe', based on a common language of Hebrew (although many Jews do not speak Hebrew; Yiddish is another language associated with Jewish people). Similarly, the word "Arab" could refer to people living in certain parts of the Middle East; or could refer to a person who speaks Arabic; or could refer to a person with a particular culture (we might expect an Arab to be a Muslim, but a member of another religion such as Coptic Christianity might also consider themselves an Arab).

In this book, I assume ethnicity can be assessed by a respondent's first language; this approach has been used in much previous research, but other methods could be used – for example, it would be possible to use racial differences such as skin colour (Fearon, 2003). Perhaps some observers assume racial differences such as height are 'objective', whereas ethnic differences such as architectural styles are 'subjective'; but there are controversies –

for example, some people claim a person should be called "black" or "African American" if they have a single drop of blood from a negro ancestor, but other people use the term 'mixed race' in such cases.

For simplicity, this book assumes there is one 'tribe' or 'ethnic group' for each language, but it could be argued that this oversimplifies ethnicity: for example, according to Fearon (2003: 197), it would be possible to include (almost) everyone in Somalia as 'Somali'; or a researcher could divide Somalis into different clans or sub-clans. Fearon (2003: 197) wrote "The nature of the concept of "ethnic group" is such that there can be multiple ways to specify the set of ethnic groups in a country, all of which include more-or-less equally valid "ethnic groups" ".

In Nigeria and Cameroon, the DHS and WAS surveys include dozens of ethnic groups; if we study small samples, we might be misled by random variation. For this chapter, I only report data on a tribe if at least 2,000 members of that tribe were interviewed, in DHS and WAS surveys combined (in that country). I chose this minimum sample of 2,000 cases because it makes tables and figures in this chapter look clear. If this minimum sample size were changed from 2,000 to 1,000 respondents, it would mean more rows on the tables, and more lines on the figures (in this chapter). For example, the 2004 DHS survey in Cameroon interviewed 18 respondents who described themselves as being members of the 'Efik' tribe; but these 18 people may not be typical of the Efik tribe as a whole.

In DHS and WAS surveys, I have not found any variable which (in my view) perfectly measures the extent of female seclusion in an ethnic group. To estimate which tribes practice female seclusion, I chose several 'proxy' measures, as explained below for Tables 18 and 20. For all tables in this chapter, I round each percentage to the nearest whole number (except that I use a decimal fraction, if a number is less than 1).

SURVEY EVIDENCE FROM CAMEROON

Cameroon is a country in central/west Africa, on the Atlantic coast. It is predominantly Christian (including Protestants and Roman Catholics), but a large minority are Muslims (about a fifth of the population). Over two hundred other languages are spoken in Cameroon; in some regions, English or French or Ewondo is often spoken as a second language, to improve communication. Cameroon is a poor country, but less poor than most African countries; it is geographically diverse, but no region is very developed economically.

To begin this investigation of ethnicity in Cameroon, let us assess whether or not there are noticeable differences between ethnic groups (as regards GBV). To study the link between GBV and ethnicity, first consider Figure 22.

It shows the respondent's education level on the horizontal axis, using a similar method to Figure 16 in chapter 7. On the horizontal axis, the number of years in education is grouped into four categories (least educated on the left, most educated on the right); this grouping makes the figures look clearer. Figure 16 had data on several countries, including Cameroon; whereas Figure 22 has data on Cameroon only, but dividing the Cameroon sample into seven tribes. Note an important distinction between figures in Chapter 7 and in this chapter: the vertical axis of Figure 16 showed attitude to GBV, whereas Figure 22 shows experience of GBV.

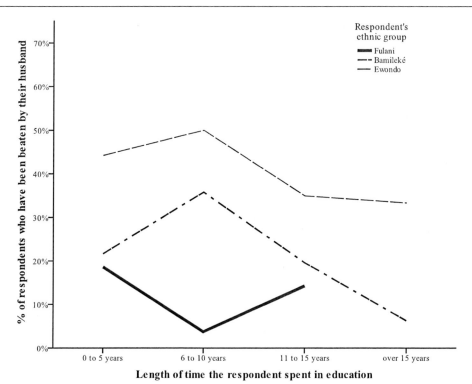

Source: DHS Cameroon 2004 (female respondents only).

Figure 22. GBV by ethnicity: Cameroon.

Figure 22 allows us to assess whether or not ethnicity is relevant to GBV. The answer, apparently, is yes: we can see the risk of a woman experiencing GBV is very different in different tribes, because the height of lines in Figure 22 varies between tribes. The Fulani line in Figure 22 is shorter than for the other two tribes – it does not extend to the right of '11 to 15 years', because no female Fulani respondents had over 15 years' education in the DHS 2004 Cameroon sample. Of these three tribes, Fulani have the lowest risk of GBV; and the Ewondo tribe have the highest risk.

In view of the importance of education to attitudes on GBV shown in Chapter 7, we might imagine any difference in GBV prevalence rates between tribes is due to different levels of education.

But Figure 22 controls for education level (on the horizontal axis); so education does not explain the difference between tribes. So, *why* does GBV prevalence differ between ethnic groups? Next, consider the possibility that female seclusion and/or nomadic pastoralism, as discussed earlier in this chapter, could be the explanation.

Table 18 has four numeric columns, each representing a factor which might be related to female seclusion; I call each of these a 'proxy' for female seclusion. The first such 'proxy' is the fraction of respondents who describe themselves as 'Muslim'. As discussed earlier in this chapter, many writers associate female seclusion with Islam (although other writers question this association: complications include the fact that seclusion may have occurred in some tribes before Islam began; many Hindus in India practice seclusion; and many Muslims do not practice seclusion – such complications are discussed below).

Table 18. Different proxy measures of female seclusion, by ethnic group: Cameroon

Ethnic group	Muslim fraction in the sample (%)	Female respondent cannot leave home (%)	Only men shop (%)	Husband manages family money (%)
Fulani	99	56	18	79
Bamileké	1	41	2	31
Ewondo	1	22	3	30

Sources: DHS 2004; WAS 2009.

In Table 18, we see a very clear distinction between the Fulani tribe, almost all of whom are Muslims; and the other two tribes (Bamileké and Ewondo), almost none of whom are Muslims.

Respondents in the 2009 WAS survey in Cameroon were asked "Are you usually allowed to go outside the house without asking someone (on your own, only with children, only with another adult, or not at all)?" For married women, I treat responses 'not at all' or 'only with children' or 'only with another adult' as implying female seclusion; and women who replied 'on your own', I classify as 'not secluded'. The second numeric column in Table 18 shows the fraction of married or cohabiting women who were 'not secluded' using this definition. There is a difference between ethnic groups – Fulani women are the most likely to say they cannot leave home alone; but the difference in prevalence of inability to leave home between tribes is nowhere near as dramatic as the ethnic differences in the Muslim column on the left. This seems to reject a simple association between Islam and female seclusion: it is not correct to claim that all Muslim women are secluded; and it is not correct to say that all secluded women are Muslims. There may be a correlation between Islam and female seclusion, but Islam is not the only influence on female seclusion.

The next proxy for female seclusion is the 'Only men shop' column, based on time-use data. In the 2009 WAS Cameroon survey, each respondent was asked the average number of hours per week they, and their spouse, spend shopping for food. For this chapter, a household is classified as 'Only men shop' if the husband spends more than zero hours per week, while the wife spends zero hours. If both spouses spend time on food shopping, or if only the wife buys food, these are not classified as 'Only men shop' households. If neither husband nor wife spends time on food shopping, the household is excluded from this column of Table 18. The resulting percentage in this column could vary from zero to 100%, but in Cameroon we only see a maximum of 18%, for the Fulani tribe. Hence, in this proxy measure, we might argue that 18% of Fulani households appear to practice female seclusion. However, other evidence in Table 18 casts doubt on this claim, as explained below. There are reasons to be wary of interpreting the 'Only men shop' column as female seclusion: for example, it is possible that both spouses are employed outside the house, but the husband passes a food shop on his way home from work each day.

The third proxy for female seclusion in Table 18 is labelled 'husband manages family money' (the right-hand column in Table 18); it is derived from Question 2 in the 2009 WAS Cameroon survey: "Which of these is nearest to the way regular household expenses are done in your household?" Respondents were asked to choose one answer, from this list: 'Husband usually looks after all expenses'; 'Wife usually looks after all expenses'; 'Husband and wife manage expenses together'; 'Husband and wife manage expenses separately'; and 'Other'.

Similar questions were asked in other WAS surveys, and in DHS surveys. To calculate the percentage in the right-hand column of Table 18, I consider the first response above to be 'husband managed'; and the other four responses to be 'not husband managed'. I use this variable as a proxy for female seclusion, because I feel household budgeting for everyday shopping is a chore – hence, most men would not do such budgeting, unless they also did the shopping. This assertion is questionable: we might consider financial management as a form of patriarchal control, in which men retain power over spending decisions – if so, husband financial management might apply in all ethnic groups, in every country. Pahl (1995) discusses such issues in the UK context. The right-hand column of Table 18 suggests that husband-managed finances occur in the majority (79%) of Fulani households, but in a minority of households in the other two ethnic groups in Table 18.

We can now consider Table 18 as a whole: in particular, have we learnt anything about female seclusion? If we ask which tribe is most likely to practice female seclusion, the three columns suggest a consistent answer: Fulani. Presumably we would not expect all members of the Fulani tribe to practise female seclusion, but it is not clear from Table 18 what fraction of women is secluded. The huge difference between percentages in different columns (Muslim; 'Female respondent cannot leave home'; 'only men shop'; and 'husband manages family money') casts doubt on this use of proxy variables: these columns cannot all be perfect estimates of female seclusion, because they differ from each other. Perhaps none of these proxies can be trusted. More research on this topic might be helpful.

The 2009 WAS Cameroon survey included a question about cattle farming (this wasn't asked in any other WAS or DHS survey): "Do men in your household take cattle away from home for several months each year?" Accepted answers were either 'yes' or 'no'. The questionnaire included an explanation for the interviewer: "This is transhumance, or nomadic pastoralism: it means taking cattle to grazing lands each year, and usually only applies in rural areas". Only 55 respondents said "yes" to this question; almost all respondents (3432 out of 3500 respondents) said "no", and 13 said "don't know". I consider this set of 55 cases is too small to analyse for this book. However, there may be some tribes in Cameroon who formerly practised transhumance; in such tribes, attitudes towards GBV today may still reflect values associated with nomadic cattle farming in previous generations (due to childhood socialisation) – even if many members of those tribes now live in cities.

Table 19. Prevalence of GBV and attitudes to GBV, by ethnic group: Cameroon

Ethnic group	Respondents who say refusing sex with husband justifies GBV (%)		Respondent has been slapped by her husband (%)	Respondent has been punched by her husband (%)	Respondent has been kicked or dragged by her husband (%)
	women	men	women	women	women
Fulani	40	20	16	7	1
Bamileké	11	8	28	13	7
Ewondo	15	12	42	24	16

Sources: DHS 2004; WAS 2009.

Table 19 reports attitudes to GBV, among male and female respondents. The first two numeric columns are attitudes of men and women, based on the question: *"Sometimes a husband is annoyed or angered by things that his wife does. In your opinion, is a husband justified in hitting or beating his wife in the following situations: If she refuses to have sex with him?"* It seems shocking that anyone would endorse this view, but many women and men in Cameroon do agree with it. We see more acceptance of GBV among Fulani, than in other tribes: 40% of women, and 20% of men, think GBV is acceptable if a woman refuses sex with her husband among Fulani respondents (compared with 15% or less, for respondents in the other two tribes).

Table 19 also reports GBV prevalence rates, for the same three tribes. Surprisingly, we now see the opposite pattern to attitudes: this time (compared to the other two tribes), Fulani women are *less* likely to experience GBV, despite the fact that Fulani women and men are both *more* likely to find GBV acceptable. I find this a surprising result; it is discussed in the following section, for Nigeria.

SURVEY EVIDENCE FROM NIGERIA

Nigeria is a country in north-west Africa, adjacent to Cameroon. Nigeria is one of the largest economies in Africa: as well as having the largest population of any African country, Nigeria is more economically successful than most African countries (due to petroleum, for example). However, Nigeria is associated with crime and corruption (often associated with the oil industry). Nigeria has a dramatic contrast, between the Muslim north and Christian south. Many of the northern states within Nigeria have adopted *sharia* law. There are sometimes religious conflicts between Muslims and Christians, such as over the 2002 'Miss World' competition; many Muslims were angered by press comments on how the prophet would have perceived the event.

To give an introduction to ethnic differences in GBV prevalence in Nigeria, consider Figure 23. In Figure 23, three lines (at the bottom of the figure) are thicker than for other tribes: I made the Fulani, Hausa, and Kanuri lines thicker, to highlight them: these three tribes have much lower GBV prevalence than the other tribes in Figure 23.

In order to process language data in WAS and DHS household surveys, I adopted the Ruhlen language classification system, as explained in Ruhlen (1987). An on-line summary of the Ruhlen language classification system is available at the website www.ling.hawaii.edu/faculty/stampe/Linguistics/Ruhlen/ruhlen.html In the Ruhlen system, there are 17 categories, each one called a 'phylum':

- Khoisan [31]
- Niger-Kordofanian [1064]
- Nilo-saharan [138]
- Afro-Asiatic [241]
- Caucasian [38]
- Indo-Hittite [144]
- Uralic-Yukaghir [24]
- Altaic [63]

- Chukchi-Kamchatkan [5]
- Eskimo-Aleut [9]
- Elamo-Dravidian [28]
- Sino-Tibetan [258]
- Austric (Miao-yao), Austroasiatic, Austro-tai (Daic, Austronesian)) [1175]
- Indo-pacific [731]
- Australian [170]
- Na-dene [34]
- Amerind [583]
- other (language isolates, unclassified, pidgins and creoles, invented)

In the above list of 17 categories, the number in square brackets at the end of the name is the number of language groups in that phylum (excluding extinct languages). For example, in the Khoisan phylum, there are 31 language groups (Hadza, Sandawe, Southern Africa, Northern, Central, Nama, Hai.n//um, Kwadi, Tshu-khwe, Northeast, North-central, Central, Northwest, Southwest, Southern, Ta'a, !Wi).

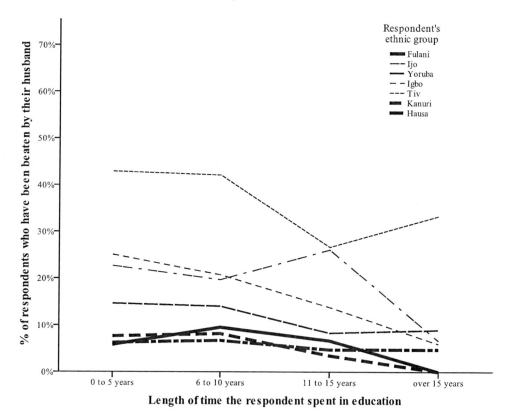

Source: DHS Nigeria 2008 (female respondents only).

Figure 23. GBV by ethnicity: Nigeria.

There is at least one language in each Ruhlen language group: for example, within the Khoisan 'North-Central' language group, there are three languages (Ganade, Shua, and Danisin). Merritt Ruhlen designed this classification for languages, rather than for cultures; if the reader rejects the assumption that there is a separate culture for each language, then this Ruhlen system may seem inappropriate. For example, Franz Boas argued that there is not always a one-to-one correspondence between race and culture; or between language and culture; or between language and race (Ottenheimer, 2009: 8). There are other methods of classifying cultures, such as the 'cultural map of the world' developed by Inglehart and Welzel (2011).

I devised a numeric system of language codes for WAS and DHS surveys, based on the above Ruhlen language classification (detals are available on the WAS website). The order of languages in the legend of Figure 23 is based on the order in which they appear in my numeric version of the Ruhlen classification system. Fulani, Ijo, Yoruba, Igbo, and Tiv are in the Niger-Kordofanian phylum (this phylum is associated with Senegal). On the other hand, Hausa is in the Afro-Asiatic phylum; and Kanuri is in the Nilo-saharan phylum. The fact that Hausa and Kanuri are adjacent in the Figure 23 legend is not meaningful, because the Hausa language is completely unrelated to the Kanuri language; and neither Hausa nor Kanuri is related to the Fulani language. Fulani and Hausa and Kanuri *cultures* seem similar to each other (see below), but they are not related *languages* – so the cultural similarity does not appear to be the result of evolution of these three languages from a common ancestral language. Hence, Figure 23 does not provide any evidence that these three cultures (Fulani, Hausa and Kanuri) evolved from a common ancestral culture, as Myres and others have claimed (in the literature review, earlier in this chapter).

Note that the order of lines in the legend of figures such as Figure 23 is not the same as the order of rows in tables 20 and 21. As explained below, I attempt to sort the rows in each table in this chapter according to the fraction of women who are secluded in that tribe.

Table 20. Different proxy measures of female seclusion, by ethnic group: Nigeria

Ethnic group	Muslim fraction in the sample (%)	Only men shop (%)	Husband manages family money (%)	Respondents saying a wife without children should not work outside home (%)		Own cows (%)
				Woman	Man	
Kanuri	97	43	83	22	33	43
Hausa	98	45	82	26	41	33
Fulani	99	36	81	34	55	65
Yoruba	41	6	36	2	4	1
Tiv	0	3	35	9	12	1
Ijo	0	9	33	3	6	0
Igbo	0	4	28	4	6	1

Sources: DHS 2008; WAS 2003 and 2005.

Next, Table 20 reports evidence on different ethnic groups in Nigeria, using a similar approach to the method used for Cameroon (in Table 18). Table 20 has data on seven tribes (the same seven tribes as in Figure 23). The four columns on the left of Table 20 are defined in the same way as the columns in Table 18; with the addition of three extra columns, which are explained below. The rows in Table 20 are sorted by the fourth column, i.e. the fraction of households which use financial control by husbands.

Beginning with the Muslim column in Table 20, we see dramatic differences between tribes. Three ethnic groups are almost entirely Muslim: Kanuri, Hausa, and Fulani. In the other four tribes in Table 20, Muslims are a minority – and usually a very small fraction of the population (Yoruba is unusual, in that about half of the tribe are Muslims).

The 'only men shop' column suggests three tribes at the top of Table 20 (Kanuri, Hausa and Fulani) are most likely to practise female seclusion; these three tribes also have a large fraction (over 80%) of households with 'husband managed' finances. There is a fairly close match between these three tribes, and the fraction which are Muslim; but this match isn't perfect (there is more variation in the Muslim column, than in the other columns).

The fifth, sixth, and seventh columns in Table 20 contain data which are not in Table 18 (because such data are not available in DHS or WAS surveys in Cameroon, but were included in Nigeria surveys). The fifth and sixth columns of Table 20 are responses to attitude question in WAS Nigeria 2003 and 2005 surveys: *"Please tell me if a woman should work outside the home full time, part time, or not at all ... after marrying and before having children"*. Possible answers were *'not at all'*, *'part time'*, or *'full time'*. I assign a code of 1 for 'not at all', or a code of zero for 'part time' or 'full time'. If a respondent approved of female seclusion, we might expect them to say 'not at all'; but note that respondent's *preferences* on female seclusion are not the same as whether or not the household *practised* female seclusion (for example, a husband might force his wife to practice seclusion against her wishes).

If we now consider which ethnic groups consider women's employment inappropriate, three tribes stand out: Kanuri, Hausa and Fulani – the top three rows in Table 20. Hence, there seems to be a reasonably close match between this attitude question, and other columns in Table 20. I think this attitude question could be used as a proxy for female seclusion; but the match between these two attitude columns and the other proxy variables in Table 20 (Muslims; only men shop; and husband manages family money) is far from perfect.

The right-hand column in Table 20 is intended to explore the possibility (discussed in the literature review of this chapter) that female seclusion is somehow related to cattle farming: in particular, nomadic pastoralism. The right-hand column includes the fraction of respondents who said their household own cattle; but according to VerEecke (1989: 54), cattle are owned by both Fulani nomadic pastoralists, and settled Fulani farmers. I am not aware of data in DHS or WAS surveys in Nigeria which would tell us which, if any, of these households practise *nomadic* pastoralism, as opposed to settled cattle farming. We see an apparent match between the right-hand column, and the 'only men shop' column, of Table 20: in both columns, the top three tribes stand out.

Table 20 is generally consistent with previous research in Nigeria. It has been reported that female seclusion is practised by several tribes (in northern Nigeria), including Hausa (Kritz and Makinwa-Adebusoye, 1999: 403; Werthmann, 2002; Yeld, 1960: 128); Fulani (Kintz, 1989: 14); and Kanuri (Kritz and Makinwa-Adebusoye, 1999: 403). Kintz (1986: 13) claimed that some Yoruba women practise seclusion, whereas other Yoruba women do not. Among other Nigerian ethnic groups, I have found little evidence of female seclusion.

GBV is considered more acceptable in north Nigeria than in the south of Nigeria, according to Oyediran and Isiugo-Abanihe (2005). Ogunjuyigbe et al. (2005: 227) contrast the fraction of men who considered GBV acceptable in southwest Nigeria, 22%, with the much *lower* fraction considering GBV acceptable (6%) in eastern Nigeria (Okemgbo, cited in

Ogunjuyigbe et al., 2005: 227). The Ogunjuyigbe et al. fieldwork was in Osun and Ondo states; DHS and WAS data (combined) suggest about 55% of Osun residents, and about 9% of Ondo residents, are Muslims. If there are regional differences in acceptance of GBV within Nigeria, we might expect to find regional differences in GBV prevalence. Ogunjuyigbe et al. (2005: 227) contrast the relatively low GBV prevalence of 19% they found in southwest Nigeria, with the much *higher* prevalence (79%) Okemgbo found in eastern Nigeria; it is not clear if this is related to Muslim versus non-Muslim populations. This evidence is complicated, but suggests it may be worth investigating differences in GBV within Nigeria. This question can be studied using Table 21.

To interpret Table 21, it is helpful to consider the similarities between Kanuri, Hausa, and Fulani rows in Table 20 (the three Muslim tribes). If we look at these top three tribes, we see from the three columns on the right of Table 21 that they are *less* likely to experience GBV (compared with the other four tribes). This applies to each type of GBV in this table: women being slapped, punched, or kicked/dragged by their husband.

By considering Tables 20 and 21 together, it can be argued that lower risk of GBV in Nigeria is associated with (proxies for) female seclusion, and with ownership of cattle. Hence, Table 21 is similar to Figure 23. Looking at the two attitude columns of Table 21, the top three tribes in the table (Kanuri, Hausa, and Fulani) have a higher acceptance of GBV among women, compared to the other four tribes (except that Tiv is slightly higher than Kanuri).

It appears that women are *more* accepting of GBV, among the three Muslim tribes which use *less* GBV. I find this counter-intuitive, and I cannot explain it; but a similar pattern is clear in Cameroon, in Table 19.

The pattern in male attitudes to GBV, as regards Kanuri, Hausa, and Fulani tribes (compared with the other four tribes in Table 21), is weaker than for female attitudes; but again, men in tribes with lower GBV prevalence tend to be more likely to consider GBV justified, if the wife refuses sex.

Table 21. Prevalence of GBV and attitudes to GBV, by ethnic group: Nigeria

Ethnic group	Respondents who say refusing sex with husband justifies GBV (%)		Respondent has been slapped by her husband (%)	Respondent has been punched by her husband (%)	Respondent has been kicked or dragged by her husband (%)
	women	men	women	women	women
Kanuri	38	46	7	1	2
Hausa	46	16	6	1	1
Fulani	48	21	6	1	1
Yoruba	10	6	13	4	4
Tiv	39	24	41	10	25
Ijo	18	9	25	8	9
Igbo	15	8	22	9	9

Source: DHS (1998 and 2005); WAS (1997, 2002 and 2007).

In summary, it appears that there are differences between tribes in Nigeria, as regards GBV prevalence. These differences do not seem random – rather, there is strong a tendency for the three tribes with most female seclusion to have low GBV prevalence, but more acceptance of a man's right to use GBV.

SURVEY EVIDENCE FROM INDIA

India is the second-largest population in the world (after China). Despite a rich cultural heritage, India has been poor for centuries. In recent years, India has achieved impressive rates of economic growth; but there is still much inequality – and hence, much poverty – in India.

About half of India's population live in rural areas, and live similar lives to previous generations; whereas the other half of India's population live in cities, and often live lives similar to European and north America residents.

Different parts of India are very diverse – for example, there are deserts in western India; the wettest place on earth in eastern India; a polar climate in parts of the Himalayas; and extremely hot weather in southern India. India's population is mainly Hindu, with a fairly large minority of Muslims and a smaller fraction of other religions including Christianity.

Domestic violence can be understood better if seen in the context of local culture. For example, in Rajasthan, "Men feel that a woman has to be controlled and kept at home so that society does not say that women in the household are undisciplined" (Satish Kumar, Gupta and Abraham, 2002: 9); they report that in Rajasthan, masculinity is associated with a man being "provider; protector; and procreator"; other admired qualities for Rajasthani men include courage; violence (e.g. killing other men); having children, and ability to afford to bring them up (Satish Kumar, Gupta and Abraham, 2002: 8). However, other Indian states are unlike Rajasthan. For example in Kerala, a state in southern India, women have far more autonomy than women most of India (Simister, 2011a). To investigate possible differences between ethnic groups in India, I begin with Figure 24: this is similar to Figures 22 and 23.

Perhaps values in Rajasthan are comparable with 'machismo' or "macho" values (the term 'machismo' is usually associated with Latin America). Some writers use 'machismo' to refer to men who try to be aggressive and virile (ICRW, 2002: 2); such a culture expects women to follow 'Marianismo' (like the mother of Christ) and/or 'hembrismo' (strong and persevering) behaviour (Aranda, Castaneda, Lee and Sobel, 2001: 44).

Figure 24 tells us that there are clear differences between ethnic groups, even if we control for education levels of the respondent. However, it is not clear what explains these differences.

There was a relatively clear pattern in Figures 22 and 23, that the Muslim tribes had much lower GBV prevalence than other tribes; but this pattern is not found in India. Perhaps Table 22 may clarify some of these issues.

Table 22 reports some measures of female seclusion. It is a complicated table, partly because of the large number of rows. There are gaps, due to missing data: for example, the second, fourth, and fifth numeric columns (from the left) are only included in WAS surveys, which have much smaller sample sizes than the DHS 1998 and DHS 2005 surveys of India.

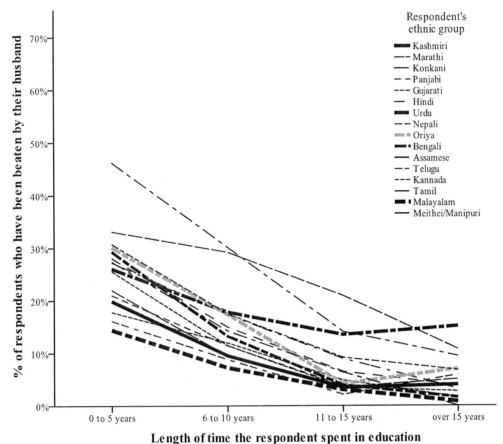

Source: DHS (1998 and 2005); WAS (2007). Female respondents only.

Figure 24. GBV by ethnicity: India.

This table is sorted in the order of 'husband manages family money' column, but (unlike the equivalent Tables 18 and 20 for Cameroon and Nigeria, earlier in this chapter) there is relatively little variation between ethnic groups in this column, for most tribes. There is little correlation between the 'Respondent cannot leave home' and 'Husband manages family money' columns (unlike Tables 18 and 20).

There is no data for Malayalam in Table 23, but this row is retained to simplify comparison with Table 22. I cannot see a pattern in Table 23, of the type seen in Tables 19 and 21 for Cameroon and Nigeria (GBV prevalence, and acceptance of GBV). Table 23 warns us not to expect a simple pattern: for research into GBV risk and attitudes to GBV, there may be differences between countries. Perhaps future research will explain why India seems unlike Cameroon and Nigeria, as regards ethnic variations in GBV prevalence and acceptance of GBV.

Table 22. Different proxy measures of female seclusion, by ethnic group: India

Ethnic group	Muslim fraction in the sample (%)	Only men shop (%)	Female respondent cannot leave home (%)	Respondents saying a wife without children shouldn't work outside home (%)		Husband manages family money (%)	Own cows (%)
			woman	woman	man		
Bengali	26	48	53	20	33	39	32
Urdu	98		70			35	7
Kashmiri	98		29			34	59
Oriya	1	45	76	24	31	33	46
Malayalam	30	27	17	4	13	33	
Telugu	3	41	53	11	21	29	17
Kannada	1		62			28	40
Hindi	14	19	62	20	29	23	43
Assamese	22		34			22	39
			woman	woman	man		
Panjabi	2	17	49	0	0	21	50
Marathi	1	8	49	17	27	20	22
Tamil	3	9	43	18	28	19	14
Konkani	2		31			17	15
Gujarati	7	0	42	31	22	15	35
Nepali	0		42			13	44
Meithei	13		24			7	16

Source: DHS and WAS.

CONCLUSION

Patriarchy is a global system, and GBV is a fundamental element of patriarchy: male violence against women is one way in which women are prevented from achieving equality with men. This is a two-way process: patriarchy also causes GBV to continue, by leading women and men to think that GBV is 'normal' or even 'appropriate' behaviour.

If we focus on Cameroon and Nigeria, there are clear differences between ethnic groups as regards their attitudes to GBV. This does not appear to be random data: the three Muslim tribes in Nigeria (Fulani, Hausa and Kanuri) seem to be associated with lower GBV prevalence, and lower acceptance of GBV, among women. This does not appear to apply in India, where ethnic differences seem more random.

If tribes differ in GBV prevalence rates, it would be useful to know why; this chapter suggests that female seclusion, associated with nomadic pastoralism – as practised by some tribes (such as Fulani, Hausa, and Kanuri) – may explain the apparently non-linear relationship between women's education and GBV prevalence, shown in Figure 24 and perhaps also noticed by some of the previous researchers discussed in the literature review of this chapter.

This chapter also tries to explain effects of ethnicity on GBV. Ethnicity seems relevant to GBV prevalence; this may be because female seclusion and nomadic cattle farming are practised in some ethnic groups. It is not clear from evidence in this paper if seclusion or pastoralism is more important; these two practices appear to be inter-related.

Societies and cultures change. Perhaps the end of patriarchy is some way off, but women have achieved some impressive steps in recent decades (for example, women can now vote in most countries). There is every reason to work for an end to GBV.

Table 23. Prevalence of GBV and attitudes to GBV, by ethnic group: India

Ethnic Group	Respondents who say refusing sex with husband justifies GBV (%)		Respondent has been slapped by her husband (%)	Respondent has been punched by her husband (%)	Respondent kicked or dragged by her husband (%)
	Women	Men	Women	Women	Women
Bengali	11	7	31	10	10
Urdu	12	5	28	7	7
Kashmiri	34	22	13	5	4
Oriya	13	7	31	11	13
Malayalam					
Telugu	24	9	31	11	12
Kannada	28	10	19	7	7
Hindi	9	6	34	11	10
Assamese	9	4	34	12	8
Panjabi	15	7	23	9	8
Marathi	13	10	27	5	8
Tamil	15	7	43	12	21
Konkani	9	7	15	5	4
Gujarati	18	12	24	6	9
Nepali	10	8	15	6	6
Meithei/Manipuri	15	6	43	9	8

Source: DHS and WAS.

Chapter 9

GBV Is Associated with Childhood Socialization

[In India], "Socialization ensures that women accept their subservient roles in the household and perpetuate the discrimination against their female offspring [..] ideology stresses male superiority within the household and places the women under the control of men throughout her life" (Bhattacharya, 2000: 22).

Abstract

Many researchers have found an association between the way a child is brought up, and the way that person behaves when she or he is an adult. For example, CDCP and ORC Macro (2003: 213) wrote "history of witnessing or experiencing abuse as a child is a well-known predictor of adult violence". This chapter reports evidence on the effect of childhood socialisation on attitudes held by the person when they become adult. In particular, this chapter considers the importance of role models as influences on children. The type of role models considered here are female political leaders, but it seems plausible that other types of role model (such as film stars, or sportsmen and women) may also have influences. Another type of evidence is based on whether or not an adult says they experienced domestic violence between their parents.

Introduction

This chapter assesses the claim (made by various writers discussed in this chapter) that the risk of GBV is related to the experiences children have when young. In this chapter, two aspects of childhood socialization are discussed. The first topic is that if a boy sees GBV happening on a regular basis (for example, if his father hits his mother), then he is likely to think of GBV as normal behavior; this may make him more likely to grow up to become a man who hits his wife. Similarly, if a girl sees GBV occurring frequently, she may come to think of GBV as acceptable, and (when she grows up to become a woman) accept GBV from her husband.

A second aspect of childhood socialization discussed in this chapter is the possible influence of a female head of state. The example studied here is Indira Gandhi in India; it seems plausible that women prime ministers and presidents in other countries may also act as important influences on children in their formative years.

Johnson and Ferraro (2000: 955) claim that psychologists studying GBV can be divided into two groups: some of these psychologists use feminist analysis; the other psychologists focus on the childhood development of boys who go on to become violent to their partner when they become adults. However, analysis of data by previous researchers suggests that the fraction of GBV explained by childhood socialization is small: only 1% or 2% in some studies (Johnson and Ferraro, 2000: 958) – hence, childhood socialization may be a useful topic to study, but we should not expect it to explain most GBV. Johnson and Ferraro (2000: 958) disagree with the assumption (by many social scientists) that violent men have children who will become violent when they grow up.

IIPS and ORC Macro (2000: 71) wrote "In patriarchal societies such as India, women are not only socialized into being silent about their experience of violence but traditional norms teach them to accept, tolerate, and even rationalize domestic violence". This chapter discusses some possible remedies to the problem of GBV being passed from one generation to the next.

No doubt there are many other aspects of childhood socialization which are relevant to GBV, but which are not examined in this chapter. This book does not go into details on adult socialization, but this is (in my opinion) also highly relevant to the risk of GBV occurring in a particular household.

GBV RISK AND WITNESSING GBV WHEN A CHILD

There is compelling evidence that ideas absorbed by children will go on to affect their behavior, when they become adults. For example, referring to data from Eastern Europe and Eurasia, CDCP and ORC Macro (2003: 213) wrote "Among ever-married women who reported having witnessed abuse in the home as a child, the prevalence of having been physically abused during the past 12 months was almost three times as high as the prevalence among those who had not witnessed abuse in their childhood home". The following Table 24 also uses DHS data to assess this – but for more countries.

Hindin et al. (2008: 23) wrote "Nearly all studies that have included a variable on witnessing interparental violence have found this experience to be a risk factor for women experiencing violence". This claim is confirmed by Table 24, which indicates a dramatic difference in GBV prevalence rates among respondents, depending on whether or not the (female) respondent had seen her father beat her mother.

Using a weighted average of all countries in Table 24, among respondents who had *not* seen her father beat her mother, 20% had experienced GBV herself; among respondents who *had* seen their father beat their mother, this prevalence rate more than doubled to 41%. For every country in Table 24, the risk of the respondent experiencing GBV is much higher if she said her father beat her mother. This appears to suggest childhood socialisation is relevant to GBV; but it is not proof – there are many other possible factors, which might mislead us. For example, if GBV prevalence rates were very different in working-class and middle-class families, we might find a respondent had a similar experience of GBV to her mother because both respondent and mother were in the same social class.

Table 24. GBV prevalence, by country and if respondent's father beat her mother

Country	Whether or not the (female) respondent's father beat her mother	
	No	Yes
Azerbaijan	8%	22%
Bangladesh	40%	70%
Cameroon	30%	52%
Colombia	25%	41%
Dominican Republic	15%	29%
Ghana	17%	33%
Haiti	11%	17%
India	21%	48%
Kenya	22%	46%
Cambodia	11%	23%
Liberia	27%	51%
Moldova	14%	32%
Mali	1%	4%
Malawi	15%	26%
Nigeria	12%	37%
Peru	26%	42%
Philippines	10%	20%
Rwanda	20%	33%
Sao Tome and Principe	24%	36%
Ukraine	9%	32%
Uganda	36%	54%
Zambia	34%	49%
Zimbabwe	21%	35%
Total	20%	41%

Source: DHS.

GBV AND CHILDHOOD EXPERIENCE OF FEMALE PRIME MINISTER

This section studies GBV, and acceptance of domestic violence, in India, using data from DHS India 2005. It investigates the effects of childhood socialisation on attitudes towards domestic violence against women, and considers evidence that children are socialised at about 5 years old in their attitudes to GBV. For this section on child socialisation, the Indian subcontinent is a fascinating place to study, when considering possible effects of female role models. The world's first woman Prime Minister was Sirimavo Bandaranaike of Ceylon; other pioneers included Indira Gandhi, Prime Minister of India; Benazir Bhutto, President of Pakistan; and female prime ministers in Bangladesh. The following figures and tables are based on household surveys in India, described above. Note that some figures refer to President Bandaranaike of Ceylon (now called Sri Lanka), because the attitudes of people in India may be affected by women in positions of power in a neighbouring country.

Figure 25 is based on data on female respondents. The horizontal axis is the age at which the respondent's husband was 5 years old (based on the year and month of interview, and age of husband at the time of interview): my research (not reported here) suggests that this is a critical age.

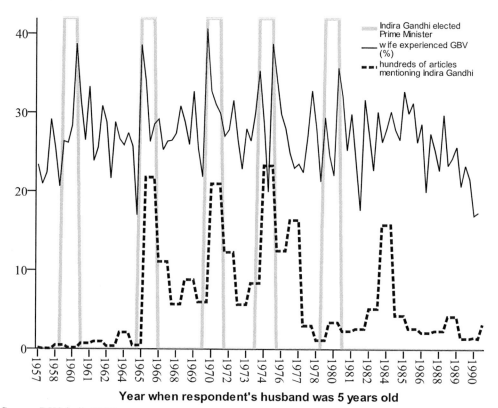

Source: DHS India 2005.

Figure 25. GBV prevalence, by year of birth of husband.

The grey vertical bands indicate the years when Indira Ghandi became Prime Minister of India – in 1966, 1971, 1975 (when she declared a state of emergency), and 1980. I also show another marker for 1960, when Sirimavo Bandaranaike was elected prime minister of Sri Lanka, on the assumption that this was comparable in its effects on childhood socialisation. I show each one as a 12-month interval ending in the date of her election, on the assumption that the process of canvassing (making speeches, etc.) is a time when she was in the news. The dotted line in Figure 25 suggests this is a reasonable approach: it reports the number of times the name 'Indira Ghandi' appeared in a newspaper article, based on my search of 'Google News'. There is not a perfect match between Indira Ghandhi's election and newspaper articles about her: the peak in articles about her in 1984 was due to her assassination.

The thin continuous line in figure 25 represents the fraction of men who have been violent to their wife. I think there is an association between the spikes in this line, with the periods of Indira Gandhi's election. There may even be two spikes for the same election – perhaps one about a year before the election (1965, 1970, 1974, and 1979), when TV, radio, and newspapers followed her campaigns; and at the time of her election (1966, 1975, and 1980). In this context, we don't need to believe Indira Gandhi was a feminist who would empower women: rather, it is a question of whether 5-years-old boys felt her election indicate a change to the tradition gender roles in India. It appears that if a boy was five years old when Indira Gandhi was elected, he is more likely to use GBV when he grew to be an adult.

This section also considers respondents' attitudes to domestic violence: does childhood socialisation affect attitudes of adults? Acceptance of GBV is defined as agreement with the question: "Sometimes a wife can do things that bother her husband. Please tell me if you think that a husband is justified in beating his wife in each of the following situations: [..] If she goes out without telling him" (IIPS and ORC Macro, 2000: 420-1). Answers to this question are shown in figure 26, using a similar method as for figure 25. There is an important difference between these figures: figure 25 is based on answers from female respondents, whereas figure 26 is based on attitudes of male respondents.

When interviewed in the 2005-6 DHS survey, it was long after the death of Indira Gandhi – we might suppose that this female prime minister is not relevant to attitudes of adults, so many years later. But figure 26 suggests there <u>are</u> lasting effects of childhood socialisation: there are spikes in 1961, 1965, 1971, 1975, and 1980 (note that the 1961 spike is probably due to Mrs Bandaranaike, not Indira Gandhi). These spikes are less clear than for figure 25, but appear to confirm that childhood socialisation has taken place.

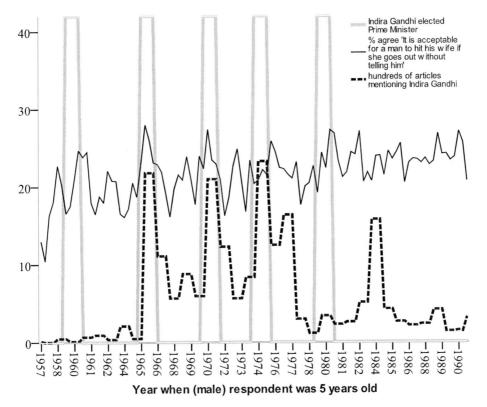

Source: DHS India 2005.

Figure 26. Male attitudes towards Gender-Based Violence, by year of birth.

In summary, figures 25 and 26 suggest that 5-year-old boys have been affected by the election of a female prime minister. It is not clear how the process happens – for example, it may be because there was more domestic violence when Indira Gandhi was elected, as men tried to reassert their authority over their wife: a man might feel threatened if a woman is elected to a position of power, and respond by criticising women who seek power. We cannot easily identify if there was an increase in domestic violence against women in the years Indira Gandhi was elected, because such crime data has only been made available by the Indian government in recent years. Indeed, for most of the time-period of Figures 25 and 26 (1957 to 1990), domestic violence was not a crime under Indian law unless it was extreme violence – such as murder.

Attitudes held by adults might be influenced by many factors, such as adult socialisation (in which adults are discouraged from accepting violence, by other people they meet); or by childhood socialisation (in which children absorb ideas current at the time of their childhood); or by other factors, such as watching role models on television or cinema. Note that other types of socialisation might occur at different ages.

REMEDIES FOR HARMFUL EFFECTS OF CHILDHOOD SOCIALISATION

This chapter has reported some evidence that childhood socialisation is relevant to the risk of an adult male using GBV. It seems that childhood socialisation can lead some adults to behave badly, apparently affected by their experiences as children. But childhood socialisation can also be beneficial, encouraging appropriate behaviour.

If child socialisation is important, we might want to assess at what age a child is socialised, in this particular respect; this could be useful information for teachers, who wish to ensure children grow up without prejudices against women. Psychologists and sociologists could research more on how to influence child development in a more positive direction. This chapter suggests that children are absorbing ideas on gender roles about age 5, when most children start their formal education. Hence, school teachers and other educationalists may be able to guide these children to become well-behaved adults.

It seems likely that role models are important for children and adults. Media can be encouraged to portray positive images of women – not only in politics, but in all areas where the public are enthusiastic about individuals. Hence celebrities such as musicians, sports stars, and television personalities can all play a positive role, by making clear their opposition to GBV to the public. Activists may wish to consider helping getting positive stories about women into public awareness by media such as television, radio, newspapers, and websites.

CONCLUSION

Some women in the Indian subcontinent are powerful role models; examples include Indira Gandhi in India; Sirimavo Bandaranaike in Sri Lanka; and Benazir Bhutto in Pakistan. Men in India appear to react negatively to such changes, perhaps turning to violence in an effort to retain male power. Boys who were about 5 years at the time of a woman taking power appear more likely to turn to violence against their wife; this appears to be a result of childhood socialisation. Further research on this subject could use data from other household surveys (e.g. from Pakistan and Bangladesh) to assess if similar childhood socialisation effects can be found. Research on childhood socialisation of girls, as well as boys, could be helpful.

One possible explanation is that when women were elected, fathers felt threatened and responded to this by sexist behaviour such as violence towards women; if such sexist behaviour was witnessed by a 5-year-old boy, he was more likely (when he himself became an adult) to see such behaviour as 'normal'. It seems that children learn from adults; we should all be careful what we say to children who are about five years old.

This chapter reports evidence that the experiences of children can go on to affect them for the rest of their life. For example, if a child sees men hitting women on a regular basis, then the child may conclude that this is normal human behaviour. This makes it even more urgent to reduce the prevalence of GBV in the current generation. Childhood socialisation may keep future generations 'locked in' to GBV, if each set of parents passes on a set of values to their children. It is important to consider how childhood socialisation can be overcome: perhaps by adult socialisation, or by consciousness-raising groups. Such ideas are discussed in the last few chapters of this book.

Chapter 10

GBV IS BULLYING, IN WHICH A STRONGER PERSON HITS A WEAKER PERSON

"The fact that one person, usually the woman, is smaller and weaker, is a crucial consideration in determining who is potentially at greater risk" (Hamel, 2005: 21).

ABSTRACT

GBV is (by definition) a way in which some men control their partner. If a wife is physically stronger than her husband, he may be unable to use violence to force her to obey him (unless he has a weapon, such as a gun). Hence in a family where GBV occurs, we would expect the wife to be physically weaker than her husband. This chapter examines the suggestion in some previous research that women who are victims of GBV are likely to be shorter than average women.

INTRODUCTION

This book focuses on domestic violence. The term 'Gender Based Violence' is used by many writers, because most victims of such violence are women. It would be helpful to understand this pattern: why are most victims of domestic violence women, rather than men? Various reasons can be put forward – for example, perhaps girls and women are socialised to be obedient, whereas boys and men are socialised to be aggressive. This idea is investigated in the 'patriarchy' section of this book (chapter 7). Another possible explanation is biological: perhaps men, in general, tend to be physically better able to fight than women, because men have more muscles. It has been claimed that victims of GBV tend to be shorter and lighter than non-victims. For example, Nicoletti et al. (2010: 278) claimed "It is generally understood by experts of gender violence that because of their greater height, weight, and muscular build, most males have a greater propensity to inflict harm on women than vise versa".

If men in general do have more muscles than women, we may then wish to investigate why men are more muscular than women – for example, perhaps men are more likely than women to use weight-training in a gym to strengthen muscles, because it is seen as 'appropriate' for men to be more muscular than women. It may be worth discouraging a 'machismo' culture, in which men are encouraged to be aggressive.

NEW EVIDENCE ON HEIGHT AND WEIGHT OF WOMEN

This chapter studies DHS data from 6 countries. These were chosen because among DHS surveys which asked about GBV and measured women's height or weight, these six countries had the largest sample sizes: each survey interviewed over 5,000 people. These large samples make them more reliable, and there is less risk of being misled by random variations. The decision on whether or not to include data on a country in this chapter is purely based on the DHS sample sizes in each country (I exclude data from the 2003 Bolivia survey, because it does not have data on two of the four columns in Tables 25 and 26; but it shows similar patterns to other Latin American countries in these two tables).

DOES A WOMAN'S HEIGHT AFFECT HER RISK OF GBV?

It would be desirable to assess the heights and weights of men, when considering the risk of GBV. We might find that GBV is more likely to occur if the husband is taller than the wife. However, most DHS surveys do not include husband's height; the only DHS survey I know of which includes husband's height is India 2005, and for that survey husband's height is in a separate file to GBV. This book does not examine if husband's height is related to GBV risk, but it may be a useful topic for future research.

For clarity in Table 25, I divided women into groups according to their height, such as '160 to 164'; this is an abbreviation for '160 or more, but less than 165' (for example, it could include 164.7 cm).

Table 25 indicates a general trend that the taller a woman is, the less likely she is to be hit by her husband or partner. The fraction of women who experienced GBV tends to be lower if she is taller, for each of these three types of violence. For example, among the tallest women in India (165cm or more), 8% had been kicked or dragged by their husband; this fraction rose to 13% for the shortest group of women in India (up to 144cm). This pattern applies to all three columns showing GBV risk. India is by far the largest of the five samples in table 25, so we would expect it to be the most reliable. But we do not see the same pattern for the African countries in table 25, Malawi and Nigeria: instead, we see the opposite pattern, that tall women are *more* likely to experience GBV (compared to short women). It is not clear why this is the case; but it might be related to the high GBV prevalence in the southern half of Africa, which is apparent in figure 2.

Another column of table 25, which gives us more insight into life in a typical household, is the right-hand column: this indicates the fraction of women who said they had hit or beaten their husband. This is not GBV (by definition, GBV is attacks by men against women). There are blanks in this column for Bolivia, Colombia, and Nicaragua, due to missing data. In the case of Peru (the 2004 survey), this column shows a dramatic change as we look down the column: the tallest women are almost twice as likely to hit their husband, compared to the shortest women (11% and 6%).

Table 25. Risk of Experiencing GBV, by Woman's Height, in Six Countries

Survey	Height of wife (cms)	husband slapped wife (%)	husband punched wife (%)	husband kicked /dragged wife (%)	Wife hit Husband (%)
India 2005	165 or more	26	8	8	1
	160 to 164	26	7	7	1
	155 to 159	29	9	9	1
	150 to 154	32	10	10	1
	145 to 149	35	11	11	1
	up to 144	37	12	13	1
Colombia 2005	165 or more	25	6	9	
	160 to 164	28	8	11	
	155 to 159	28	9	11	
	150 to 154	32	11	13	
	145 to 149	31	11	14	
	up to 144	37	17	19	
Nicaragua 1997	165 or more	10	14	4	
	160 to 164	11	13	6	
	155 to 159	12	15	7	
	150 to 154	13	14	7	
	145 to 149	13	16	7	
	up to 144	15	18	8	
Peru 2004	165 or more	18	7	4	11
	160 to 164	25	19	12	11
	155 to 159	27	23	16	9
	150 to 154	27	25	18	9
	145 to 149	28	26	20	8
	up to 144	27	27	20	6
Malawi 2000	165 or more	15	8	7	3
	160 to 164	16	9	6	3
	155 to 159	16	8	6	3
	150 to 154	16	7	5	2
	145 to 149	13	8	4	2
	up to 144	16	6	5	2
Nigeria 2008	165 or more	17	4	6	2
	160 to 164	16	4	6	2
	155 to 159	15	4	5	2
	150 to 154	16	4	6	2
	145 to 149	15	3	5	1
	up to 144	12	3	3	2

Source: DHS (female respondents only).

The other countries for which data are available (India, Malawi and Nigeria) are much less clear than Peru. This right-hand column is consistent with the idea that if a person is taller than their spouse, they are more likely to be violent against their spouse.

IS A WOMAN'S WEIGHT RELATED TO HER RISK OF GBV?

It may seem plausible that a woman is more at risk of GBV if she is thin, because a thin woman is likely to have fewer muscles – and may be more vulnerable to being bruised. However, it is difficult to be confident about the cause and effect: perhaps GBV leads to some women going hungry (because GBV allows her husband to control household spending), so we might find GBV victims are thin due to lack of food. This section examines whether or not the weights of women seem relevant to her chance of experiencing GBV.

Table 26. Risk of experiencing GBV, by woman's *weight*, in six countries

survey	Weight of respondent (Kg)	husband slapped wife	husband punched wife	husband kicked or dragged wife	Wife hit husband
India 2005	70 or more	20%	5%	5%	1%
	65 to 69	22%	6%	6%	1%
	60 to 64	23%	6%	6%	1%
	55 to 59	25%	7%	7%	1%
	50 to 54	29%	8%	9%	1%
	45 to 49	33%	10%	11%	1%
	up to 45	39%	13%	14%	1%
Colombia 2005	70 or more	29%	10%	11%	
	65 to 69	29%	10%	12%	
	60 to 64	31%	10%	13%	
	55 to 59	30%	10%	14%	
	50 to 54	30%	10%	13%	
	45 to 49	31%	11%	13%	
	up to 45	27%	9%	11%	
Nicaragua 1997	70 or more	13%	17%	8%	
	65 to 69	12%	15%	7%	
	60 to 64	13%	15%	7%	
	55 to 59	12%	14%	7%	
	50 to 54	11%	14%	6%	
	45 to 49	13%	14%	8%	
	up to 45	14%	14%	7%	
Peru 2004	70 or more	28%	24%	17%	10%

survey	Weight of respondent (Kg)	husband slapped wife	husband punched wife	husband kicked or dragged wife	Wife hit husband
	65 to 69	29%	26%	20%	10%
	60 to 64	27%	24%	18%	9%
	55 to 59	26%	24%	18%	8%
	50 to 54	27%	25%	18%	7%
	45 to 49	28%	25%	20%	7%
	up to 45	25%	24%	20%	5%
Malawi 2000	70 or more	12%	9%	5%	3%
	65 to 69	15%	5%	6%	2%
	60 to 64	18%	9%	6%	3%
	55 to 59	16%	9%	6%	3%
	50 to 54	15%	8%	6%	3%
	45 to 49	14%	7%	5%	2%
	up to 45	16%	7%	5%	2%
Nigeria 2008	70 or more	17%	4%	6%	3%
	65 to 69	16%	5%	6%	3%
	60 to 64	17%	5%	7%	3%
	55 to 59	18%	5%	7%	2%
	50 to 54	15%	4%	5%	2%
	45 to 49	14%	4%	4%	1%
	up to 45	13%	3%	4%	1%

Source: DHS (female respondents only).

Table 26 suggests a similar pattern for weight, as table 25 showed for height. The clearest pattern in table 26 is for India, which shows a lighter woman (up to 45 Kg) is much more likely than a heavier woman (70 or more Kg) to experience GBV. Latin American countries are not clear: weight seems to have little effect on the risk of GBV (perhaps larger samples would produce clearer results). Nigeria seems to have the opposite pattern to India: a Nigerian woman is *more* likely to be a victim of GBV if she is heavier. It is not clear whether or not this pattern applies to Malawi, perhaps because the Malawi sample is much smaller than the samples in India and Nigeria. Other African countries are excluded from Table 26 because they have smaller samples (and hence may be unreliable). Further research would be desirable, to shed more light on this puzzling topic.

Table 26 also reports data on husbands hit by their wife, but here the evidence is less clear. Perhaps the clearest patterns are for Peru and Nigeria, where a woman is more likely to hit her husband if she is heavier: for example, in Peru, a man's risk of being hit falls from 10% (among women who weigh over 70 Kg), down to 5% (among women who weigh up to 45 Kg). For other countries, there seems to be little sign of a connection between a woman's weight and her risk of experiencing GBV.

CONCLUSION

This chapter has analysed the possibility that a woman's height, or her weight, may be related to her risk of being hit by her husband or partner. There does appear to be such a link, in some of the six countries studied in this chapter. I also examined data from other DHS surveys, and found similar patterns; but the sample sizes in some DHS surveys are much smaller than the DHS samples in these six countries, so my findings not shown in this chapter may be unreliable.

If we focus first on the largest of these six samples, India, there appears to be a clear pattern: GBV is more likely if a woman is short (e.g. under 145 cm in height), or if she is light (e.g. under 45 Kg in weight). There is not such a clear pattern for these Latin American countries. The African countries examined in this chapter (or at least Nigeria) seem opposite to India. This paper does not explain why African countries seem so different to India, but perhaps future research will explain this. The high prevalence of GBV in Africa, shown in Figure 2, may be related to this; perhaps future research will explain this pattern.

Some women are physically better able to fight than their male partner. For example, if a man is ill, or shorter than most men, or in poor physical condition, then it may be possible for his wife to beat him if a fight occurs. This may partly explain why some men are victims of domestic violence.

A lesson from this chapter is that the ability to fight may give some men greater potential to use GBV. Women might be advised to consider the possibility that she should not choose a partner who is (for example) a professional boxer, because she may be at great risk of harm if he becomes violent. But there are complications: for example, some men (and women, if she is stronger than him) choose not to utilise the fact that they are physically stronger than their spouse.

This chapter investigates the possibility that some men are violent because they can use violence effectively; but it should be seen as just one of many influences on GBV.

Chapter 11

GBV and Women's Earnings

"Lack of economic resources underpins women's vulnerability to violence and their difficulty in extricating themselves from a violent relationship. The link between violence and lack of economic resources and dependence is circular. On the one hand, the threat and fear of violence keeps women from seeking employment, or, at best, compels them to accept low-paid, home-based exploitative labour. And on the other, without economic independence, women have no power to escape from an abusive relationship" (Kapoor, 2000: 7-8).

Abstract

Many victims of GBV are not passive – they choose to leave the violent relationship; other women who remain in an abusive relationship manage to limit the abuse (Ellsberg and Heise 2005; Johnson and Ferraro 2000). This chapter considers the possibility that if women earn enough, they can protect themselves from GBV by leaving, or threatening to leave, a violent husband or partner. For such a threat to be credible, she would need to earn enough to support herself and her children (if she has any).

The second half of this chapter concentrates on a specific type of household: where the wife earns more than the husband. This is called 'gender deviant', because in traditional families, the husband is expected to be the main earner for the household. If a wife earns more than her husband, we might expect the husband to do most of the domestic work: the wife has less time for housework than the husband, if she works more hours per week (note, however, that a woman could earn more than her husband and spend less hours at work, if her wage-rate is much higher than his). Also, if a wife is the main earner, she may be in a stronger position to 'bargain' with her husband: for example, she could be cope (financially) better than her husband with divorce, so she can threaten to leave him if he didn't do more housework – this is examined in the section on 'economic bargaining models' below.

Introduction

Many factors affect the likelihood of leaving a violent husband; perhaps a woman is more likely to remain with a violent partner if she thinks violence is widespread (because it is likely that her next partner will be violent). The victim's interpretation of what level of aggression is 'violence' is also relevant: "The social construct surrounding the ideal of the "good woman" clearly sets the limits for acceptable norms beyond which verbal and physical assaults translate into the notion of violence. Thus, beating is not seen as an excessive reaction if the woman gives cause for jealousy or does not perform her "wifely" duties adequately, such as having meals ready on time" (Burton et al., 1999: 5).

According to Johnson and Ferraro (2000: 958), "Research focusing specifically on low-income women has uncovered an extraordinarily high level of interpersonal violence". Studies in some countries found many women stay in an abusive relationship because they do not have their own income (Ellsberg and Heise, 2005). Barnett (2000) and Johnson and Ferraro (2000) found some violent men don't let their wife do paid work – this means she cannot leave her husband. Kapoor suggests a circular relationship between GBV and women's employment: "Lack of economic resources underpins women's vulnerability to violence and their difficulty in extricating themselves from a violent relationship. The link between violence and lack of economic resources and dependence is circular. On the one hand, the threat and fear of violence keeps women from seeking employment, or, at best, compels them to accept low-paid, home-based exploitative labour. And on the other, without economic independence, women have no power to escape from an abusive relationship" (Kapoor, 2000). Krishnan (2005: 772) claimed "Women's ability to resist violence hinged on access to economic and social resources".

Regarding Peru, Flake (2005: 366) found from regression analysis that a woman is more likely to be abused by her husband if she is employed, than if she is unemployed. Hindin et al. (2008: 26) claim women in Bolivia are more likely to report GBV if they are employed, whether in agricultural or non-agricultural work; but in Kenya, Malawi, Moldova, and Zimbabwe, women in agricultural jobs were more likely to report GBV than women in non-agricultural jobs, or women who were not employed.

ECONOMIC BARGAINING MODELS

In recent decades, most economic theories of household decision-making are based on (game theory) 'bargaining models'. These models assume that a husband and wife sometimes disagree with each other; in such cases, each spouse can threaten to divorce, unless they get their own way. A spouse is in a stronger bargaining position if they are better able to cope, should a divorce occur; economists focus on money. If a man is the main earner in a household, he can threaten to divorce because he knows he can afford to live comfortably without his wife (and presumably he can marry someone else). A wife in such a situation is in a weak position, because if a divorce occurred, her standard of living would fall; so she might be prepared to let her husband make decisions she disagreed with, to avoid being left in poverty. Economic bargaining models treat a household decision as a battle between husband and wife; the outcome is determined by each spouse's "threat point", related to that person's income – the more a person depends financially on their partner, the less power that person has (Haddad and Reardon, 1993).

Several economists have dropped the assumption of symmetry between men and women (implicit in early economic bargaining models), sometimes by including 'Extra Environmental Parameters' in bargaining models, to reflect asymmetry such as lower average wages for women than for men. "The generalized Nash bargaining solution is obtained by dropping symmetry from this second list of axioms, to reflect differences in previous or current assets, income, or social customs determining the "bargaining power" of each adult. Dropping symmetry seems appropriate since traditional gender roles may affect the bargaining ability of the two adults" (Martinelli and Parker, 2003: 528).

Many social scientists claim a woman's earnings do not always give her power; this view seems incompatible with economic bargaining models. Engle and Menon (1999: 1318-9) wrote "Working for income, however, does not automatically mean that women control their incomes; in many societies, income is automatically assumed to be the property of the husband". Other empirical research, such as Turner (2000: 1032), also casts doubt on economic bargaining models; *"The household bargaining theory has scant empirical support as far as children are concerned"* (Purkayastha, 2003: 604; emphasis in original).

GBV AND ABILITY TO AFFORD SUFFICIENT FOOD

Several writers claim that children are more likely to be underfed if GBV occurs in the household. Hindin (2008: 71) reports that among children aged 4 years or younger, there is more risk of being 'stunted' (shorter than expected) if the child's mother experienced GBV, in Haiti and Kenya – after controlling for other factors which might influence the child's height. Similarly, there is more risk of children being 'wasted' (of lower weight than expected) if the child's mother experienced GBV, in Haiti and Kenya. In India, children tend to receive less food if their mother is beaten by her husband (Heise et al., 1994: 28). Pahl (1985: 33-4) found male violence against women often gives men control of household financial decisions – many British women who had left a violent husband or partner became 'better off' on state benefits, than when they lived with a rich partner: a woman could feed children more easily if she controlled a small income, rather than having little or no control over a large household income.

According to Flake (2005: 358), research in North American indicates that the risk of GBV is reduced when women are employed, have similar levels of education as their husband, and share in household decision making. It isn't clear which is 'cause', and which is 'effect': perhaps women's share in decision-making is increased in households where GBV does not occur.

To assess poverty, I use a 'household equivalence scale', which takes account of the number and ages of members of each household. In the 'OECD' income equivalence methodology (Hagenaars, de Vos and Ziadi, 1994: 18), the first adult in each household is given a score of 1; each subsequent adult adds 0.7 to the score; and 0.5 is added for each child. This score is added up for every household. I divide total household income by this score, to calculate equivalent incomes. I use this equivalent income to split each survey into six income bands for Figures 27 to 29.

Information on inability to afford food in WAS surveys is based on the question "In the last 12 months, how often did you or anyone in your household cut the size of meals or skip meals because there wasn't enough money for food?" Respondents were asked to choose one answer from this list: 'almost every month', 'some months but not every month', 'only one or two months', or 'never'.

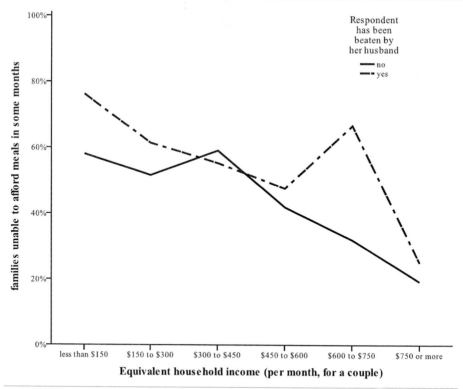

Source: WAS Cameroon 2009.

Figure 27. Inability to afford food, by household income and GBV: Cameroon.

Figure 27 indicates two patterns in Cameroon, which help us to understand why some families can't afford enough food. The first pattern is predictable: as we go from left to right, i.e. if the household is richer, there is generally less risk of being hungry. The second pattern is more relevant to this book: there is a tendency for more hunger in households where GBV has taken place. Similar evidence for Chad and Kenya are shown in Figures 28 and 29.

In Figure 28, we see a dramatic effect of GBV, when controlling for household income (on the horizontal axis). Households where GBV occurred are far more likely to report that they were sometimes unable to afford food.

The effect of GBV seems most obvious where the 'equivalent household income' is in the range $450 to $600 per month per couple (a couple with children would need a higher income than a couple, to reach the same standard of living): in such households, a husband might wish to spend money on luxuries for himself (such as eating away from home, running a car, or hiring prostitutes) – and using GBV may give him more control over spending decisions. In the poorest households (under $150 per month for a couple, or the equivalent income for a larger family) there may be little spare money to argue about – even if he was able to control household spending, that control would not bring him a high standard of living.

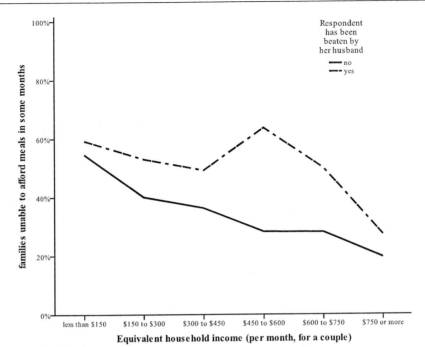

Source: WAS Chad 2008.

Figure 28. inability to afford food, by household income and GBV: Chad.

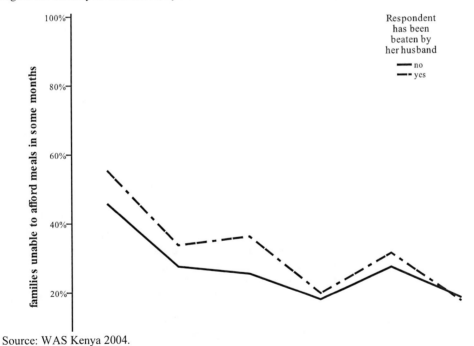

Source: WAS Kenya 2004.

Figure 29. Inability to afford food, by household income and GBV: Kenya.

Figure 29 suggests GBV tends to increase the level of hunger in Kenyan households, if we control for their level of household income. If we consider households with an income of $300 to 400 per month per couple (or equivalent for larger households), we see an increase in the risk of going hungry from 25% to 36% if GBV occurs.

Testing the 'Children Fare Better' Hypothesis

Some researchers (e.g. Haddad and Reardon, 1993; Simister, 2009) claim that many children suffer undernutrition because their parents spend a large fraction of their money on non-food items. Such items might include alcohol, cigarettes, illegal drugs, restaurant meals, clothes, cars, and prostitutes. There is evidence from Côte d'Ivoire, Guatemala, Jordan and Mali (cited in Engle and Menon, 1999: 1318), and from Rwanda and The Gambia (cited in Kennedy and Haddad, 1994: 1081), that children fare better when mothers have more control over household decisions. Evidence reported by Lundberg and Pollak (1996) indicate that children benefit more when their mother, rather than their father, are responsible for household spending decisions.

The evidence in Figures 27, 28 and 29 is consistent with the 'children fare better' hypothesis: the idea that many husbands mis-spend household money. This hypothesis makes various assumptions, such as that the wife and children would generally prefer to spend money on essentials such as food, whereas many husbands would prefer to buy luxuries such as alcohol. This is consistent with conventional economic analysis, which assumes that everyone is selfish: economic analysis suggests that every man on earth would want to control household spending to suit his own preferences, if he could (in bargaining models, explained earlier in this chapter, women and men both seek control). But economists generally assume parents care about children, and hence most men would not wish to spend money on alcohol if their children were starving. There are various complexities to consider: perhaps some men spend excessively on alcohol, or drugs, or gambling, because they are addicted? Note, however, that women – like men – can be addicted. The 'children fare better' hypothesis is not so crude as to assume all men are addicts, or all women angels. Instead, the 'children fare better' view suggests that in general, women tend to care more than men for children (childhood socialization may explain why men behave differently to women).

This section considers evidence on whether or not the hypothesis is supported by the evidence; it is not a formal test of the 'children fare better' viewpoint (for scientific testing, regression analysis is usually used; but that is inappropriate in a book for the general reader, such as this book). Instead, this section reports some evidence on whether or not this hypothesis seems plausible. Ideas tested in this section include: in households with children, do men appear to spend more than women on personal spending? And do some men spend prefer to money on luxuries while the household is unable to afford enough food?

Consider the following evidence, based on WAS surveys. Male and female respondents were asked how often they and their spouse visited bars per week; this number was converted to number of visits per year, for clarity. Results are shown in table 27. For all five WAS surveys which asked this question, the sample is limited to respondents who lived in households containing at least one child, and where the respondent was married, cohabiting, divorced or separated. Table 27 suggests bars and similar venues are visited by both women and men, but men attend more often than women.

Table 27. Number of visits to bars, by men and women

Survey	Number of times husband goes out to bar/club (per year)	Number of times wife goes out to bar/club (per year)
Cameroon	62	26
Chad 2008	74	27
Kenya 2004	58	27
Nigeria 2003	46	23
Nigeria 2005	22	7

Source: WAS (limited to households with children, excluding unmarried respondents).

Table 28 considers the question of whether or not all men who spend on luxuries (such as cars, alcohol, etc.) do so without harming other household members; it is based on answers to the following question (in some WAS surveys): 'Do you [if male] / does your husband [if female] prefer car/drink/etc. spending even if child hungry?'

Table 28 is complicated, and the three countries studied (Cameroon, Chad, and Nigeria) appear to differ from each other: there seem to be more men in Nigeria (than Cameroon or Chad) who prefer luxuries to food even if food is scarce. The question on mis-spending was not included in the WAS surveys in Kenya 2004, or Nigeria 2003.

Table 28. Association between men preferring luxuries to food, and hunger

Survey	Does the husband prefer car/drink/etc. spending, even if children are hungry?		*Frequency of cutting meals in the last year*			
			Never	only 1 or 2 months	some months, but not every month	almost every month
Cameroon 2009		No	98%	96%	97%	97%
		Yes	2%	4%	3%	3%
	Total		100%	100%	100%	100%
Chad 2008		No	98%	94%	98%	91%
		Yes	2%	6%	12%	9%
	Total		100%	100%	100%	100%
Nigeria 2005		No	81%	86%	80%	84%
		Yes	19%	14%	20%	17%
	Total		100%	100%	100%	100%

Source: WAS.

Regarding the 'children fare better' hypothesis, a key lesson from table 28 is that there seems surprisingly little connection between husbands preferring luxuries to food, and shortages of food: for example, the fraction of men who prefer luxury spending to food in Nigeria is 19% in households which never went without food, and 17% in households which went without food almost every month. One possible explanation is that some men are addicted to drugs or drink, and will prioritise spending on drugs and drink whatever happens to the affordability of food. In households where the family goes hungry but the husband prefers luxuries, we might expect women and children to complain to the husband; perhaps some such men are able to use GBV to ensure that most of the household spending is on alcohol or drugs, rather than food. My research (not included in this book) suggests that only a small fraction of men are addicted to this extent; and in many cases, women leave such violent and addicted husbands, taking their children with them (Gwagwa, 1998).

SURVEY EVIDENCE ON GBV AND WIFE'S EARNINGS

The WAS Egypt 2005/6 survey asked women (but not men) respondents the following set of 3 questions:

"Why was your husband violent?
'arguments over spending/money'
'arguments over children'
'arguments about going to work' "

For each of the above three questions, respondents chose from answers "*yes*", "*no*", or "*don't know*" (respondents who said 'don't know' are excluded from this analysis). When women answered the above three questions, they gave the following responses: 80% said yes to *'arguments over spending/money'*; 38% said yes to *'arguments over children'*; and 4% of women said *'arguments about going to work'*. Regrettably, this set of three questions was not asked of men (because men are the violent partner, their opinions might help us to understand the causes of GBV). But I think it probable that women who suffer violence from their husband have a good understanding of why the violence happens. If these women (GBV victims) are correct, most male violence is associated with household spending or other financial issues.

Table 29. Reason for violence, and prevalence of violence, by household poverty

How often was the family unable to afford food in the last 12 months?	Wife has been hit by her husband	(GBV victims): Husband's violence was over spending/money
Never	14 %	69 %
Only 1 or 2 months	32 %	79 %
Some months, but not every month	25 %	85 %
Almost every month	28 %	89 %

Source: WAS Egypt 2005/6 (female respondents).

The middle column of table 29 shows that the risk of a woman being hit tends to increase as we look down the table, i.e. in households where hunger is more frequent (this pattern is not very clear – a larger sample size is desirable). As we look down the right hand column of Table 29, there is an increasing fraction of women who said the reason for violence was arguments over money and spending decisions. These findings suggest a link between hunger and arguments, but it is not obvious what the link is. One possibility is that for households where money is scarce, women are less likely to accept their husband's spending decisions, and start to argue; in response, some men use violence to ensure he can continue to dominate household spending decisions.

Table 30. GBV prevalence, by country and whether or not wife is employed

Continent	Country	Wife is in a paid job	
		no	yes
Sub-Saharan Africa	Congo Dem Republic	41%	53%
	Cameroon	28%	38%
	Ghana	12%	21%
	Kenya	27%	37%
	Liberia	34%	36%
	Mali	1%	2%
	Malawi	16%	20%
	Nigeria	10%	18%
	Rwanda	19%	27%
	Sao Tome and Principe	25%	29%
	Chad	27%	29%
	Uganda	32%	48%
	South Africa	9%	12%
	Zambia	39%	44%
	Zimbabwe	24%	29%
Americas	Bolivia	40%	49%
	Colombia	25%	35%
	Dominican Republic	16%	18%
	Honduras	3%	7%
	Haiti	10%	13%
	Nicaragua	16%	23%
	Peru	27%	38%
Middle-East/Asia	Bangladesh	45%	55%
	Egypt	21%	16%
	Indonesia	5%	6%
	India	18%	27%
	Jordan	19%	21%
	Cambodia	13%	14%
	Philippines	11%	14%
Europe	Azerbaijan	11%	14%
	Moldova	18%	23%
	Ukraine	10%	15%

Source: DHS and WAS.

Table 30 is generally consistent, in that in every country (except Egypt) there is a larger risk of GBV for a wife is she is in a paid job. I am unable to explain why Egypt is unlike other countries in Table 30; a larger sample size would be more reliable.

In South Africa, the 1998 DHS survey interviewed 11,702 women; of these women, 1,628 said they had experienced GBV from their current or former partner. Of the women who had experienced GBV, 664 women had left their husband or partner because of this violence. In the WAS 2011 Congo-Brazzaville survey, 30% of women interviewed said they agree with the statement "I want to leave my husband because he is violent, but I can't afford to live on what I earn".

ARE HOUSEHOLDS 'RATIONAL' IF THE WIFE IS THE MAIN EARNER?

In this chapter, housework is used to give insights into the balance of power between husband and wife. We could start by considering 'rational' behaviour, regarding housework, in a household where a woman earns more than her partner. There are a number of theories, such as economic 'bargaining' models of the household, which might explain this. There are several reasons why we would expect men to do more housework, and women to do less housework, if the wife is the main earner:

- If a woman is employed full-time whereas her partner is employed part-time or unemployed, she has less time she could spend at home (compared with her husband); it should be easier for him (than for her) to find enough time to do the housework.
- We might expect that a woman would specialise in paid work and her partner in unpaid work (Halleröd, 2005). For example, if she works as an accountant, she may need to keep in touch with changes in the law – but her partner need not concern himself with such legal changes, if he is a full-time househusband.
- If a woman is the main earner, she may be able to 'get her own way' more often – insisting her husband contributes more in terms of unpaid work. Newman (2002: 394), describing empirical research in Ecuador, claimed "higher women's wages enabled women to bargain for a redistribution of housework in which men did more than they otherwise would have".

Hence, if there are households where women earn more than their partner, we might expect to see her partner doing most of the domestic work. But much previous research found households do not behave as the above 'rational' behaviour suggests. Zuo and Bian (2001: 1131) wrote "the husbands' participation in housework still does not measure up to that of their wives, given that 90% of the wives hold full-time jobs. Husbands' domestic labor seems unrelated to their relative economic resources, a similar pattern noted by previous research".

'GENDER DEVIANCE NEUTRALIZATION'

If the division of housework (and household decisions in general) don't follow predictions of 'rational' behaviour, how can we explain how households behave? The 'doing gender' approach argues that a woman's earnings, wealth, and other resources (relative to those of her husband) have only a limited effect on her decision-making power; a woman who is the main earner in her household may find her earning-power a curse, rather than a blessing. Pyke (1994: 88-9) suggests women may be less powerful if they earn more: a husband might be ungrateful if his wife earns too much. Some men feel a sense of failure if they have a less successful career than their wife: "The effect a particular resource has on marital power depends on whether couples consider it as a gift or a burden. Those men who are denied a sense of occupational success are less likely to view their wives' market work as a gift. Sensitive to their husbands' feelings of failure, some wives respond by not resisting their husband's dominance to "balance" his low self-esteem" (Pyke, 1994: 89). Zuo and Bian (2001: 1131) claim "Neither men of "failed aspirations" who increase performance in domestic tasks nor woman of "excessive" career orientation who climb the corporate ladder in both salary and status are able to easily turn their work into valued resources in marital exchange. On the contrary, their work is viewed as a debt to their spouse because they have breached gender boundaries". Perhaps GBV (or the threat of GBV) is a reason why many women who earn more than their husbands still defer to their husband.

The 'gender deviance neutralization' view suggests men and/or women reduce stress caused by 'gender deviance'. A wife who is the main earner tends to do more of the housework than her earning power suggests. For example, "when American men were economically dependent on their wives, they "displayed gender" by lowering their time in housework" (Evertsson and Nermo, 2004: 1274). Evertsson and Nermo (2004: 1279), studying households in USA and Sweden, found "a man is likely to do more housework when he and his spouse have equivalent earnings, as compared with when he either provides for or is economically dependent on his wife". A similar comment was made by Shelton and John (1996: 304): "In studies of the impact of earnings on the division of household labor, most researchers find that the smaller the gap between husbands' and wives' earnings the more equal the division of household labor".

According to Stamp (1985: 546), a woman who is the main earner often gives financial power to her husband: "women think they ought to be less powerful than men because of cultural norms, and will see themselves that way whether they are or not – or, as in some of these cases, retreat from the exercise of power they could have. Money isn't everything, even in marriage!" (Stamp, 1985: 554). Similarly, "some women are careful not to exploit their greater potential power to the fullest, despite their increased economic resources [..] expectations in marriage operate as a form of subtle coercion that undermines the relationship between women's resources and their power in marriage [..] In a society in which breadwinning is a social representation of manhood, wives whose husbands are not good providers often submit to their husbands' dominance because they feel guilty for contributing to their husbands' sense of failure" (Lim, 1997: 34-5).

There is evidence from time-use data that most housework is done by women, and most paid work is done by men (e.g. Newman, 2002: 384; Peters, 1999: 342; Voicu, Voicu and Strapcova, 2008). The reasons for this gender inequality in time spent on housework are not clear, and beyond the scope of this book; presumably this is one of the many types of gender inequalities in every society. Social scientists have reported evidence that women experience numerous kinds of discrimination, such as being paid less than men for the same job (Mumford and Smith, 2009: i56).

Evertsson and Nermo (2004: 1274) wrote that in the "doing-gender" approach, a husband and/or a wife see housework as a symbol of gender relations. In an (unconventional) family in which the woman has the higher income job, time availability doesn't seem to explain the division of housework between spouses: "gender trumps money [..] When men have difficulties in sustaining their traditional family roles (i.e., being the main breadwinner working the most hours, or being employed at all), both women and men may act in a way that neutralizes this presumed violation of gender norms".

If a man feels his gender identity is threatened by his partner earning more than himself, then he might do more than refuse to do housework: he may also become violent to his partner. Atkinson et al. (2005: 1139) wrote: "From the perspective of gendered resource theory, wives who are primary breadwinners and who have traditional husbands are at the greatest risk of abuse".

The rest of this chapter focuses on data from four countries: Cameroon, Chad, Nigeria, and India. I limit the sample (in each of these four countries) to married or cohabiting respondents, and I exclude polygamous households (if a man had more than one wife, he would have less time spend on housework with each of his wives). The definition of 'housework' in this chapter includes cooking, cleaning the house, laundry, shopping for food, and childcare. Married or cohabiting respondents were asked how much time they, and their spouse, spend on each of these five tasks. For each survey, the WAS website www.was-survey.org reports the exact question wording. Bittman et al. (2003: 195) refer to the approach used in WAS surveys (asking respondents how many hours of work they do) as the "stylized question" method; they argue that although such time-use data are less accurate than time-use data from diaries kept by respondents, it can still be used for research on 'gender deviance neutralization' (Bittman et al., 2003: 194-5). For this chapter, I exclude households where neither spouse does any housework (presumably all housework is done by paid help such as a maid, in some households).

The earnings variable (used to calculate the wife's relative earnings, shown on the horizontal axis) refers to usual earnings, after tax. For each figure in this chapter, I divided the horizontal axis into six categories: where the wife earns nothing; where the wife earns something, but less than a quarter of combined (husband + wife) earnings; where the wife earns at least a quarter, but less than half (of her and her husband's earnings); where she earns at least half, but less than three-quarters of their joint income; where she earns at least three-quarters of the combined earnings, but was not the only earner; and finally, where the wife is the only earner. I simplify labels on Figures 31 to 35, to improve clarity – for example, the penultimate category is shown as "75 to 99%", but strictly speaking this should be '75% to just under 100%': it would be more accurate to put "75 to 99.99%" on the horizontal axis.

For this chapter, I exclude from my analysis households where neither husband nor wife earned anything. I assume earnings of other household members (e.g. children) are zero, or small enough to be ignored; this assumption is questionable, because many households are extended families. As a check, I limited each sample to nuclear families, and obtained similar results (not shown in this book). WAS surveys do not ask earnings of children of the respondent, so it isn't possible to assess the effects of children's earnings. To assess possible effects of GBV, the variable I use for this chapter is 'ever experienced GBV' (as opposed to 'experienced GBV in the last year', or 'experienced GBV in the last month').

Figure 30 shows the number of hours per week which husband and wife spend on housework, at different levels of wife's relative earnings. The horizontal axis goes from wife not employed (on the left), to husband not employed (on the right). Around the mid-point of this scale is where husband and wife have approximately equal earnings.

On the left of Figure 30, almost all housework is done by women: typically a wife does about 55 hours per week, and her husband does about 12 hours per week, if the husband is the only spouse employed. We see a gradual change in this pattern as we go from left to right:

there is a more equal distribution of housework, in which men do more housework and women do less. This tendency continues up to the point (toward the right-hand-side of the Figure) where the wife earns between 75% and 99% of the combined earnings of both spouses: at this point, husbands and wives do a fairly similar amount of housework (although the wife still does more: about 28 hours per week, compared to about 21 hours per week from her husband). If we go a further step to the right, to the situation where the husband earns nothing, there is a retreat from this relatively egalitarian sharing of housework: the husband then does less housework, and the wife more. Note, however, that the situation where the wife earns between 75% and 99% (of husband + wife earnings) should not be called 'fair' to women: it implies a woman earning almost all the household income, and yet still doing noticeably more housework than her partner.

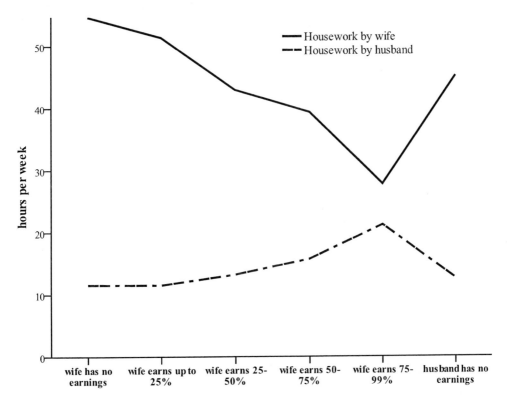

Source: WAS Cameroon 2009.

Figure 30. Husband's and wife's housework by wife's relative earnings: Cameroon.

My research (not all shown in this book) indicates Cameroon is fairly typical of the WAS surveys completed so far, as regards women's share of the housework. The sample sizes of some WAS surveys, such as Brazil 1994, could be considered too small to trust; so I only examined figures like Figure 30 for six countries. Of these six, only one – Nigeria – showed a pattern of the average husband doing more housework than the average wife (this was where the wife earned between 75% and 99% of the combined income). It is possible to compare Figure 30 with Australian and U.S. data shown as 'Fig 1' and 'Fig A1' in Bittman et al.

(2003), but their two figures are based on estimates of time-use by husband and wife from their regression analysis: whereas my Figure 30 is 'actual' data (not 'fitted values', based on regression estimates).

We can consider Figure 30 from the viewpoint of 'gender deviance neutralization', discussed in the literature review of this chapter. We are assessing the possibility that husbands do less housework than expected, and women do more, if the wife is the main earner. This means considering the three categories on the right of Figure 30: where the wife earned between 50% and 75% of the combined income; where the wife earned between 75% and 99% of the combined income; or where the husband didn't earn anything.

Bittman et al. wrote "the American data suggest that, in most of the population, which men (and which women) will be doing more housework fits exchange theory quite well, although the higher base level of housework done by all women is consistent with strong gender effects. We will look for both of these *gender effects* in our data – a higher base level of housework for women, net of hours of employment, and the nonlinearity by which couples respond to the gender deviance of men's earning less than women by increasing the traditionality of their housework allocation" (Bittman et al., 2003: 194; emphasis added).

Bittman's comments suggest two features in which we could look for effects of gender in Figure 30. One feature is that there is a non-linear pattern, when we go from 'wife earns 75 to 99%' to 'husband has no earnings'; this is referred to as 'nonlinearity' or a 'curvilinear' relationship, and I believe this is the meaning of 'gender deviance neutralization' in previous literature. Another feature, which Bittman et al. call the 'base level', is whether or not husbands do less housework, and wives do more housework, than we would expect – at <u>any</u> level of husband's and wife's earnings.

If there were complete gender equality in Cameroon, we would expect men to do *less* housework than women on the left of Figure 30, and men to do *more* housework than women on the right of Figure 30. And we'd expect to see a symmetrical pattern for women in Figure 30, where the line for women (sloping down) is the mirror image of the line for men (sloping up). These two lines would cross in the middle of Figure 30: husband and wife would spend the *same* number of hours on housework, if husband and wife have similar earnings. However, we see a very different picture in Figure 30: perhaps the most striking difference is how much more housework is done by women than by men, in general (Bittman et al. call this the "base level of housework", in the above quote).

For the rest of this chapter, I adopt a simpler method to assess if GBV is relevant to housework: I convert the two lines (in Figure 30) into one line, by calculating the husband's share of housework: i.e. the fraction of total housework by husband and wife, which is performed by the husband (expressed as a percentage).

This percentage is shown on the vertical axis of Figures 31a, which uses the same data as Figure 30, but replaces two lines by one. This approach is simpler than most previous research (which often uses a figure like Figure 31). However, my method has a drawback: if we observe what appears to be 'gender deviance neutralization' or 'gender effects', we cannot tell (from the figure) if this is due to the husband doing less work, or the wife doing more.

Figure 31 is a simple representation of how husband's unpaid work is related to his share of the household income. We see a pattern that husbands do the largest share of housework if the wife earns between 75% and 99% of joint (husband plus wife) income.

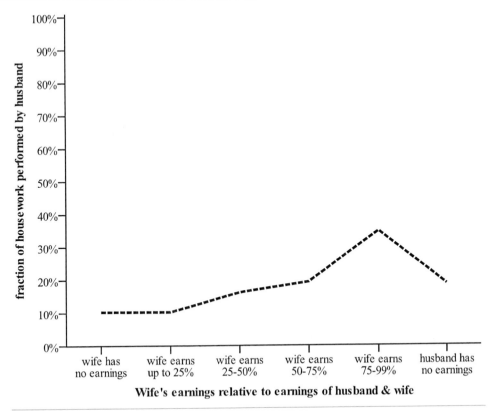

fraction of housework performed by husband

Wife's earnings relative to earnings of husband & wife

Source: WAS Cameroon 2009.

Figure 31. Husband's share of housework by wife's relative earnings: Cameroon.

Each of the next four figures is similar to figure 31, in using wife's relative earnings on the horizontal axis, and husband's share of housework (by husband and wife) on the vertical axis. They differ from Figure 31 in that the next four figures all add an indicator of GBV risk. Hence, the next four figures help us to assess if GBV is relevant to the amount of housework done by men and women.

First, consider Figure 32, for Cameroon. If there were no sexism, we would expect to see a diagonal line from the bottom-left corner (wife does no paid work, and almost all unpaid work) to the top-right corner (wife does all paid work, and almost no unpaid work) in Figure 30; if husbands and wives have similar earnings, we'd expect this line to be about 50% on the vertical axis (husbands and wives do similar amounts of housework). A world without sexism would be a world without GBV (there might still be domestic violence, but men would not use violence to control women). This ideal world is in sharp contrast to what we actually see in Figure 32. The right-hand-side of Figure 32 shows a clear difference between households where GBV occurred, and households with no GBV. The right-hand-side of the figure is where we might expect a woman's greater earnings to give her power over her husband: for example, she could threaten to divorce him unless he does more housework (because she would cope better than he would, financially). But this does not happen, if the husband was violent: a woman who earns 75-99% of her household's income still does most of the housework. One way to interpret Figure 32 is to say GBV gives men power, which can counteract the power a woman gains if she is the main earner. The left-hand-side of figure 32 suggests GBV has little or no effect on how much housework is done by men, if the wife has relatively low earnings. Perhaps a man doesn't need GBV to get his own way, if he is the main earner.

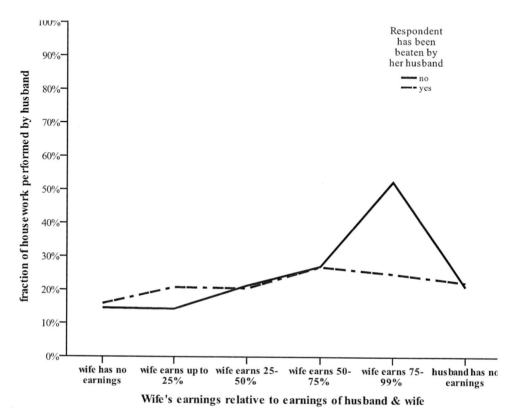

Source: WAS Cameroon 2009.

Figure 32. Husband's housework share by wife's relative earnings: Cameroon.

At first glance, Figure 33 (for Chad) looks quite different to Figure 32 (for Cameroon): Figure 33 looks more like two horizontal lines. In general, men appear to do a smaller fraction of housework in Chad, than men in Cameroon do. But Figure 33 is similar to Figure 32 in a key aspect: for the line for households without GBV, the line is higher on the right-hand-side (than for households with GBV).

This is consistent with the idea that some men use GBV to avoid doing housework, if his wife is the main earner. The effect of GBV in Figure 33 is mainly visible on the right side of Figure 33, where the wife is the main earner; on the left side of Figure 33, the husband does only a small share of housework whether or not he uses GBV. Overall, Figure 33 suggests that for higher-earning women, her earning power tends to give her power to persuade her husband to do more housework; but some men can override this financial power by using GBV. Figure 35 (for India) is similar, generally, to the three preceding figures. Most male housework (as a fraction of husband's plus wife's housework time) occurs in households on the right of Figure 35, where the wife earns between 75% and 99% of the joint husband-and-wife income, and where GBV does not occur.

This suggests that if a man earns less than his wife, he tends to do more housework. There were no households in WAS India 2007 where GBV occurred, and where the wife earned between 75% and 99% of the combined income of herself and her husband. This explains why the dashed line appears broken on the right hand side of Figure 35. In general, larger samples are desirable; but in India (and in most countries), there are only a small fraction of households in which the wife earns more than her husband.

In Figure 35, a woman's earnings do not appear to offer her much help with domestic work in India. In Figure 35, even if a woman earns between 75% and 99% of the combined (husband + wife) income for that household, the husband only does about 30% of the housework – if he doesn't use GBV. We might have expected the husband to do between 75% and 99% of the unpaid work, in this situation.

A similar finding applies to Figure 33, for Chad. It could be argued that if a woman wants to reduce the time she spends on housework, she might benefit more from hiring a maid or buying labour-saving devices (such as a washing machine and vacuum-cleaner), rather than trying to persuade her husband to do more housework: "it is the washing machine, not the vote, which is the true liberator of women" (Oakley, 1982: 171).

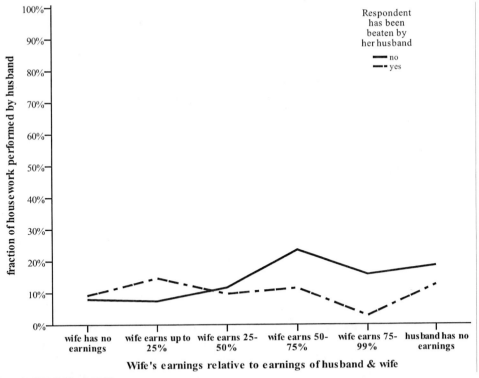

Source: WAS Chad 2008.

Figure 33. Husband's housework share by wife's relative earnings: Chad.

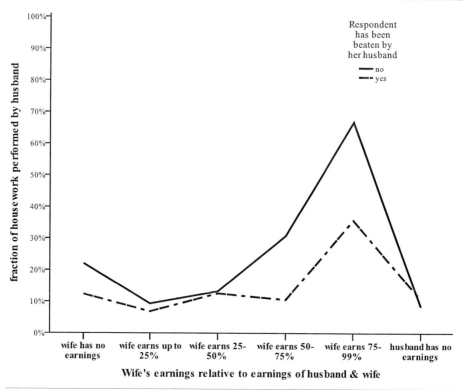

Source: WAS Nigeria 2005.

Figure 34. Husband's housework share by wife's relative earnings: Nigeria.

But presumably male reluctance to do housework is cultural, not biological: women in future could aspire to have the same status as men, where household chores are shared equally between men and women.

Figure 34, for Nigeria, has similarities with Figures 32 and 33: in households where the wife is the main earner (the right-hand-side of the figure), men tend to do a larger share of the housework. And also like Figures 32 and 33, we see a tendency for violent men to do less housework than non-violent men, on the right-hand-side of Figure 34. It seems that in Nigeria, a woman's earnings tend to help her persuade her husband to do a larger fraction of the domestic work; but that this power can be reduced by a husband using GBV. In Nigeria (unlike Cameroon and Chad, in the two previous figures), a man generally seems to do slightly more housework if his wife earns 75 to 99% of the combined (husband + wife) earnings, even if he uses GBV. It seems from the above four figures, using WAS survey data, that GBV may sometimes be a response by a man who considers himself to be 'gender deviant'. WAS surveys have the advantage of including time-use data: there is little time-use data in DHS surveys. But DHS surveys have much larger sample sizes than WAS, so it is appropriate to use DHS data where possible; hence, I include figure 36, based on DHS data, to show the link between wife's relative earnings and GBV.

Figure 36 shows data on three of the four countries studied in this chapter: the missing country in Figure 36 is Chad, because DHS surveys in Chad did not include questions on experience of GBV. Figure 36 does not include time-use data, unlike previous figures in this chapter. DHS does not have earnings data for women and men, from which the variable on the horizontal axis of the previous figures were calculated; instead, DHS reports answers to the question: "Would you say that the money that you earn is more than what your husband earns, less than what he earns, or about the same?" (IIPS and Macro International, 2007: 119). Hence, Figure 36 uses a smaller number of categories on the horizontal axis than do the earlier figures in this chapter.

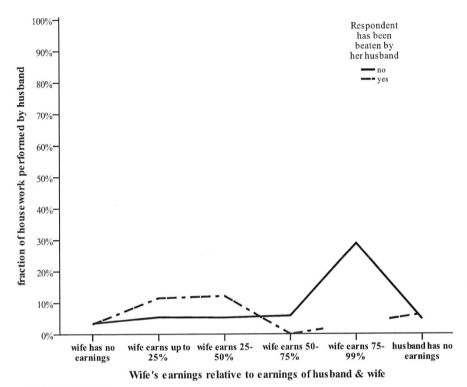

Source: WAS India 2007.

Figure 35. Husband's housework share by wife's relative earnings: India.

Figure 36 (based on DHS data) shows similarities with the previous figures in this chapter (based on WAS data). In particular, there is a tendency for more GBV on the right-hand-side of the figure, where the female respondent earns more than her partner. This apparent effect of earnings on GBV is not dramatic: the risk of experiencing GBV does not fall to zero among households where a woman earns less than her partner, so the woman's relative earnings are clearly not the only cause of GBV. The pattern in Figure 36 is not entirely consistent between countries: in Cameroon and Nigeria, the highest GBV risk is where the wife earns 'more than half' of the combined earnings of herself and her partner, whereas the highest risk in India is where the wife is the only earner in the relationship. If any reader understands why India differs from Cameroon and Nigeria, I would be grateful if you contact the author: despite researching such topics for years, there is much I do not understand. But despite these complications, Figure 36 appears to support the idea that 'gender deviance neutralization' may be a cause of GBV: if the theory of 'gender deviance neutralization' (discussed in this chapter) is correct, then a man who earns less than his wife may feel the need to correct this 'deviance', and respond by using violence – perhaps to make him more powerful than his wife.

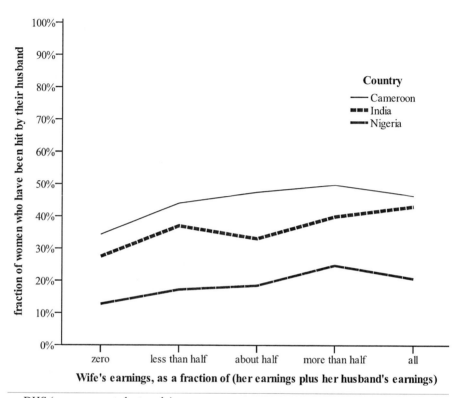

Source: DHS (women respondents only).

Figure 36. GBV prevalence by wife's relative earnings, and by country.

Respondents in the 2005 WAS Nigeria survey were asked if they agree or disagree with the statement "If a woman earns more than her husband, it's almost certain to cause problems". 57% of respondents agreed with the statement (18% said 'neither agree or disagree'; 25% disagreed). It appears that in Nigeria at least, most people think it normal for a husband to earn at least as much as his wife, and consider any deviation from this norm to be a potential cause of difficulties. This question does not make clear *what* problems may be caused if a woman earns more than her husband, but it seems plausible that GBV is one such problem: this is consistent with the higher risk of GBV on the right hand side of Figure 36.

Many social scientists have observed gender inequalities in paid and unpaid work. To some extent, we might explain these differences in terms of society-level factors, such as male-dominated trade unions. But the 'gender deviance neutralization' hypothesis suggests some of the gender difference in housework is due to the way an individual spouse feels. If a man has been socialised since childhood that the main earner in a household should be the male head of household, he may feel stressed if he finds his wife earns more than himself. In response to this, according to previous research, many men refuse to do much housework. This is complicated by gender influences on women's behaviour: women who are the main earner have often been found to do a larger share of housework than we would expect (in terms of fairness, or in terms of her bargaining power).

It would be helpful to know if there are systematic differences between countries regarding 'gender effects', such as 'gender deviance neutralization'. Bittman et al. (2003: 210) suggest USA differs from Australia: "It is as if Australian wives and American men are trying to neutralize the deviance of the husband's economic dependence. The response by the Australian wives is larger, perhaps because women's employment is still more secondary in Australia and hence the deviance to be neutralized more striking". Evidence in this chapter supports this claim by Bittman et al. of differences between countries; but we cannot generalize from the four countries in this chapter to the world as a whole. My research (not all reported here) suggests that we can only assess 'gender deviance neutralization' reliably if the sample is large. This type of research focuses mainly on households where a woman earns more than her partner, and this is only a small fraction of households; to get a reasonably large number of households in the sample where a woman earns more than her partner, the total sample size should be several thousand respondents.

If 'gender deviance neutralization' does occur, it would be helpful to understand more about it. For example, how can some men get away with doing very little housework, if they don't earn much money from paid work? This chapter has put forward evidence of a possible explanation, in Figures 32 to 35: GBV. It seems that among households where the husband is the main earner (i.e. the right-hand-side of figures in this chapter), the fraction of housework done by the husband is much lower if he uses GBV.

In this chapter (and in much social science), we cannot be sure of which factors are 'cause', and which are 'effect'. I suggest that a plausible explanation for the appearance of Figures 32 to 35 is that some men use GBV to persuade their wife to do a larger share of the housework. But there are other possible explanations, which I do not explore in this chapter: for example, an educated man may be less likely to use GBV, and more likely to do a fair share of housework. More research is needed; but it seems difficult to be sure of the causality, because there are so many factors which could be relevant – such as social class, personality, role models, and education.

Figure 36 confirms the impression (in previous figures in this chapter) that GBV is more likely to occur if a woman earns more than her husband, for three of the four countries considered in this chapter (DHS surveys do not tell us whether or not GBV occurs in the fourth country, Chad).

CONCLUSION

Many writers have claimed a woman's risk of GBV is much lower if she earns enough money 'in her own right' (i.e. from her own earnings, or from savings which she controls) to support herself (Simister, 2009). In such cases, a woman can afford to leave a violent husband. A woman may be able to achieve a similar effect by having the potential to earn money (for example, a highly educated woman may be able to obtain well-paid work if she chooses, even if she is currently not employed). But poor women may find themselves vulnerable to GBV.

A possible remedy for the problem of women being economically dependent on her husband or partner is a welfare state, as is widespread in rich countries such as Europe and north America. Poorer countries may find it difficult to provide such benefits, but there are encouraging signs in countries such as South Africa. Where payments such as child benefits are paid, they should be paid to mothers, rather than to fathers, to give mothers some protection against GBV.

Chapter 12

ALCOHOL INCREASES THE RISK OF GBV

"Beedu, which is a village of about sixty families, has three arrack shops. We found it impossible to stay in the village after six in the evening due to the risk of being harassed by dozens of drunken men on the streets. Drunkenness was only a little less common in Halli and Ooru. Not surprisingly, most women who were beaten complained that the problem was exacerbated by the drunken fits of their husbands. Sometimes drunkenness acted as catalyst, in the sense that arguments that would otherwise have passed uneventfully would turn violent if the husband was drunk. But drunken husbands would also assault their wives without any other provocation" (Rao, 1998: 6).

ABSTRACT

In previous research on GBV, there are many stories of women being beaten by their husband or partner when the man is drunk. This chapter provides more evidence of the link between alcohol and GBV. Alcohol has complicated effects on households: for example, alcohol can change the behaviour of men, which may make some men more violent; but sometimes arguments between spouses can result from husbands demanding money from their wife, to buy alcohol (Gwagwa, 1998): alcohol may be part of a 'vicious circle', in which some men become more dependent on alcohol, becoming less employable and losing the respect of their family, causing the man to be even more reliant on alcohol.

INTRODUCTION

It is often claimed that alcohol consumption causes an increase in the risk of GBV occurring. Husbands consuming alcoholic drink are more likely to commit domestic violence, in India (Visaria, 1999: 13), South Africa (Parry, Myers and Thiede, 2003: 266), and USA (Kantor, 1997). Analysing a southern India community, Rao (1997) found the risk of wife abuse increases when husbands are alcoholic.

For some poor families, alcohol is a large fraction of household spending. Some men are unable to obtain paid work, because they are seen to have an alcohol problem. This can lead such men to demand their wife earn money, to pay for alcohol for himself as well as supporting other household bills such as food. If this happens, a woman may lose respect for her partner; men may only be able to persuade women to pay for alcohol if he uses, or threatens, violence (Gwagwa, 1998). However, this is not the only way in which alcohol can lead to violence: it is sometimes claimed that alcohol can 'disinhibit' a person: this may lead to a man being more likely to use violence when he has consumed alcohol.

This chapter considers evidence (from DHS and WAS surveys) on whether or not alcohol is associated with the risk of GBV occurring. It focuses particularly on alcohol consumption by the husband, on the grounds that a man may beat his wife when he is drunk.

DOES ALCOHOL INCREASE THE RISK OF GBV?

According to McKenry et al. (1995: 309), clear evidence of links between alcohol consumption and domestic violence have been found, but it is difficult to assess the exact nature of the link. Perhaps violence is more common after alcohol consumption because alcohol 'disinhibits' some types of behaviour (a pharmacological explanation); or perhaps violence is more likely because some men blame alcohol for their behaviour (a sociocultural explanation) (McKenry et al., 1995: 309).

Gwagwa's (1998) study of South African families found evidence of a 'vicious circle', in which men who drink increasing amounts of alcohol cannot get paid work, so they use GBV to obtain money from their wife to buy drink. Gwagwa suggests that a man may be seen by his wife as a failure, if he doesn't want to work, or he can't find a job; and some employed men don't support their families financially – often spending on drink, or on other women. If a husband is unemployed, or withholds earnings from his family, a woman in the household may need to earn money to support herself and her children. Gwagwa found there is often a downward spiral: the husband feels he is a failure; he turns to drink; he does not support his family financially; so he loses his wife's respect. Gwagwa's study was a small sample, using qualitative research methods – such data are seen as unscientific by researchers from a quantitative background; but Gwagwa's analysis is the best evidence I know of, if we wish to make sense of "cause and effect". Another excellent source of insights into the link between GBV and money, in the UK context, is Pahl (1985). If we were to use data from a more scientific source (such as the World Bank's 'Living Standards Measurement Study'), we could be precise about average spending on alcohol, and estimate correlations; but if we find a correlation (between alcohol spending and GBV, for example), cross-section data does not tell us which is "cause" and which is "effect". LSMS data do not include data on GBV, so we cannot assess if such a correlation exists; WAS surveys are the only quantitative data source I know of, which could be used to assess such a correlation. The WAS 2000 survey of South Africa did not include data on GBV. It would be useful to use time-series data from a panel study, to assess this: if we found some households where the wife became the main earner, we could see if GBV occurred before or after the increase in alcohol spending. I am not aware of a panel survey in any country which could answer this question. So for the time being, it appears that qualitative research by academics such as Gwagwa and Pahl are the best evidence we have: the best way to understand GBV is to ask the women who are victims of GBV. Future researchers might ask violent men why they are violent, to shed more light on this issue.

Gwagwa's view is supported by McKenry et al. (1995: 310): they report evidence that alcohol consumption interacts with family conflict. If a couple become less intimate, they are more likely to experience domestic violence – and alcohol may increase the risk of conflicts becoming violent. Hindin et al. (2008: 24) point out that GBV and alcohol are inter-related, but give a completely different explanation to Gwagwa. Hindin et al. claim that GBV is more likely to occur if a husband consumes more alcohol, citing evidence from China, Kenya, Peru, South Africa, Uganda, and USA. Flake (2005: 366) concludes that a woman in Peru is about nine times as likely to be abused by her husband if he regularly gets drunk (compared to a husband who never gets drunk). There is a possibility that an association between alcohol and GBV is misleading, because increased alcohol consumption may be a response to stress (Umberson et al, 2003: 234).

Perhaps alcohol may sometimes *reduce* a man's ability to use GBV. Ward et al. (2005: 108) report the story of a survivor of GBV: "he started taking drugs and drinking alcohol. He started to insult me and beat me. At first, I didn't do anything but then I started fighting back – but only when he was drunk and weaker than me".

DHS surveys do not give details on alcohol spending. In some DHS surveys, if the female respondents had experienced GBV, she was asked if her husband was drunk, or on drugs, when he hit her. Table 31 reports evidence from four surveys (as far as I know, these are the only surveys which ask GBV victims about use of drugs/drink by the person who beat them). Table 31 helps us to assess whether or not GBV is related to the consumption of alcohol or drugs. For GBV, this means the husband; but table 31 refers to domestic violence in general (including women who were hit by one of their parents, for example).

Table 31 is of limited help, because we cannot tell how many men became drunk but did not beat their wife. Another limitation is that it does not distinguish between violence caused by alcohol, and violence caused by an illegal drug such as heroin. But evidence in table 31 is consistent with the idea that alcohol is relevant to the risk of GBV. The experience of Egypt may seem to disprove this hypothesis, because few of the violent men were affected by drugs or drink; but Egypt is a predominantly Muslim country – and Islam forbids the consumption of intoxicants such as alcohol. Hence, we would expect few Egyptian men to be drunk; the fact that any Egyptian men were drunk (or on drugs) when they were violent could be taken to suggest that a large fraction of the (few) Egyptian men who got drunk then became violent.

Colombia is not a Muslim country, but there seems little evidence that alcohol or drugs are associated with domestic violence there. In Bolivia and South Africa, much of the violence was carried out when the aggressor was drunk or on drugs; this appears to be a majority of times in Bolivia (69%), and a large minority of violence in South Africa (37%).

Table 31. GBV and consumption of alcohol and/or on drugs, in four countries

Survey	The person who beat respondent was drunk or on drugs		
	never	sometimes	always/frequently
Bolivia 2003	31 %		69 %
Colombia 2000	95 %	3 %	2 %
Egypt 1995	95 %	4 %	1 %
South Africa 1998	37 %	26 %	37 %

Source: DHS (female respondents only).

Table 31 makes it clear that alcohol and drugs are not the only explanation for violence: in all four countries, there are many households where violence occurred but drugs and alcohol were not used. Several DHS surveys (including India 1998) include a question on whether husband and wife ever drink alcohol. Table 32, based on India data, shows that domestic violence is associated with men drinking, rather than with women drinking.

Table 32. Fraction of women experiencing GBV, by male and female drinking

| | | Does the husband drink alcohol? | |
		No	Yes
Does the wife drink alcohol?	No	15% (38,894 households)	27% (14,280 households)
	Yes	16% (111 households)	29% (1,794 households)

Source: DHS India 1998.

Table 33. GBV risk, by how often husband is drunk

| Country | year | How often does your husband get drunk? | | |
		Never	sometimes	often
Azerbaijan	2006	9%	14%	49%
Cambodia	2005	7%	11%	36%
Cameroon	2004	34%	54%	70%
Colombia	2000	30%	41%	68%
Congo Dem Rep	2007	46%	62%	75%
Dominican Rep	2007	13%	19%	55%
Ghana	2008	16%	29%	53%
Haiti	2005	10%	26%	34%
Honduras	2005	3%	4%	5%
India	2005	24%	40%	65%
Kenya	2008	31%	38%	69%
Liberia	2007	32%	49%	65%
Malawi	2000	16%	25%	45%
Mali	2006	2%	5%	4%
Moldova	2005	12%	22%	72%
Nigeria	2008	13%	42%	59%
Peru	2004	30%	44%	84%
Philippines	2008	7%	14%	43%
Rwanda	2005	20%	37%	67%
Sao Tome	2008	20%	43%	73%
Uganda	2006	35%	57%	75%
Ukraine	2007	5%	14%	57%
Zambia	2007	36%	50%	70%

Source: DHS (most recent survey in each country).

Table 34. GBV risk, by household spending on alcohol: India and Nigeria

Household spending on alcohol:	Fraction of female respondents who have been beaten by her husband	
	India 2007	Nigeria 2005
No alcohol spending	6%	7%
up to 4% of household spending	12%	20%
5% to 8% of household spending	13%	11%
9% to 16% of household spending	23%	13%
over 16% of household spending	33%	23%

Source: WAS (male and female respondents).

In Table 32, the risk of domestic violence hardly changes as we go down from the 'no' (wife doesn't drink) row, to the 'yes' (wife drinks) row. But there is a dramatic increases in GBV prevalence as we go from the 'no' (husband doesn't drink) column to the 'yes' (husband drinks) column – the GBV prevalence rate almost doubled if the husband drinks alcohol.

Table 33 uses DHS data, to assess whether drunkenness (rather than moderate alcohol consumption) explains GBV. The table shows all DHS surveys for which appropriate data were collected; but where more than one DHS survey in the same country had data on these variables, table 33 only reports data from the most recent survey (for example, these questions were asked in both the Peru 2000 and Peru 2004-8 DHS surveys, so the Peru 2000 survey is excluded from table 33). Table 33 provides data on many countries, which makes it more reliable than tables 31 and 32. In Table 33, we see a woman's risk of GBV tending to rise, as we look from left to right: i.e. as we focus on men who get drunk more often. For example, in Zambia, the risk of a woman being beaten by her husband rises from 36% (for men who never get drunk) to 70% (for men who often get drunk). This is consistent with the idea that the risk of GBV is higher among households where the husband gets drunk. Note, however, that the risk of GBV in the 'never gets drunk' column is always above zero; this indicates that even in households where the husband never gets drunk, GBV still occurs sometimes. Table 33 suggests alcohol is not the only cause of GBV; but that husbands who get drunk are more likely to use GBV than men who do not get drunk.

Table 34 shows the proportion of household spending on alcohol, and violence; it indicates a clear pattern in which violence rises from 6% or 7% (in households not buying alcohol) to 33% or 23% (in households where alcohol spending is over 16% of total spending). As we look down Table 34 from low to high alcohol spending, the risk of GBV tends to increase. Table 34 is consistent with the idea that if a man spends more on alcohol, he is more likely to be violent to his wife. Table 34 analyses data on alcohol spending; it refers to spending by the household as a whole, not just by the husband; but data in Tables 32 and 33 suggest GBV is associated with alcohol consumption by the husband, rather than by the wife.

DO SOME MEN SPEND TOO MUCH ON ALCOHOL?

The previous section suggests alcohol consumption can lead to GBV; but it may also cause other types of harm. One example is that alcohol may lead to hunger, for some or all household members. Imagine a household in which the total income after tax is just sufficient to buy enough food, if all disposable income (after paying the rent) is spent on food. In such a household, every Rupee (or Rand, or Naira, or other currency unit) spent on alcohol means there is now not enough money left to buy enough food. If a man gains more control of household spending, he may be able to increase his own alcohol consumption by reducing the food consumption of his wife and children.

It is sometimes suggested that some (but not all) men spend too much money on drink, which can lead to hunger for members of their household. This is sometimes referred to as the 'children fare better' hypothesis – meaning that children will tend to be better fed if their mother is earning money herself, rather than relying on her husband's income. Hoddinott and Haddad (1995), and Phipps and Burton (1992), found that higher female income is associated with lower expenditure on alcohol and tobacco; this suggests men and women have different spending priorities – many men consider alcohol spending a high priority, whereas many women consider the children to be more important. There is no evidence (as far as I know) that this pattern is inevitable: it appears to be cultural, and hence could be changed. School teachers could warn pupils (especially male pupils) about the dangers of excessive alcohol consumption, and the need to behave responsibly – especially for people with dependent children. Education of adults could be achieved by media campaigns, such as reporting examples of men who are good fathers.

It would be useful to identify the effects of the husband's priorities, as distinct from the effects of the wife's priorities, regarding household spending. One way is to study male-headed and female-headed households, on the grounds that the 'head of household' can be assumed to be influential in household decisions. Previous research has found differences between male-headed and female-headed households, regarding household spending. Male-headed households in Accra (Ghana) spent more than female-headed households on alcohol (Levin et al., 1999). A Malawi study (cited in Kennedy and Haddad, 1994: 1080) found that female-headed households spend 25% to 50% less on alcoholic drink than male-headed households; and "The lower level of malnutrition among female-headed households, particularly among de facto female-headed households, is striking given these households' significantly lower incomes" (Kennedy and Haddad, 1994: 1082). Further evidence that female-headed households fare better than comparable male-headed households has been found in Kenya (Kennedy and Peters, 1992). Pahl (1985) found similar patterns in UK: a mother with a low income may be able to provide better for her children, because she can prioritise spending on food for the children; whereas a mother in in a relatively rich household may see her children go hungry, because her husband decides how the family's money is spent.

Kerr (2005: 74) criticises mainstream economic analysis, for assumes rational behaviour by each spouse: "The bargaining approach to examining intra-household relations, although identifying the co-operative or conflictual nature of household relations, does not describe many of the structural aspects of household relations in northern Malawi". Alcohol and violence do not appear consistent with conventional economic analysis – Kerr (2005: 72) wrote "Wives openly dispute some decisions made by husbands, particularly regarding alcohol use or insufficient funds given to the household, but they appear to have few avenues to change their situation. The high level of physical abuse clearly creates a climate of fear and uncertainty for wives. Thus, to characterise the household relationship as simply that of 'bargaining' ignores the broader structural context that gives men more access to entitlements and in which social norms reinforce unequal power relationships within the household".

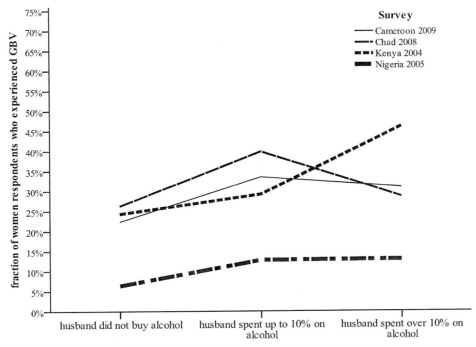

Source: WAS.

Figure 37. GBV by country and husband's spending on alcohol.

Figure 37 uses WAS data, to assess if there is a link between alcohol consumption by a husband, and shortages of food in his household. Note that Figure 37 uses data on alcohol spending by the husband (presumably for his own use), unlike Table 34 above – which considered spending on alcohol by all household members.

Figure 37 tells us that if the husband spends more on alcohol, the wife (or female partner) in that household is more likely to be a victim of GBV. This is shown by the tendency for the number of women who experience GBV to increase, as we look from left (husband did not buy any alcohol) to right (husband spent over 10% of household income on alcohol). This pattern appears to apply in all four countries in Figure 37 (Cameroon, Chad, Kenya, and Nigeria).

The lines are not straight, perhaps because the sample sizes in these WAS surveys is much smaller than in DHS surveys – so there is noticeable random variation. As discussed elsewhere in this chapter, the causality is unclear – some of the complexities are discussed in

Gwagwa (1998), such as a woman losing respect for her husband if he becomes alcoholic (so he cannot get paid work).

Table 35 gives some insights into household spending, and may (at least partly) explain the patterns in Figures 32 to 35. Table 35 shows the average spending on alcohol by husbands, expressed as a fraction of total household income.

Table 35. Spending by husbands on alcohol, by whether GBV occurred

Country	Whether or not wife has been hit by her husband	Husband's spending on alcoholic drink, as a percentage of total household income
Cameroon (2009)	no	6 %
	yes	15 %
Chad (2008)	no	19 %
	yes	19 %
Kenya (2004)	no	7 %
	yes	13 %
Nigeria (2005)	no	1 %
	yes	1 %

Source: WAS.

In two of these four countries, the amount of money spent on luxuries tends to increase if the wife has been hit by her husband – in Cameroon, the share of household income spent by the husband on alcohol for himself is 6% of household income among men who do not hit their partner, increasing to 15% of household income among men who do hit their partner. And in Kenya, the fraction spent by the husband rose from 7% to 13%, if GBV occurred in the household. There appears no such connection in the other two countries in Table 35: Chad and Nigeria. The influence of Islam (and the prohibition against drinking alcohol) probably explains at least partly why Nigeria is different; we would expect Nigerian Muslims, who make up most of the northern half of Nigeria, to spend less on alcohol whether or not GBV occurred – overall, 45% of the 2005 WAS Nigeria sample were Muslims. The Chad data in Table 35 seem surprising: a fairly large fraction of Chad's population is Muslim (31%, in the 2008 WAS survey), so the fraction spent on alcohol is surprisingly high; and there appears to be no association between alcohol consumption and GBV in Chad. Perhaps more research will shed light on why Chad seems unusual in this respect.

The apparent link between alcohol and GBV in Table 35, for Cameroon and Kenya, is difficult to interpret. Some writers, such as Hindin et al. (2008: 24), argue that alcohol consumption causes some men to be violent. It seems likely that causality applies in both directions: alcohol consumption causes GBV, and GBV causes alcohol consumption. For example, Gwagwa (1998) studied households in Durban (South Africa), and found a 'vicious circle' in which men who increasingly drank alcohol found themself unable to obtain work, and in many cases used GBV to demand alcohol from their wife. Presumably men who use GBV are more likely to get money from their wife, to buy more alcohol: GBV gives men power.

A Possible Remedy: Taxes on Alcohol, to Pay for Child Benefits Paid to Mothers

Taxing alcohol could reduce drink-related violence (Parry, Myers and Thiede, 2003), with tax revenue paying for refuges for battered women; or perhaps the money could pay child benefit to women, so they are less financially dependent on their husband. The idea of governments using tax revenue to pay child benefit to mothers has been adopted in several countries, such as UK; and taxes on alcohol are often high. The idea of making a direct link between alcohol tax and child benefit may be helpful, by making clear to fathers and mothers that alcohol consumption by fathers can cause problems for other members of their family. Expenditure on alcohol by mothers is generally much smaller than alcohol expenditure by fathers, according to WAS data (not reported here).

Taxation is one of many approaches which could be used to reduce the inter-related problems of GBV and alcohol consumption. Education is vital: not just in schools, but helping adults to understand the damage which can be done to a family if alcohol consumption leads to violence. Activists who are working to reduce the risk of GBV could consider media campaigns, to warn people (especially men) of the harm that can result from over-indulgence in alcohol. Qualitative research (such as Gwagwa, 1988) suggests that women have a key role here: if a man loses his job, it would be very dangerous for his partner to humiliate him because he no longer provides for his family – he may turn to drink, become alcoholic, and eventually find himself unemployable. Instead, a woman who is supportive to his wife may be able to support her partner through a difficult time, if he is out of work. But we should not ask women to be submissive: women's empowerment may be essential, in refusing to let him become dependent on alcohol. In many ways, it would be better for the family if the wife/partner has her own job – this will tend to be less stressful for the family than relying on one income (the husband).

Conclusion

As is common in social science research, we cannot be sure that there is a simple cause-and-effect relationship between alcohol and GBV. Perhaps excessive alcohol consumption is a symptom of stress, such as male unemployment, in which case it could be that the real cause of GBV is unemployment rather than alcohol.

The tables in this chapter suggest there is a fairly strong connection between alcohol consumption and GBV. This connection is apparent if we study spending on alcohol; evidence on whether or not the husband drinks; and data on whether or not the husband gets drunk.

If any reader feels we should not intervene in domestic disputes, this chapter provides a clear illustration of why activists and campaigners should pay attention to the problem of GBV. If a man uses GBV, his wife/partner suffers from the violence; the power some men get from violence may harm his partner and children, because he spends too much on alcohol, leaving little left for food. And excessive alcohol spending may harm the husband, if he becomes alcoholic – this can often lead to breakup of the family. GBV is a problem which society should not ignore.

Chapter 13

GBV MAY BE RELATED TO CORTISOL

"Cortisol is often called the "stress hormone" [..] Released from the adrenal cortices into the bloodstream, cortisol flows to the brain and other organs, where it mobilizes the body's physical resources in preparation for fight or flight." (Mazur, 2005: 87).

ABSTRACT

Cortisol is a stress hormone, which is often at higher levels in a person's blood early in the morning. Daly et al. (2011: 524) claimed "Past work suggests that one function of cortisol is to energize people in the morning". There is evidence from medical research that cortisol may influence behaviour: for example, cortisol may be associated with one person dominating one or more other people. This chapter uses data from household surveys, to assess how attitudes to GBV vary, depending on the hour when the interview took place. This chapter may shed light on the hypothesis that cortisol is associated with acceptance of GBV (and violence generally) among men and women.

INTRODUCTION

Cortisol is a chemical emitted by the human body to produce certain types of response when a person is (or feels) under threat. This appears to affect human behaviour, including aggression and dominance (Anderson and Summers, 2007: 103). Cortisol is one of several hormones which, in humans, are associated with a 'fight or flight' response – preparing a human under threat (other stress hormones include adrenaline, discussed in the following chapter). There is general agreement that the level of cortisol varies over the day: it tends to rise suddenly soon after a person wakes, and then declines slowly during the day (Purnell et al., 2004).

There seems to be a complicated relationship between cortisol and aggression. There is some evidence (reported below) that a person is more likely to be aggressive if they usually have a low level of cortisol in their blood. Mazur (2005: 88) claimed cortisol level in the blood is higher when people compete – whether this competition is in physical sport, sedentary chess matches, or trading personal insults.

It would be helpful to know if more violence occurs early in the morning: I have not yet found suitable data to test this, but crime statistics may offer potential for future research. Even if data on how many crimes occurred at different times were available, it would be hard to interpret: for example, we may find more crimes in the evening due to alcohol consumption (see the previous chapter); if we find more crimes in the afternoon, it may be due to high temperatures (see the following chapter). Rather than *occurrence* of GBV, this chapter focuses on *attitudes* to GBV, so we can assess if there is any change in attitudes during the day.

PREVIOUS RESEARCH

Lindman et al. (1992) studied a sample of men arrested for domestic violence, and measured their level of cortisol. They found the level of cortisol in the blood of these violent men was higher at the time of the incident than it was a few hours later. In addition, they found that men who committed domestic violence tended to have a higher level of blood cortisol than a sample of men who were not violent. This suggests a link between cortisol and GBV, but the details are not clear – for example, alcohol may complicate any apparent link between cortisol and GBV. "The significantly elevated cortisol and glucose concentrations in offenders when sober compared to nonviolent controls could be viewed as direct effects of life stress, or as indirect effects of stress mediated by learned escape drinking" (Lindman et al., 1992: 393).

If cortisol is a stress hormone, we might expect more violence if there is a high level of cortisol in a person's blood. But some writers, such as Cauffman (2008: 128), claim violence is more common in people with *low* levels of cortisol: this pattern applies to both men and women. Perhaps a person who has a generally low level of cortisol in their blood, is better able to 'rise to a challenge': their cortisol level can rise when a crisis or conflict occurs.

Mazur (2005: 88) wrote "individuals who are chronically shy or nervous, hence usually unassertive, have relatively high cortisol levels"; perhaps a high cortisol level indicates a person under stress – cortisol could be a sign of someone being dominated. Research reported by Astbury (2006: 52) suggests that women with high levels of cortisol are more likely to experience psychological problems such as depression. Perhaps this can be explained by Mazur's claim that people who are dominated tend to have high levels of cortisol: if so, the sequence of causality could be a woman who is dominated has a higher level of cortisol (perhaps from stress, due to her husband's dominating her); and the experience of being dominated may lead the woman to be depressed. A high cortisol level may indicate a woman who is dominated, but cortisol may not be the *cause* of depression. Other causal explanations are possible – for example, a woman may be stressed (and perhaps prone to have a higher cortisol level) because her husband is violent, and this violence could cause depression for women. This book does not investigate the long-term effects of a high cortisol level in the blood. Rather, this chapter studies variation in attitudes to GBV over the course of a day, on the grounds that this may be related to changing levels of cortisol.

Cohen and Vandello (1998: 574) studied levels of cortisol in blood in a sample of people in the USA; they found the highest level were associated with men who were from southern USA and who had been 'insulted' as part of an experiment. This suggests that cortisol is linked to the experience of being insulted, but only in southern USA – which Cohen and Vandello consider to be a region with a violent culture. So a high cortisol level in someone's blood may have different effects in different cultures.

SURVEY EVIDENCE INTO EFFECTS OF CORTISOL

Previous medical research has established that there is a 'diurnal' pattern of cortisol level in the blood of a typical person. An illustration is shown in Figure 38, which I obtained by measuring the heights of points on a printout of Figure 4 in Purnell et al. (2004). Figure 38 looks clearer than Figure 4 in Purnell et al. (2004), because they report data at 30-minute intervals (I take the average of their two measurements per hour, to improve clarity).

Figure 38 indicates a very strong variation over the course of the day, for the 18 men and women studied by Purnell et al. (2004). The peak of the curve, the highest level of cortisol, is at 7am for the subjects they studied; but the time of this peak may be influenced by the time at which they normally get out of bed in the morning, which could be affected by various factors such as the time sunrise occurs.

Fuller-Rowell, Doan and Eccles (forthcoming: 2011) studied a sample of white and African American men, and found an apparent link between attitudes to race discrimination and the slope of the decline of cortisol over the day. I am not aware of any similar study on gender discrimination, but perhaps attitudes to gender discrimination are similar to attitudes to racial discrimination, in terms of the biological processes involved.

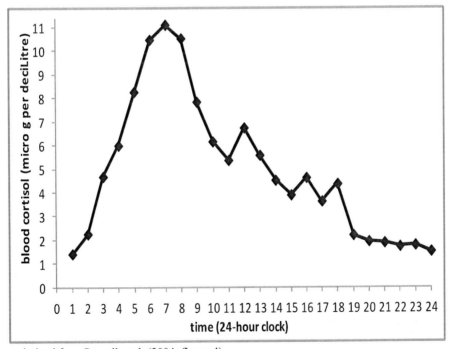

Source: derived from Purnell et al. (2004: figure 4).

Figure 38. Blood cortisol level, by time of day (average of 9 men and 9 women).

CORTISOL AND GBV

If people usually have a peak in their cortisol level in the early morning (as Figure 38 suggests), does this affect their attitudes to GBV? Figure 39 allows us to assess this topic: it uses data from the DHS and WAS survey in several countries (focusing on the surveys with the largest sample sizes, among the DHS and WAS surveys available so far). The horizontal axis of Figure 39 is the time at which the interview took place, rounded to the nearest hour (using the 24-hour clock: 24 represents midnight). Where any one survey had less than 10 respondents in any one hour (men and women combined), the data for that hour are not used to create Figure 39; hence, the earliest interviews in Figure 39 took place at 6am (shown as 6 on the horizontal axis). Figure 39 uses attitudes of female respondents; Figure 40 is the equivalent for male respondents.

Figure 39 is based on answers to the question 'Is a husband justified in hitting or beating his wife: if she argues with him?' (answers were yes or no). In Figure 39, women interviewed before mid-day were more likely to agree with the statement about acceptability of GBV. This is consistent with the hypothesis that in the morning, women are affected by cortisol; and that cortisol makes them more aggressive. Anderson and Summers (2007) use the term 'dominant', rather than violent, to describe the effects of cortisol.

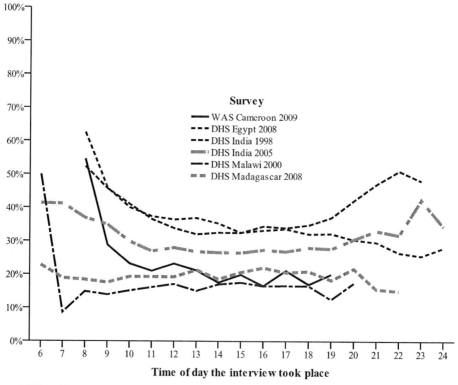

Source: DHS and WAS.

Figure 39. Attitude to husband hitting his wife, by time of day: women respondents.

If we compare Figures 38 and 39, there may be a similarity between female acceptance of GBV (in Figure 39), and cortisol level (in Figure 38). There is more acceptance of GBV among women respondents at the time we would expect cortisol levels to be high (i.e. about 7am). It is difficult to make a precise comparison between Figures 38 and 39. There were only a handful of interviews between midnight and 5am in the DHS and WAS surveys used for Figure 39, so they are excluded from Figure 39, because too few cases are available; whereas data for Figure 38 is provided by Purnell et al. (2004) for the full 24-hour period. The peak in Figure 38 is at 7am, whereas the peak in Figure 39 is at 6am (or it may be earlier, since Figure 39 shows no data before 6am). The exact time of the cortisol peak might be related to the average time at which people rise: there is some evidence that the time at which people wake affects the time at which their cortisol level peaks (Edwards et al., 2001). Roden et al. (1993) found the timing of the cortisol peak is usually similar for night shift workers as for the majority of the population. Another possible influence on when the peak cortisol level occurs is the number of hours of daylight; but Campbell et al. (1982) found a cortisol peak continues even among people who experience 24-hour daylight. Practical considerations influence the availability of household survey data on this topic. If DHS or WAS interviewed a respondent at night-time (such as midnight), then the respondent was awake at that time; this may suggest that respondent has a non-typical lifestyle, such as a night worker. This practicality does not apply to the clinical data collected by Purnell et al. (2004), which are used to create Figure 38.

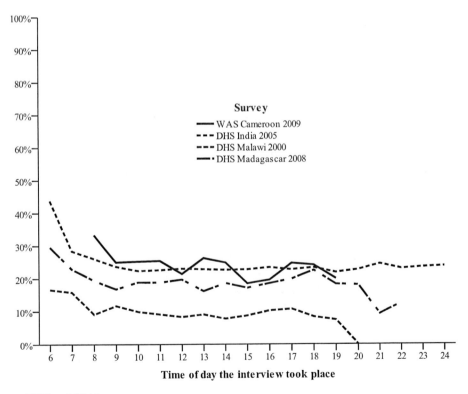

Source: DHS and WAS.

Figure 40. Attitude to husband hitting his wife, by time of day: male respondents.

Figure 40 is similar to 39, but for men rather than women. Figure 40 is based on acceptance of GBV, in the same scenario as Figure 39 (where a wife argues with her husband). There are fewer countries in Figure 40 than in Figure 39, because some DHS surveys did not interview men.

If we consider the possible influence of cortisol in Figure 40, we see a man is almost twice as likely to say GBV is acceptable (in this scenario) if he is interviewed at 6am as if he was interviewed after mid-day. In the 2005 DHS survey in India, for example, 44% of men interviewed at 6am said they agreed with the statement, compared with 23% for men interviewed at noon.

In the DHS Malawi 2000 survey, none of the men interviewed at 8pm (shown as 20, on the horizontal axis of Figure 40) agreed that GBV is acceptable if a wife argues, but this 8pm sample is not large enough to be reliable: only 7 men were interviewed in Malawi at 8pm. On the other hand, the DHS Madagascar survey interviewed 215 men at 8pm; and the DHS India sample interviewed 3,566 men at 8pm (the 2005 DHS India survey is one of the largest social science surveys ever collected, and hence is more reliable than most surveys). So while we might not wish to put too much trust in the evidence for Malawi in Figure 39, we can be more confident in the results from the Indian survey.

The fact that all four countries show increased acceptance of GBV before 9am suggests this is not just random, but indicates a real link between cortisol and (acceptance of) GBV. If there is such a link, cortisol is not the only influence on how acceptable GBV is: for example, there is much less acceptance of GBV in Malawi than in the other three countries in Figure 40, because the line for Malawi is near the horizontal axis in Figure 40. The general level of acceptance of GBV among women in Figure 39 varies between countries (as well as men, in Figure 40); this may be due to a combination of factors, such as education level and culture.

In Figure 39, there is a large increase in acceptance of GBV in the evening, in the two DHS India surveys; due to the very large sample sizes in these two surveys, it is highly unlikely that this is due to random variation. Astbury (2006: 52) claims that women respond differently to stress, if they experience GBV. In particular, women who have experienced a history of GBV tend to have higher levels of cortisol in the evening, when we would expect cortisol levels to have fallen. This seems consistent with Figures 39 and 40: women in India seem to have higher than expected acceptance of GBV, which may indicate high levels of cortisol, but this does not apply to men in Figure 40.

To investigate this, Figure 41 uses data from the 1998 DHS India survey (female respondents only), controlling for whether or not the respondent experienced GBV in the 12 months preceding the interview. If we interpret acceptance of GBV as an indicator of cortisol, Figure 41 suggests support for the claim of Astbury (2006), that experience of GBV tends to increase a GBV victim's level of cortisol in the evening. Note, however, that there are numerous other factors which affect attitudes, and hence which could make Figure 41 misleading – for example, perhaps alcohol consumption is more common in the evening, for both women and men. If women's high cortisol levels in the evening is a result of them being victims of GBV, we would not expect to see the increase in acceptance of GBV in the evening among women who did not experience GBV. It may be helpful for medical researchers in future to measure cortisol levels in the blood, at the same time as asking about attitudes to GBV.

Figure 42 uses time of day on the horizontal axis, as did the previous figures in this chapter.

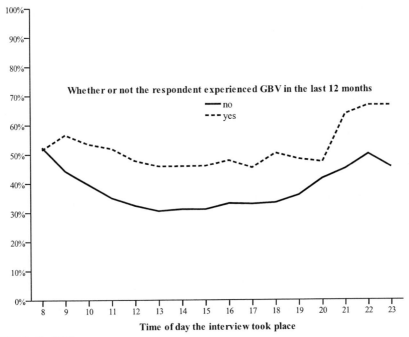

Source: DHS India 1998.

Figure 41. Attitude to husband hitting his wife, by time of day and GBV experience.

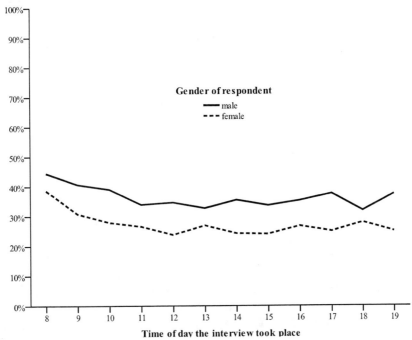

Source: WAS Cameroon 2009.

Figure 42. Respondents wanting to make decisions themselves, by gender.

The vertical axis in Figure 42 shows an index from zero to 100%, where 100% represents respondents saying they 'strongly agree' with the statement "I want to make decisions myself, without having to discuss it with my spouse"; a score of 0% represents people who 'strongly disagree' with the statement. There is an increase in support for the statement, on the left side of Figure 42 before about 11am, for women and for men. This appears to support the hypothesis that respondents are likely to have high levels of cortisol in their blood early in the morning, and that this makes them keener to achieve dominance over other people (in this case, wanting to dominate their spouse).

It may be possible to assess if more violent crime is committed in the early morning, to assess the hypothesis that cortisol is associated with aggression, by using published crime statistics. I have not found suitable data, but this may be a useful direction for future research. However, if suitable data are available, there are complications in interpreting them: for example, there may be a high crime rate in the evening, due to alcohol consumption (a topic discussed in the previous chapter); and there may be a high crime rate in the afternoon, when the temperature is high (a topic discussed in the following chapter).

CONCLUSION

This chapter reports evidence from household surveys, which suggest there may be a tendency for attitudes to GBV to be different in the early morning, due to the effects of cortisol. The evidence for this is not entirely persuasive, being based on a similarity between Figures 39, 40, and 41 with the diurnal variation in cortisol from clinical studies such as Purnell et al. (2004), which I adapt to make Figure 38 in this chapter. Women and men would be expected to have more acceptance of GBV, at times when cortisol levels in the blood of men and women tend to be high: early in the morning. But because household surveys (such as WAS and DHS) do not test levels of cortisol, this chapter can only report indirect evidence – the only persuasive way to test the effects of cortisol is in a clinical study, which involves regular testing of cortisol (usually blood tests, or saliva tests). The evidence in this chapter should only be considered tentative – as far as I am aware, this book is the first academic study which reports a link between cortisol and attitudes to GBV; more research is needed, before we can be confident of the claims in this chapter. The possibility of a link between GBV and cortisol is complicated, and there may be interactions between two or more factors (for example, some writers consider the ratio of cortisol to testosterone gives useful insights into human behaviour).

One question to consider is whether we should focus on the wife's cortisol level, or the husband's cortisol level. If we think GBV is a result of men being angry, it makes sense to see any factor which may make men angry (including cortisol) to be a cause of GBV. But perhaps a woman's cortisol level in the morning may make her aggressive – if, for example, she finds her husband spent most of his earnings in a bar the previous evening, and there's no longer enough money to buy food for their children. In such cases, GBV might be a result of the husband responding to his wife's disobedience. In such cases, it's not clear how campaigners should react: clearly we don't want to ask women to be submissive to their husband, because GBV is not the only problem. If a woman behaved in a submissive way, it might reduce her risk of experiencing GBV, but could lead to her children going hungry – if her husband then reacts to her submissiveness by spending more on alcoholic drink for himself, for example.

If there is a link between cortisol and attitudes to GBV, this may suggest a useful lesson: women should be careful in the early morning, because there is a risk that their husband or partner may be more aggressive due to a higher level of cortisol in his blood. If women also have higher cortisol at this time, there may be more risk of the argument escalating. This does not mean that women should defer to their husband in case he becomes violent; but perhaps women and men could be advised not to discuss topics (such as money) which are likely to cause conflict between them, early in the morning.

Chapter 14

VIOLENCE, AND GBV IN PARTICULAR, HAPPEN MORE AT STRESSFUL TEMPERATURES

"violence and murders have been found to increase following heat waves [..]
Temperature-induced violence includes political rebellions / riots, assaults, spouse abuse /
domestic violence, manslaughter and murder" (Simister and Cooper, 2005: 4).

ABSTRACT

Previous research has shown a strong link between temperature and several types of violent crimes. Thermal stress may cause aggression in hot countries; frequent exposure to such aggression may make it seem normal (and hence acceptable) to people who observe it. This chapter uses household survey data to study effects of hot temperatures on physical violence between husband and wife: such surveys indicate a strong link between temperature and attitudes to GBV. Respondents tend to be more accepting of a man using physical violence against his wife if the interview takes place at a high temperature, compared to moderate temperatures; this tendency applies to both male and female respondents. This tendency may be due to the effects of stress hormones such as adrenaline and noradrenaline. Ownership of electric fans tends to reduce acceptance of violence; air-conditioning is even more effective. If women are taught more about the thermal stress, they may be able to reduce their risk of violence.

INTRODUCTION

Studies in many countries indicate seasonal patterns in violent crime-rates (Anderson (1989): there is a tendency for crime rates to be higher in hot summer months, than in cooler months. Such links between extreme temperatures and violence have been reported from several countries, including the USA (Anderson, 1989; Simister and Cooper, 2005), UK (Semmens et al, 2002: 798), and India and Pakistan (Simister, 2001; Simister and Van de Vliert, 2005). If we take one location (such as Los Angeles in USA), we find more violent crime in summer than the rest of year. All temperatures in this chapter are in degrees Centigrade (°C); I round each temperature to the nearest whole number.

A different type of evidence on the link between temperature and violence can be found by comparing two different locations: this type of comparison often uses annual data in several different locations, to assess if hot places have more violent crimes than cooler places. Rosenfeld's research on USA (cited in Anderson, 1989: 79) found violent crimes such as murder significantly higher in (hot) southern cities. Van de Vliert et al. (1999: 300) claim there is more violence in hot climates, and they argue this is due to 'cultures of masculinity': in hot places, men are usually expected to dominate women. Some writers suggest a 'culture of violence' may be responsible for more aggression in areas such as southern USA; note, however, that such a culture may be an effect of temperature, rather than a cause of violence (Anderson, 1989: 79).

Simister and Cooper (2005) report evidence that there is more violence in hot places, but they explain this in terms of stress hormones such as noradrenaline. Humans find very hot or very cold weather stressful. Each human must keep their blood temperature in a narrow range of temperatures: 37°C is a typical temperature in the inner 'core' of the body (Brück, 1999: 642). Roberts (1986: 238-9) suggests that for a naked man, 29°C is comfortable (Roberts does not indicate whether a woman has different preferences to a man); Brück (1989: 631) suggests a seated, lightly clothed person in 50% humidity will prefer a temperature around 25 to 26°C (but other factors such as work and acclimatization also affect preferences). Humphreys (1995: 8) claims that humans prefer temperatures ranging from 17°C to 33°C. Roberts (1986: 238-9) describes an "efficiency range", in which the body can control temperature by physical means (such as vasodilatation and sweating); if the temperature is hotter or colder than this efficiency range, the body augments physical cooling with an emergency response, to increase the metabolic rate. Perhaps adrenaline levels may rise when temperatures exceed the lower end of the efficiency range. Roberts (1986: 238-9) suggests the lower end of the efficiency range is about 27°C for a naked man, not much below the optimal temperature of 29°C (Roberts doesn't state the upper end of the efficiency range).

Humans need stress hormones, to cope with the stressful environments in which we live; but these hormones can have undesirable side effects. The human body reacts to extreme temperatures by producing stress hormones. Cortisol is one stress hormone, discussed in the previous chapter. Mazur (2005: 88) claimed that it takes minutes for cortisol to suffuse through the body and reach the appropriate organs, so "If we had to wait for a cortisol response before responding to a sudden threat, we would have a poor chance of survival".

Some writers suggest testosterone may be related to violence. Testosterone levels are higher in summer (Andersson et al., 2003); Andersson et al. claim that air temperature accounts for this seasonal variation of testosterone in men. However, Anderson (1989: 85) reports that increase in rapes occurs earlier in the year than the rise in testosterone levels. Kemper suggests that the interaction of noradrenaline and testosterone cause aggression; but testosterone may be an effect – rather than a cause – of violence (Kemper, 1990: 29-33). Testosterone levels are much higher in men than in women (ten times higher, on average, according to Kemper, 1990: p. 134); but women and men are not as different to each other, when it comes to rates of violence – as explained in chapter 2 of this book. This casts doubt on the importance of testosterone in violence. Mazur (2005: 110) claimed "It may be the case that testosterone is related primarily among men and not to aggression except in situations where dominance happens to be asserted aggressively". McKenry et al. (1995: 309) claim that the interaction of testosterone and alcohol is associated with domestic violence. Terburg et al. (2009) claim that the ratio of testosterone to cortisol is important: "High levels of testosterone and low levels of cortisol have been associated with social aggression". Van Honk et al. (2010: 67) add a third factor to testosterone and cortisol: serotonin, to create a 'Triple Imbalance Hypothesis' (TIH), where "The TIH suggests that reactive aggression is differentiated from proactive aggression by low brain serotonergic function". Mehta et al. (2010: 898) claim "Because dominance is related to gaining and maintaining high status positions in social hierarchies, the findings suggest that only when cortisol is low should higher testosterone encourage higher status. When cortisol is high, higher testosterone may actually decrease dominance and in turn motivate lower status." It is possible that cortisol and/or testosterone may be related to aggression; but as far as I am aware, there is no direct or compelling evidence. The next section considers two other hormones: adrenaline and noradrenaline.

Adrenaline level in the blood is higher if the temperature is very hot, in men and women (al-Hadramy, 1989; Jezova, Kvetnansky and Vigas, 1994). Blood adrenaline level is not raised by cold weather (Frank et al., 1997; Sramek et al., 2000). Effects of adrenaline include vasodilatation (expanding peripheral blood vessels, to cool the body); increasing the heartbeat rate; raising the blood pressure; and stimulating respiration. According to Barrington (1983: 1081), these effects of adrenaline probably help to regulate body temperature in mammals.

Noradrenaline blood levels are higher in extreme heat or extreme cold, in both men and women (al-Hadramy, 1989; Frank et al., 1997; Jezova, Kvetnansky and Vigas, 1994; Sramek et al., 2000). Kukkonen-Harjula et al. (1989) found more noradrenaline in blood of heat-stressed people.

In very cold weather, noradrenaline contracts blood vessels, reducing heat loss through the skin (Pocock and Richards, 1999: 541); noradrenaline also lowers the heartbeat rate, and slightly raises blood sugar level and metabolism (Barrington, 1983: 1081). Hence, noradrenaline has some similarities to adrenaline; but in other respects, noradrenaline has the opposite effect to adrenaline.

A person under threat receives a rapid first response in the form of a shot of adrenaline (within seconds of the threat being detected by the human); adrenaline is often associated with a 'fight or flight' response: to fight against an aggressor, or to run away. Adrenaline is associated with aggression (Simister and Cooper, 2011); noradrenaline could have similar effects – Haller, Makara and Kruk (1998) claim noradrenaline causes aggression. Research by Kemper (1990: 31) suggests a relationship between noradrenaline and "anger, which is a frequent precursor of aggression".

Types of violence which seem to be affected by temperature include political rebellions and riots, assaults, manslaughter and murder, and domestic violence (Anderson, 1989; Rotton and Cohn, 2001). If violence in general is more common in hot climates, this may apply to GBV also. This chapter investigates the hypothesis that very high temperatures are associated with a higher risk of GBV, and with more acceptance of GBV.

Researchers disagree on the precise effects of temperature on violence. Some writers, such as Van de Vliert et al. (1999) and Anderson and Anderson (1984) discuss the 'curvilinear hypothesis': this claims that violence tends to increase with higher temperatures, up to a point, but then declines with further increases in temperature.

Simister and Cooper (2005) disagree, arguing that there's more violence at very hot temperatures. Despite such controversies, there are areas of agreement: over a range of roughly 8°C to 24°C, most researchers in this field claim violence tends to increase if the temperature rises.

DATA AND METHODS

For some of the countries studied in this book (such as Egypt and Nigeria), I estimate temperature in each part of the country, and in each month, using data from Weatherbase (2006). I use 'maximum' temperature, i.e. the average (for all available years) of the maximum temperature for that month and that weather station; and 'minimum' temperature, the average minimum temperatures at each station and month.

This data source has limitations – for example, for interviews in January 2006, it would be better to use the January 2006 temperature rather than the average January temperature in recent years, if it is available. If there is more than one weather station in a governorate (Egypt) or state (Nigeria), I use the station in the largest town/city; for governorates or states with no weather station data in Weatherbase, I use data from adjacent governorates/states.

Most household surveys do not report the temperature at which the interview took place. For this chapter, the temperature at the place and time of each interview is estimated by the following formula, assuming a sine wave is an approximation of hour-to-hour temperature variation:

$$temperature = ((Tmax + Tmin)/2) + ((Tmax - Tmin)/2)*sine(pi*(H - 8)/12)$$

where $Tmax$ is the hottest temperature at that governorate and month;
             $Tmin$ is the coolest temperature in that governorate and month;
             H is the time of interview (using the 24-hour clock).

I assume the maximum temperature is 2pm (not noon, when the sun is overhead, because homes retain heat). Malinda Anthony (2002: 14) found the hottest indoor temperature about 3pm to 5pm, in the case of hospital buildings; but there will tend to be less thermal inertia in smaller buildings such as a family home, or outdoors.

Consider, for example, a Cairo household interviewed in January: the above formula assumes a respondent interviewed at 2pm experienced $Tmax$ (the maximum Cairo temperature recorded in January in recent years); if anyone were interviewed at 2am, they'd be expected to experience $Tmin$ (the minimum January Cairo temperature, averaged over recent years).

For someone interviewed at 8am or 8pm, the temperature estimate is exactly halfway between $Tmin$ and $Tmax$. The increasing ownership of fans and air-conditioning in recent decades is another complication; this is discussed below. This paper does not assess the influence of other factors such as humidity or wind speed, but future researchers could control for them. This temperature estimate is used on the horizontal axis of Figures 46 and 47 below.

The three most recent WAS surveys (in Chad, Cameroon, and Congo-Brazzaville) are innovative in that each interviewer measured the temperature using a thermometer, about mid-way through the interview (as far as I know, these are the only social surveys which measured temperature).

This information is used on the horizontal axis of Figures 43, 44 and 45. The temperature on the horizontal axis of these three Figures is probably more accurate than the estimated temperature using the method in the previous paragraph.

APPARENT LINKS BETWEEN ATTITUDES AND TEMPERATURE

The previous chapter investigated the possibility that cortisol may be associated with acceptance of GBV (by men) and rejection of GBV (by women); and that this can be assessed by comparing attitudes to GBV in interviews at different times of day. Figure 43 offers more evidence on this, using WAS data from Cameroon.

Figure 43 is based on answers to the question "In your opinion, is a husband justified in hitting or beating his wife in the following situations: If she argues with him?" Figure 43 is limited to male respondents only. It appears to show a difference between respondents' attitudes and the temperature at the time of the interview (in Figure 43, the temperature is grouped in intervals 5 degrees Centigrade apart, to clarify the chart). But a key aspect of Figure 43 is that if the respondent was interviewed before 10am, there is a clear increase in the chance of them stating GBV is acceptable – even if we control for temperature. This evidence is consistent with the hypothesis that cortisol tends to increase the likelihood of a respondent considering GBV acceptable, as examined in the previous chapter. It is not possible to provide a thorough test of this using WAS or GBV data, because neither set of surveys carried out blood or saliva tests to assess the respondent's cortisol level. But I consider Figure 43, and figures in the previous chapter, sufficiently persuasive to exclude data from all interviews which were carried out before 10am, in Figures based on DHS or WAS surveys, in the remainder of this chapter.

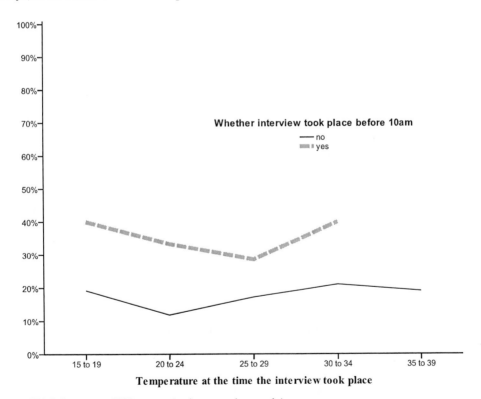

Source: WAS Cameroon 2009 survey (male respondents only).

Figure 43. Attitudes to GBV, by temperature and if interviewed before 10am.

Early-morning interviews may be influenced by cortisol; and this would make it more difficult to assess whether or not there is a link between temperature and (attitudes to) GBV. If early-morning interviews were included in data used for this chapter, we might find respondents interviewed at relatively cool (morning) temperatures had a tendency for more acceptance of GBV (men) or more rejection of GBV (women) because of the intervening effect of cortisol on attitudes. This might lead us to conclude that cold temperatures are associated with accepting GBV, whereas the real cause is cortisol rather than temperature.

The decision to exclude data collected before 10am is arbitrary: Figures 38, 39, 40 and 41 in the previous chapter suggests there is no obvious time to distinguish between interviews which may be influenced by cortisol, and interviews which are not influenced by cortisol. It would be possible to exclude data collected before 9am (for example), rather than exclude data collected before 10am.

In the three WAS surveys which measured temperature during the interview, respondents were asked if they agree with the statement "is a husband justified in hitting or beating his wife in the following situations: [..] if she argues with him?" (Respondents answered yes or no). The fraction who answered 'yes' at each temperature are shown on the vertical axis of Figure 44. The horizontal axis in Figure 44 shows the temperature to the nearest degree Centigrade. This makes the figure prone to vertical 'spikes' (such as 44°C for Chad, on the right of Figure 44).

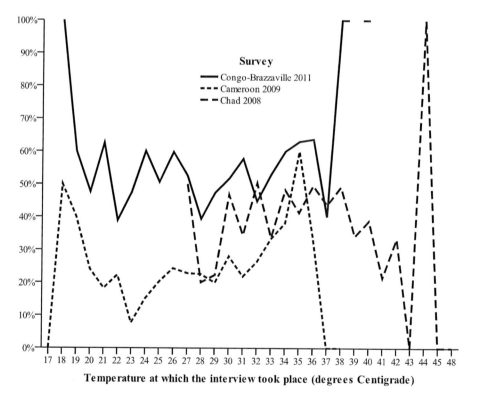

Source: WAS.

Figure 44. Acceptance of GBV if wife argues, by temperature and country: men.

The sample sizes in these WAS surveys is much smaller than most DHS surveys (including a temperature measurement adds to the cost of the survey; so it tends to reduce the sample size, if the budget for the WAS survey is fixed). Larger sample sizes would be desirable, in future.

There is much more acceptance of GBV in Congo-Brazzaville than the other two countries, as shown in the line for Congo being vertically above the lines for the other two surveys (in Figure 44); this indicates that temperature is only one of the many influences on GBV. Each of the three lines on Figure 44 indicates an upward trend, as we go to right (hotter temperature). This supports the hypothesis that among women, attitudes to GBV is affected by temperature. In Figure 44, there is also a tendency for acceptance of GBV to increase on the left of the figure (at a cooler temperature – especially at 18°C). This seems to support the idea that extreme temperatures, hot or cold, are associated with more acceptance of GBV; this might be explained by the presence of adrenaline in the blood of respondents (men and women) at stressful temperatures.

Figure 45 is for female respondents, but in other respects is comparable to Figure 44 (for male respondents). Results are fairly similar for men (in Figure 44) and women (in Figure 45): both figures show a general tendency for acceptance of GBV to increase, as we go from left to right – i.e. as we go from cooler to hotter temperatures. There may also be a tendency for more acceptance of GBV at cold temperatures, for women in Figure 45 (in Congo-Brazzaville, at least).

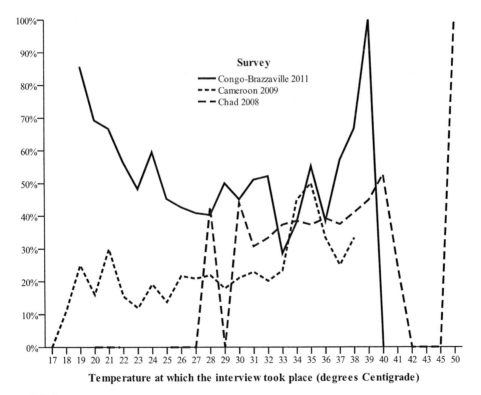

Source: WAS.

Figure 45. Acceptance of GBV if wife argues, by temperature and country: women.

More data are needed, before we can be confident about the results in Figures 44 and 45. But if we take these two figures at face value, they suggests some support for the 'curvilinear hypothesis' discussed earlier in this chapter; but they imply that the temperature at which the peak acceptance of GBV occurs varies, from one country to another. I would suggest that for women, the highest acceptance of GBV occurs at about 35°C for Cameroon; 39°C for Congo-Brazzaville; and 40°C for Chad (I treat the spike at 50°C as spurious, due to the small sample at this temperature). The reason for this variation between countries may be due to acclimatisation: residents of each country get used to a particular temperature range, and are stressed when the temperature gets towards the top end of that range). But the evidence of a curvilinear effect is not very persuasive: a larger sample size might produce clearer results. Another complication is the possibility that in the hottest parts of a country, households are more likely to buy an electric fan – this could give the impression that very high temperatures tend to reduce acceptance of GBV, but this would be a misleading impression if fan ownership is the real cause. Another factor which may influence GBV is the presence of fan or air-conditioning in the home. I now turn to figures using Nigeria data, which use estimated temperature (as calculated in the 'data and methods' section, earlier in this chapter) on the horizontal axis. DHS Nigeria 2008 has an impressively large sample; DHS India surveys in 1998 and 2005 are even larger samples, but neither of them includes data on air-conditioner ownership. Estimated temperatures are used rather than actual temperature, because DHS surveys do not measure the temperature at the time and location of the interview (as three recent WAS surveys do). Figure 46 reports attitudes to the question "Sometimes a husband is annoyed or angered by things that his wife does.

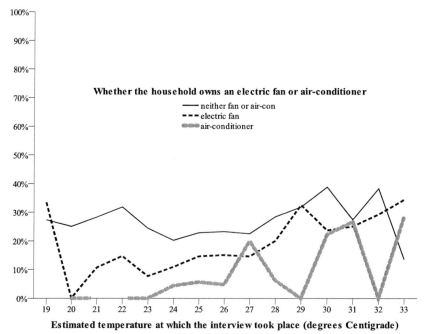

Source: DHS Nigeria 2008.

Figure 46. Attitude to GBV by temperature in Nigeria, by fan or AC: men.

In your opinion, is a husband justified in hitting or beating his wife in the following situations: If she goes out without telling him?" We see a general tendency for more agreement with this statement, as we go from left to right (cooler to hotter temperatures: 19 to 33°C). Figure 46 uses a more precise measure of temperature than Figure 43: this is possible because of the much larger sample size in DHS Nigeria 2008 than in WAS Cameroon 2009.

A key feature of Figure 46 is that there seems much less acceptance of GBV (in the case of a wife going out without her husband's permission) if the household owns a fan, or air-conditioning. Air-conditioning seems to be much more effective than a fan in reducing the acceptance of GBV, according to Figure 46. This may be because the respondent in an air-conditioned room (or a room with an electric fan) does not feel as hot as a respondent without either of these devices, at any given temperature.

There appear to be limits to the effectiveness of fans and air-conditioning, at least in Nigeria: if they were able to maintain a constant temperature in the home regardless of the outside temperature, we would expect temperature outside to have no effect on attitudes. But even in households with air-conditioning, there seems to be a tendency for more acceptance of GBV if the temperature is higher. This may be partly due to practical issues: for example, if the respondent was interviewed on the doorstep, we would expect hot air to enter the home – and hence reduce the effectiveness of the fan or air-conditioner.

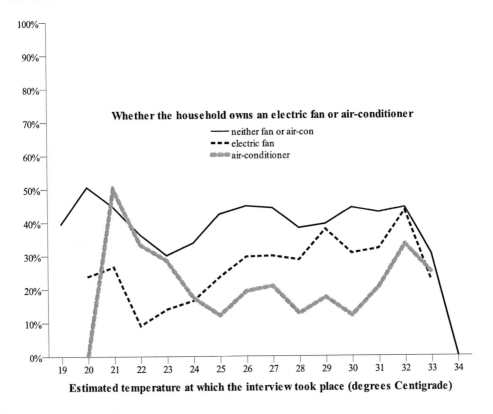

Source: DHS Nigeria 2008.

Figure 47. Attitude to GBV by temperature in Nigeria, by fan or AC: women.

Table 36. Attitudes to GBV, by fan/air-conditioner ownership: Egypt

Survey	Is there a fan or air-conditioner in the respondent's home?	Agree that domestic violence is justified, if a wife refuses sex with her husband	
		Male respondents	*Female respondents*
DHS 1995	no fan		84 % (3,270 cases)
	fan		72 % (3,631 cases)
DHS 2005	no fan		50 % (2,201 cases)
	fan		35 % (16,189 cases)
	air-conditioner		26 % (719 cases)
DHS 2008	no fan		36% (1,280 cases)
	fan		25% (14,507 cases)
	air-conditioner		9% (583 cases)
WAS 2005/6	no fan	27 % (309 cases)	27 % (433 cases)
	fan	19 % (2,016 cases)	16 % (1,962 cases)
	air-conditioner	10 % (93 cases)	1 % (69 cases)

Source: DHS and WAS.

Figure 47 is similar to Figure 46, but Figure 47 uses data from female respondents (whereas Figure 46 uses data from male respondents). There is a clear reduction in acceptance of GBV (in this scenario) for women, if the household owns a fan or air-conditioning. But despite the influences of fans and air-conditioners, it seems women in hotter temperatures are more likely to say GBV is acceptable (if a woman leaves home without her husband's permission).

In view of the effects of fans and air-conditioning on attitudes in Figures 46 and 47, it may be appropriate to investigate households whether GBV prevalence is higher or lower in households which own either a fan or air-conditioner or both.

Many surveys (such as DHS surveys in India) do not ask about air-conditioner ownership; this may not always represent a major problem for studying the effects of temperature, because few Indian households own air-conditioners (among WAS India 2007 respondents, only 3% lived in homes with an air-conditioner).

Table 36 uses data from household surveys in Egypt, to investigate whether or not owning a fan or air-conditioner seems to affect GBV prevalence. DHS surveys do not ask men about their attitudes to GBV, so male responses are only reported for the WAS Egypt survey.

The evidence in Table 36 suggests ownership of an electric fan or air-conditioner makes a large difference to the chance of a man or woman in that home accepting GBV. In the 2008 DHS Egypt survey, for example, 36% of women with neither fan nor air-conditioner accepted GBV; this fell to 25% for households with fan but no air-conditioner, and down to 9% among households with air-conditioners (some, but not all, of these households owned a fan as well as an air-conditioner). This evidence is consistent with the pattern in Figures 46 and 47, for Nigeria. Attitude data in Table 36 suggest that women and men react in similar ways to stressful temperatures: people become more accepting of GBV if they are under stress.

Table 37 is similar to Table 36, but with a key difference: Table 37 reports whether or not the respondent *experienced* GBV (rather than accepted GBV as reasonable behaviour). In

DHS and WAS surveys in Egypt, experience of GBV was only asked of female respondents; GBV was not asked in DHS 2008 (whereas DHS 2008 did include questions on attitudes to GBV).

Table 37 suggests that fans and air-conditioners are beneficial, in that they reduce the risk of GBV occurring: in DHS 2005, for example, the risk fell from 36% (if neither fan nor air-conditioner is owned) to 12% (if an air-conditioner is owned). This result is consistent with the evidence in Table 36: there is less GBV if the temperature is less stressful. As always in research, we need to be careful to avoid being misled by other variables. It is possible that the apparent effects of fans and air-conditioning is really due to education – there is a tendency for fans and air-conditioners to be owned more by rich households than by poor households; and rich households tend to be better-educated.

Table 37. Risk of GBV, by fan/air-conditioner ownership: Egypt

Survey	Is there a fan or an air-conditioner in the respondent's home?	Respondent reported that they had experienced GBV *Female respondents*
DHS 1995	no fan	19 % (6,728 cases)
	fan	14 % (8,050 cases)
DHS 2005	no fan	36 % (663 cases)
	fan	30 % (4,735 cases)
	air-conditioner	12 % (208 cases)
WAS 2005/6	no fan	29 % (441 cases)
	fan	19 % (1,988 cases)
	air-conditioner	6 % (69 cases)

Source: DHS and WAS (women respondents only).

CONCLUSION

The links between hormones and behaviour is a complicated topic, and this chapter does not attempt to report all medical evidence published so far. In this research area, knowledge is accumulating fast, and I am confident that scientists' understanding on this topic will continue to make impressive progress in the next few years. I hope the epidemiological evidence in this chapter may help researchers at the frontiers of scientific knowledge to make more rapid progress.

Theories based on culture as a cause of violence (such as Van de Vliert et al., 1999) might explain why some countries have more violence than others; but they cannot explain the seasonal changes in crime rates at one location; and they cannot explain why GBV (or acceptance of GBV) is less likely in a household with a fan or air-conditioning. In my view, the association between extreme temperature and violence is more likely to be stress hormones than culture. However, it is entirely plausible that extreme temperatures in a country (or part of a country) can cause violence to be more frequent; so the research by Van de Vliert et al. (1999) may help us to understand the effects of hormones.

In countries or regions where very hot temperatures are experienced, an electric fan seems to reduce the risk of GBV; an air-conditioner is even better. Another approach is for a family member who is too hot to be given a cool drink, such as water. It is not clear if very cold temperatures also lead to more aggression. If future medical research gives a better understanding of how stress hormones lead to aggression, we might be able to offer more advice to women, to help them reduce their risk of GBV.

Chapter 15

WE NEED A GLOBAL INTERVENTION TO REDUCE GBV

"This is how things happen in movements for social change, in revolutions. They start small and curiously, an unexpected flutter that is not without precedence, a barely observable ripple that heralds a return to the unfinished business of prior generations. If conditions are right, if the anger of enough people has reached the boiling point, the exploding passion can ignite a societal transformation. So it was with the Women's Liberation Movement in the latter half of the twentieth century" (Brownmiller, 2000: 1).

ABSTRACT

GBV is one of the biggest problems worldwide: "the sheer scale of violence against women forces the question of what it will take to translate increasing recognition of the global prevalence of this abuse into meaningful, sustained, and widespread action" (Watts and Zimmerman, 2002: 1237).

Ward et al. (2005) suggest the battle against GBV can be compared with campaigns such as the anti-slavery movement; efforts to prevent genocide, and the Nazi holocaust. Manning (1990: 257) estimates that between 1500 and 1900, about 12 million people were sent from Africa in the slave trade. Eckardt and Eckardt (1980: 166) claim about six million Jews were murdered by Nazis during the Second World War. Readers of this book were born too late to help the campaign to make slavery illegal in the 19th century. Many readers were not alive when the holocaust occurred (millions of Jewish people were murdered, during the Second World War). No doubt you and I could have done more to bring Apartheid to an end in South Africa. But we can help to end GBV. The scale of the GBV problem seems to dwarf most previous problems in human history: perhaps a billion women have suffered already, and many more women are threatened by the spectre of violence from their partner. It is hard to think of a more serious problem facing the human race.

INTRODUCTION

Heyzer (1998: 18), discussing some of the landmarks in the struggle to prevent GBV, wrote "At the beginning of the United Nations World Decade for Women (1976-85), the issue of violence against women was not on the agenda [..] it was the World Conference on Human Rights in Vienna which really brought the issue of violence against women on to the international agenda". This suggests the *global* battle to end GBV is a relatively new one; but local groups have been working to improve women's situation for much longer.

In terms of numbers, the estimate of a billion women suffering from GBV makes the reduction of GBV seem a daunting task. Sadly, it seems difficult to imagine a time when there will no longer be GBV. Even struggles which are widely seen as completed, such as the anti-slavery campaign in previous centuries, still have work to do: Ward et al. (2005: 96) give an example of modern-day slavery. After the Nazi holocaust, there was widespread agreement that genocide should never be permitted against any group; but there have been many attempts at genocide since the Nazis were defeated, such as the 1994 Rwandan genocide.

WOMEN'S GROUPS

There is widespread agreement that services to protect GBV victims should be organised by women, for women. Many writers report evidence that government-run agencies fail to provide adequate help for victims, and may try to persuade a GBV victim to go back to her violent husband (e.g. Kosambi, 1993: 42). In many countries, there are networks of women's groups, who are actively working to make women safe. An example is Women's Aid, in the UK (their website is www.womensaid.org.uk). Such organisations provide many types of help, but one of the most important is refuges for victims of GBV – where a woman (and her children, if she has any) can stay in a place of safety until she can find a new home. Such shelters have been found to be very beneficial to many women who stay there, although they may not be appropriate for all GBV victims (Berk, Newton and Berk, 1986).

If we were to see the struggle to end GBV as a movement (like the suffragette movement or anti-Apartheid movement), it may be important to acknowledge tensions within it. Various groups of people who oppose GBV may see such violence very differently – for example:

- It is sometimes alleged that religion contributes to the problem of GBV, and of women's subordination generally. As an example, traditional Christian marriage vows required a wife to 'love, honour and obey' her husband, whereas a husband did not promise to obey his wife.
- Some women's groups are often associated with lesbianism, which is unacceptable to many religious people.
- Some people with radical political views (e.g. feminism) are opposed to hierarchies, and hence object to a conventional political group, or to a church-based group – especially if it were headed by a man, as most religions are.
- In some groups (such as collectives which run hostels for battered women), only women can be members.

Such tensions have applied to other struggles: for example, in the campaign to win votes for women in the UK, the suffragists were a women-only group, whereas the suffragettes accepted women and men as members. The suffragists and suffragettes were successful: UK women can now vote.

It may seem unsurprising that many women who have experienced GBV do not trust men, and do not feel safe in the company of men. In such cases, we should not criticise women for excluding men from their group. But men can join other groups which campaigns against GBV. As a white Christian man, I object to racism, despite not being black. I object to persecution of Jews, despite not being a Jew myself. And I object to GBV, despite the fact that I will never experience it. I believe there should be at least one group of people who campaign against GBV which accepts men as members; but women-only groups can also be formed.

It seems unlikely that we will see a single organisation which can represent everyone opposed to GBV. This has advantages, in that there is less risk of an organisation being taken over by one or more individuals who prevent the organisation from being effective.

Many writers encourage campaigners and activists to work together, to gain strength from a supportive network. Ellsberg and Heise (2005: 155) point out that working with victims of violence can be upsetting for researchers: "Just as violence research raises special issues around respondent safety, the emotional sensitivity of the topic raises special issues for building and sustaining your field team. Working on a violence project can be extremely taxing, and it is important – both for ethical reasons and to ensure the quality of the data – that researchers take active steps to protect the emotional well-being of team members. This means that research plans and budgets need to include specific measures for addressing the emotional consequences of doing gender-based violence research."

POSITIVE ROLE MODELS

Leaders such as Martin Luther King, Nelson Mandela, Mahatma Gandhi, and Aung San Suu Kyi can inspire people, whether or not the role model has political power. Sports personalities, television personalities, film stars, and musicians can act as positive role models by making their opposition to GBV clear.

Sometimes, press, radio, and television can be persuaded to publicise campaigns against violence. It may be a good idea to persuade role models (such as sporting celebrities, film stars, and musicians) to publicly state their opposition to GBV. By making their opposition to GBV clear in public, this can encourage victims of GBV to come forward and seek help.

LOCAL, NATIONAL, AND INTERNATIONAL ORGANISATIONS

UN (1948) wrote "No one shall be subjected to torture or to cruel, inhuman or degrading treatment or punishment". The national government of almost every country in the world has signed the UN 'Universal declaration of human rights', which should – in theory – guarantee everyone 'freedom from fear'. This, and other international agreements, suggests every government should be working hard to ensure the safety of citizens. Where governments fail, it may be appropriate for activists to demand more action. In democratic countries, one way to achieve this is to persuade politicians that they're more likely to be elected if they work to keep women safe.

Source: Shutterstock (2011).

Figure 48. A female police officer makes an arrest.

There is much evidence that police forces in many countries should do more to protect victims of GBV, as discussed in chapter 4 of this book. Activists and campaigners may be able to persuade the police to do more, to enforce the laws of that country.

UN Women (formerly UNIFEM) seem to offer hope for GBV victims in their campaign 'Say no: unite to end violence against women': website www.saynotoviolence.org has helpful insights and ideas for activists. In my opinion, 'UN Women' is doing excellent work in working to prevent GBV in future. But if all actions against GBV were organised into one group (such as a UN agency), then the leader of that group would have too much control – they might prevent the organisation from being effective. The battle to prevent GBV is too important for us to rely on one hierarchy; it seems unwise to put all our trust in any one organisation (McMillan, 2007). An alternative approach is to have many smaller organisations, so there's less risk that the leaders of an organisation will take the organisation in an inappropriate direction. There are similarities between the 'separatist feminist' organisations and the 'separate but equal' approach in Islam (in which girls are expected to have a female teacher, a female doctor, etc.); but it may be more effective for Muslim women to campaign against GBV in a different organisation to separatist feminists, because most feminists do not accept every aspect of Islamic culture. If a person feels more comfortable in (for example) a Christian socialist organisation, perhaps they will be more effective in overcoming GBV if they work with other members of their Christian socialist group.

It may be helpful for local groups to begin their own media campaign – which can be tailored to suit local culture and religion. Regional organisations can accelerate the process of change – for example, SANGAT is a group in Asia: www.sangatsouthasia.org In Africa, the GBV Prevention Network is a helpful focus for activists: www.preventgbvafrica.org It is also possible to form a group within one country, or a part of one country.

INTERVENTION: A THREE STAGE PROCESS

Ward et al. (2005: 124-5) wrote "To date, very few programmes have been assessed for their effectiveness. In fact, monitoring and appraising interventions is one of the crucial steps toward improving local, national and international capacity to address the problem". Without such research, it's not clear which interventions are effective in reducing GBV.

GVHC (2009: 6) describe an intervention to reduce the prevalence of GBV and HIV in a group of poor women in South Africa: over a two year period, they found a 55% fall in the prevalence of intimate partner violence as a result of this intervention. This is encouraging, because it tells us that the risk of GBV can be reduced. But another point to note about this GVHC intervention is that they were able to <u>tell</u> that it worked.

Campaigning against GBV might be best achieved by a three-stage process: first a 'baseline' study, to assess the original problem; then the intervention; and finally a follow-up study, to assess whether or not the intervention was effective. The baseline study should include as many countries as possible, to establish current GBV prevalence rates, using consistent questions in each country. The second stage would be an intervention, such as UN WOMEN's campaign, or a series of concerts like 'Live Aid'. The third stage would be a follow-up survey a few years later, in the same countries, to assess if GBV prevalence rates fell due to the intervention. It seems likely that some interventions are more successful than others; it would be important to compare data from the first and third stages, to learn lessons about which countries (and which regions within a country) made progress – and which did not. Future campaigns against GBV can then be made more effective.

UNECE (2010) seeks to improve international comparability of GBV data; Ramirez et al. (2010) discuss standardising questionnaires between countries. Perhaps UNECE and 'UN WOMEN' can persuade agencies such as DHS, CDC, and WHO to share a consistent methodology, and organise their next surveys as a global baseline survey. An alternative approach is to set up a new study (perhaps based on the methodology of one of these organisations): this may make it easier to ensure comparability of results between different countries.

Survey data can make a difference to campaigns. In East Europe and Eurasian countries studied by DHS surveys, "Traditionally, none of these countries had established laws and mechanisms to protect women from spousal abuse. Survey data have produced the first population-based nationally representative information on violence against women ever available. Dissemination of these data can have important implications in mediating changes in the legal and support service environments of these countries. Dissemination of findings, however, needs to reach potential users outside the health community, which may require extra efforts. There are already several examples from some countries of specific uses of the data in making legislative changes" (CDCP and ORC Macro, 2003: 219).

CONCLUSION

In my opinion, the struggle to bring an end to centuries of GBV will not be primarily due to a single individual who passes laws against GBV. Presumably some politicians will be persuaded to pass laws, because they think it will get them re-elected (persuaded by anti-GBV activists, perhaps by arranging petitions). Some police forces will be persuaded to enforce laws against GBV, but it will be an uphill struggle for groups – who may need to visit their local police station many times, to persuade police officers to do their job. I think the real difference will be made by millions of ordinary people (almost all women), who care enough about their friends and neighbours to work together in small groups to stop GBV. History won't record your name; perhaps nobody will say "thank you"; many people you meet will consider you a nuisance; but you will bring the nightmare of GBV under control, forever.

Chapter 16

CONCLUSION: WHAT SHOULD WE DO NOW?

"A fascinating paradox emerges regarding women's status and domestic violence. On one hand, these data indicate that women should increase their status to reduce the likelihood of being abused. Women who attend postsecondary school and who delay union formation are far less likely to experience violence than are women whose status is lower. On the other hand, these data also suggest that whereas high status protects women from abuse, it can also have the opposite effect – it can increase the likelihood of partner violence – if their status exceeds that of their partners. Women who are employed, have more education than their husbands, and are the dominant decision makers are more likely to be abused than are women whose status is equal to or lower than their husbands' status" (Flake, 2005: 368).

ABSTRACT

There is no easy way to end GBV. But GBV is a huge global problem, and it is vital that campaigners and activists find a way to bring change. This chapter gives some ideas of what has been achieved so far, and what can be done in future, by ordinary women, celebrities, politicians, community leaders, religions leaders, etc. This chapter contains a few of the types of work being done to reduce GBV. There is not enough space in this book to list all the work being done to reduce GBV. The work by organizations such as UN Women is helping to build a world where women are less at risk of violence.

Many researchers claim GBV can be reduced or prevented, by various types of intervention. Some victims of GBV might prefer to remain in the same relationship, but to stop her husband/partner from being violence. There are many ways in which this might be achieved, such as education (of husbands and wives); creation and enforcement of laws to prevent domestic violence; and persuasion by role models.

INTRODUCTION

Some readers of this book may be surprised to find how often GBV occurs; presumably many other people remain unaware of the scale of the problem. GVHC (2009:4) claim "Violence against women is often hidden, and policy makers and communities may not fully appreciate the true magnitude of the problem, or its implications for health and development.

Rigorous evidence on the levels of violence that women experience and its causes and consequences is important for advocacy and policy making."

The status of women in India was described by Kosambi (1993: 45) as follows: "The conservative approach to prostitution rests on the premise that society is divided into two sets of women: the good and the bad. The good women are within the homes – the submissive docile wives and daughters who need to be protected from the outside world (though they may be battered, burnt or assaulted within the home). The bad women are out on the streets and deserve to be treated with contempt. And while one set of women needs to be protected from the other, the men can have access to both". In India, as in other countries, GBV is a part of the social structure; reducing the risk of GBV may require other changes, such as empowering women. This chapter suggests some ways in which activists have sought to improve the lives of women; but perhaps new ways are also needed, to end violence against women.

At a local level, perhaps women's consciousness-raising meetings (popular among some feminist groups) could give women the strength to halt male violence, for example by informing the police.

CONTRADICTIONS

In chapter 2, it was argued that most victims of GBV are women. This argument can be used to publicize the problem of GBV, and may persuade politicians to pass laws which will protect women from GBV. In this context, it may seem inconvenient to find many women are violent to their husbands: it makes it more difficult to portray women as helpless victims, who need protection from their husband (perhaps by politicians, police officers, and judges – most of whom are male). But there is a positive side to this: women are not always weak, and this is a helpful basis for the future. For example, if women are taught self-defence, they need not always end up being controlled by their husband.

Many campaigners express dissatisfaction that so many women choose to stay with a violent partner. Rather than seeing a woman who experiences GBV as a passive and helpless victim, perhaps we should see her as a survivor. Some women are murdered by their husband, and police forces should ensure such men spend a long time in prison. But for women who experience GBV, it may be more appropriate to respect the victims – in many cases, it may be a woman's own ingenuity which keeps her alive. GBV victims are often creative and ingenious. But these women deserve a better life, free of violence; and we should not abandon women who do not leave a violent partner.

GIVE CHOICES TO GBV VICTIMS

Perhaps activists should aim to give every GBV victim a whole set of choices, so that each woman can decide what she wants to do next. Some women might choose to forgive their husband, if there are networks to ensure her safety (e.g. if he agrees to accept 'anger management' counseling, and a local women's group is ready to rescue her and take her husband to the police, if he is ever violent again). Another GBV victim may decide her husband is not worth the effort, and choose to leave him (if she has support when making the transition, such as transport to another city and help in finding a home and a job). A third woman might wish to live separately from her former husband or partner, but stay in touch with him – perhaps so her children can stay in contact with their father.

Here are some ideas which seem to have been effective in combatting GBV. It's not a complete list.

- A GBV victim may choose to leave a violent husband; a network of refuges for battered women is often an essential step for a woman (and her children) to reach safety.
- In India and other countries, the police are unwilling to help victims of domestic violence (Kosambi, 1993: 42). A specialist government-run organisation such as a women's police force may help encourage GBV victims to seek help. But groups of anti-GBV activists might persuade their local police station to support GBV victims.
- Some women might find it helpful to have the option of marriage counselling, or other forms of support. Some marriages and cohabiting relationships are worth saving.
- Some men could benefit from 'anger management' counselling. It might be offered by volunteers, if the government cannot afford such a service.
- Medical and psychological treatment could help a man control his addiction to alcohol.
- Tax and benefit systems can encourage some types of behaviour (such as feeding children properly), and discourage others (such as drinking alcohol).
- Health care providers "should be made aware of the prevalence of IPV and the reluctance of victims to seek treatment, and should initiate inquiries about domestic violence experience during routine health visits. Such screening may contribute to reducing the frequency and severity of intimate partner violence and could provide early interventions for domestically abused victims" (CDCP and ORC Macro, 2003: 219).
- Self-defence classes could help a woman protect herself from a violent husband or partner. Schools could play a role in this.
- Some women may find earning money in their own right is vital to give them bargaining power: a woman with enough income might be able to say to her husband 'if you hit me, I will leave you'.
- Female education is vital, to reduce GBV in future. Cultural barriers prevent female access to education in many countries: in India for example, "Boys are educated because they must fulfil their role as providers, but girls will do household work and thus do not need advanced schooling" (Satish Kumar, Gupta and Abraham, 2002: 8).
- Education of boys and men can reduce the risk of GBV in future.
- Working with small groups of men may help. Bird et al. (2007: 113) wrote "Working with men on the prevention of GBV against women may seem like an impossible task or a naïve proposition, considering the small number of men currently willing to participate in prevention projects. But not to work with men is to stop short of affecting real and lasting change. [..] Men are not born violent". Ward et al. (2005:

125) support such programmes, but warn "their reach and impact is sorely inadequate when compared with the number of men who abuse their partners".

- The 'white ribbon campaign' is an example of a large-scale organisation of men against domestic violence; it began in Canada, but has spread to dozens of other countries.
- "Most women suffering current physical abuse were more likely to talk about the abuse with a family member or a friend than to seek legal or medical help" (CDCP and ORC Macro, 2003: 218). Perhaps campaigners can find creative ways to help women experiencing GBV – for example, a café or other drop-in centre could be part of the process by which women start to seek help.
- Family members, friends, and neighbours can be encouraged to intervene if a woman is being abused (Ward et al., 2005: 230).
- Some women gain strength from the support of other women. One such approach is women's empowerment groups, popular among some groups of feminist women (Brownmiller, 2000). Self-help groups for women can be very beneficial, such as SANGAT: www.sangatsouthasia.org
- Jeffrey (1989: 32) claims that in India, the women's movement must play a central role in helping women to make progress: women can act more effectively if they are united, so that campaigns can be co-ordinated.
- Various types of professionals such as medical staff, police officers, and social workers can play a vital role in recognising the signs that GBV has taken place, and advising GBV victims of possible solutions.
- Role models may be important, for child socialisation and adult socialisation. It would help if the contributions of successful women were recognised (in, for example, science and medicine).
- The media can be encouraged to portray positive images of women and girls, and help ordinary women to see that GBV is not inevitable. Television and radio are among the options for activists to publicise problems and solutions.
- More women in politics may be important in most countries. Helping more women to become elected as Members of Parliament, cabinet ministers, prime ministers, and presidents could be a way to make laws more supportive of women's interests.

Often, a person acting as an individual can achieve a lot. But it is clear (from research reported in this book) that a women's group is often a very effective way to help GBV victims.

A HISTORICAL PERSPECTIVE

It is difficult to assess public opinion on GBV, if we look back a long way in history: household surveys such as DHS have only asked about GBV in recent decades. In 1992, I asked academics (sociologists) about how to include domestic violence questions in my first household survey; I was told (with absolute certainty among the academics) that it was impossible to ask about domestic violence in a quantitative survey, because of the sensitivity of the subject. It is now clear that those academics were mistaken. The first quantitative survey to ask about domestic violence, as far as I know, were DHS surveys, but several other large-scale surveys also ask respondents about GBV (see appendix).

In the late twentieth century, there seems to have been a change in public attitudes to GBV. For example, Counts et al. (1992: 1) wrote "Our purpose is to provide a unique and innovative perspective on a complex problem that has only recently generated public concern in Euro-American society: wife-beating. The present volume is the first collection of ethnographic explorations (largely first hand) devoted to the subject".

Ward et al. (2005: 124) wrote "The last 20 years of activism on the part of women's and human rights groups has laid firm the foundation to combat intimate-partner violence. Evidence suggests that in the majority of countries across the globe, there are at least some small efforts being made to identify and address the issue. In some settings, those endeavours are widespread. While strategies vary according to culture, commitment and the availability of resources, almost all involve legislative and policy reform, as well as grassroots initiatives that support women's rights".

To achieve progress, a whole array of techniques will be needed – tailored for the political and cultural context of that country. For example, in Saudi Arabia, it might be appropriate to use religious leaders to remind Muslims that education of girls is a religious requirement; and reminding men of Islam's prohibition against alcohol might reduce the risk of GBV. In a democracy, on the other hand, it might be better to remind politicians that about half of the voters are women – and hence policies which support women are likely to help politicians to get elected.

Researchers can help to identify problems and solutions. Survey data may persuade politicians and government officials about the need to support GBV victims. For example, DHS data were very important in setting up a centre for abused women in Romania; DHS findings were used in a for two month nationwide campaign (sponsored by the Ministry of Health and UNFPA) to raise awareness of domestic violence on radio, TV, and newspapers; and the Ministry of Health distributed educational materials about GBV to the public health community (CDCP and ORC Macro, 2003: 220).

STOPPING VIOLENCE

Many women successfully leave a violent or abusive husband; but some women put up with domestic violence for years, or decades. Reasons why a woman chooses to stay in a violent marriage may include social pressure; fear of being unable to survive financially without their husband; and childhood socialisation. If a woman leaves a violent husband, she may end up in extreme poverty, be shunned by her own family, and be a social outcast. But if a GBV victim understands the risks and wants to create a new life for herself (and perhaps her children), she should be empowered to break away from her abuser. Every country needs a network of refuges, for women (and their children) who wish to leave a violent partner.

Women's groups have achieved impressive results in setting up networks of shelters for battered women. Ward et al. (2005: 139) wrote "Evidence suggests that there is a great demand for services, including shelters, for abused women. But even where shelters are available, there is often little they can provide in terms of concrete assistance because of the limited rights and opportunities afforded to women by the prevailing culture".

Governments could be very helpful to campaigners and activists against GBV: for example, the state can choose to provide funding for hostels for battered women, and provide more legal rights for women. But will governments help? There have been disagreements in women's groups about whether it is better for a women's group to rely on state-funding, or retain independence (McMillan, 2007: 38-9).

Carrillo (2000: 11) wrote "In the early 1990s, violence against women was still a taboo issue for many, including most governments. A few would not even admit that it took place within their borders, let alone acknowledge responsibility for devising policies or allocating funds for the programmes and services to address it." But politicians want to be (re-)elected; maybe they can be persuaded to support campaigns to end violence, if they think women (who are about 50% of voters) want them to.

CAMPAIGNING

The 'Just Say No' campaign by UN Women (formerly UNIFEM) is inspiring; I believe it is changing the world for the better. An advantage of such a global campaign is that it unites women in different countries in a common struggle, and may lead to women's rights being enshrined in national and international laws. However, national campaigns (as well as international campaigns) can be effective, for example to change the laws of that country.

New technologies, such as mobile phones and internet, may be helpful to help a group of friends work together. If you think of a new way to reduce violence, maybe you should tell someone about it.

DATA

Statistics can help some campaigns – for example, if you want to persuade your government to protect women (as they should: almost every country has signed the UN Declaration of Human Rights, for example). You are welcome to contact the author of this book at the e-mail address contact@was-survey.org if you want help with obtaining information for your campaign to reduce violence against women.

More research is needed. With so much data available (for example, GBV statistics are reported by several governments including India), you may be able to gain new insights into GBV, and publish your findings. This book uses quantitative methods, but many authors writing on GBV use a qualitative approach (such as in-depth interviewing, or focus groups). A more accurate understanding of GBV could include both quantitative and qualitative research.

CONCLUSION

Violence against women should end. This won't happen unless activists, campaigners, and researchers make it happen. Collaboration between groups of law-makers (such as members of parliament), law-enforcers (such as police officers), and citizens can bring change. There may be a billion women who are at risk of GBV; that's a billion reasons for us to act.

APPENDIX: STATISTICS ON GBV PREVALENCE WORLDWIDE

The map in Figure 2 (chapter 4) uses data on all countries in Table 40 (the 'ever' experienced GBV column), below. The GBV prevalence shown on the map for each country is a weighted average of all surveys on that country, in Table 40; the weights are the sample size in each survey, shown in Table 40. In some surveys, I cannot identify the sample size (shown as a blank in the fourth column of Table 40) – in these countries, I use only the national sample if one exists (ignoring surveys in local areas), or calculate the unweighted average if I do not know of a national sample.

Prevalence rates for DHS and WAS are analyzed by the author; all other GBV prevalence rates are reported in published sources, shown in table 41 (the code in the right-hand column of Table 40 indicates which row in table 41 to look at, for the source).

DHS SURVEYS

This book relies mainly on evidence from the 'Demographic and Health Survey' (DHS); in India, DHS is called the 'National Family Health Survey' (IIPS and ORC Macro 2000). In each country studied, DHS interview a sample of people representative of the whole country: urban and rural locations, in various parts of the country. DHS India 2005 is one of the largest social surveys ever carried out. Most DHS respondents are women, age 15 to 49; in most DHS surveys, a smaller sample of men are also interviewed, but they are not usually asked about GBV. For this appendix, the DHS sample is restricted to women only.

DHS surveys are provided with weight variables, to allow researchers to correct for known imperfections in the sample, or for deliberate oversampling in the selection of people to interview. For example, DHS Kenya 2003 over-samples urban households, and under-samples North Eastern Province (CBS et al., 2004). Analysis in this book does not use weighting to correct for such imperfections, assuming DHS and WAS and samples are representative of Kenya as a whole. There is disagreement among social scientists over whether or not weighting is appropriate in such cases. For example, weighting exaggerates the impact of some cases; if there are typing errors in cases which have a weight above 1, the effect of these typing errors may be amplified by the weighting process.

Table 38 gives an outline of some DHS surveys. Note that these are just a small fraction of the DHS surveys which have been collected so far; they are intended to help the reader compare DHS and WAS surveys – Table 38 (for DHS) can be compared with Table 39 (for WAS).

Table 38. Sampling details of selected DHS surveys

Survey	Data Collection Agencies	Sample Size	Field Work Dates	Gender
Cameroon 2004	Institut National De La Statistique, Ministry Of Public Health, Comité National De Lutte Contre Le SIDA	32,186	Feb – Sept	Female
Chad 2004	Institut National De La Statistique, Des Études Économiques Et Démographiques	13,607	July –Dec	Male And Female
Egypt 2005	Ministry Of Health And Population, National Population Council, El-Zanaty And Associates	33,325	April –July	Female
India 1998	International Institute For Population Sciences, And 13 Fieldwork Organisations	123,329	Nov 98- Jul 2000	Female
Kenya 2003	Central Bureau Of Statistics, Ministry Of Health, And NCPD	17,722	April –Sept	Male And Female
Nigeria 2003	National Population Commission	15,995	March – August	Male And Female

Source: DHS documentation, available at www.measuredhs.com such as NPC and ORC Macro (2004).

WAS SURVEYS

The 'Work, Attitudes and Spending' (WAS) surveys were commissioned by the author of this book. This section gives an overview of the survey methods used. In every WAS survey, the fieldwork agency decided fieldwork details such as how to select the sample, and also selected and trained the interviewers. Every WAS survey used 'cluster sampling' (locations were chosen at random, and several interviews – typically about a dozen – were carried out at each location). In each WAS survey, about half of the sample was men, and the other half women: no children were interviewed. Different WAS surveys used different age-ranges of respondents; the definition of adult varied from one WAS survey to another. There was no upper age limit for respondents in WAS surveys (unlike DHS surveys). One respondent was interviewed, in each of the households chosen by the fieldwork agency.

The following list gives more details about the differences between WAS surveys in different countries.

- In India, 'Work, Attitudes and Spending' (WAS) surveys were carried out in 1992 (2654 respondents) and 1997 (1003 respondents) and 2002 (1651 respondents) and 2007 (2475 respondents). These WAS surveys are intended to be nationally representative of India, but are limited to urban households (Ahmadabad,

Bhubaneswar, Chennai, Delhi, Kochi, Kolkota, Lucknow, Ludhiana, Mumbai, Patna, and Vijayawada).

- In Brazil, fieldwork was carried out in August and September 1994 by 'Marplan Brasil'. Only two cities were sampled (Rio de Janeiro, and Sao Paulo), and both cities were in the relatively prosperous south of Brazil, so the WAS Brazil survey should not be considered a national sample. The questionnaire was translated from English into Portuguese.

- In South Africa, the WAS survey was carried out in 11 metropolitan areas in September 2000, as part of the Markinor 'Year 2000 Syndicate' survey (www.markinor.co.za). In South Africa, WAS is a quota sample (50% female; the ethnic composition is 50% black, 32% white, 12% coloured, 6% Indian), stratified by ethnicity, town, and suburb. Quota sampling was not used in any other WAS survey – ethnicity seemed important in South Africa in the year 2000, because the Apartheid system only formally ended in 1994, and there were still huge gaps in income and wealth between black and white people. The sample-size in South Africa is 2,000 households.

- In Indonesia, the fieldwork and data entry were carried out by the 'Demographic Institute' in the 'University of Indonesia' (based in Jakarta). Only four cities were sampled (three of these four cities are on the island of Java), so this cannot be considered a representative sample of Indonesia; it would be expensive to produce a representative sample, because there are so many islands in Indonesia. Nevertheless, a large fraction of Indonesia's population lives on the island of Java, so it may give an approximation to the attitudes and behaviour of Indonesians in general. Fieldwork was carried out in October 2001 (1,003 households) and May 2002 (1,000 households).

- Interviews for WAS Kenya were carried out by SBO Research Ltd (SBO, 2009); the fieldwork took place in November 2004. WAS Kenya includes urban and peri-urban households (peri-urban refers to the region near a town or city; this was a compromise, because a truly rural sample would have increased travel time and costs). WAS Kenya aimed to produce a nationally representative sample of Kenya's urban and peri-urban population; it is a stratified sample, covering all eight of Kenya's standard regions. WAS Kenya used cluster sampling, in 47 locations. SBO interviewed 1,564 women and 1,527 men, including adult ages up to 65.

- In Nigeria, WAS surveys in 2003 and 2005 were carried out by Research Marketing Services Ltd., as part of their 'Omnibus' series of surveys. RMS interviewed men and women aged 18 or older, selecting their sample using a modified form of multi-stage random sampling. RMS interviewed in urban and rural households: the rural households were between 50 and 100 Kilometres from the nearest town or city. Fieldwork took place in November 2003, and in February 2005. The target sample was 5,000 households, in each year. The WAS Nigeria sample sizes were 2,618 men and 2,430 women, in 2003; and 2,643 men and 2,368 women, in 2005.

- In Egypt, the University of Cairo organized and carried out all fieldwork and data entry. They produced a sample which reflected the main populated regions along the Nile (upper and lower Egypt); no samples were carried out in desert regions (but few people live in those areas). Sampling was carried out in 5 out of the 27 governorates of Egypt. Half the interviews were carried out in 2005, and the remainder in 2006.

- The 2008 Chad survey was carried out by a commercial market research firm, Cible Ltd (www.groupe-cible.com). It was intended to carry out a national survey, but there were problems interviewing in Eastern Chad due to fighting spilling over from the civil war in Sudan. Nevertheless, the resulting sample should be a fairly effective representation of the national situation in Chad. Questionnaires were translated by Cible from English into French, Swahili, and Gambaye; where appropriate, the interviewers translated questions into a local language.

- In Cameroon, the June 2009 survey was carried out in all ten of the provinces of Cameroon, in urban and rural locations. Cible Ltd carried out fieldwork and data entry – the same survey organization as performed the 2008 Chad survey. Questionnaires were produced by Cible in English, French, and Fulfulde; interviewers translated the questions into local languages where needed (Cameroon has hundreds of languages).

- In Congo-Brazzaville, fieldwork was carried out by Cible Ltd. in five locations: Brazzaville (1,000 respondents); Pointe-Noire (800 respondents); Cuvette (200 respondents); Pool (350 respondents); and Kouilou (650 respondents). The first three of these locations are urban, and the last two rural or semi-rural. Interviews took place in June to July 2011. The questionnaire was translated by Cible from English to French, Lingala and Kikongo.

In my opinion, WAS surveys in Kenya, Nigeria, Egypt, Cameroon, Chad, and Congo-Brazzaville can be described as nationally representative. The WAS surveys in India (2002 and 2007) and South Africa can be described as nationally-representative, but only for urban areas. WAS surveys in India (1992 and 1997), in Indonesia, and in Brazil are only urban samples, and are of just a few cities – so they are not nationally representative. Table 39 below summarizes the above information on WAS sampling. The WAS website www.was-survey.org has more information on each WAS survey.

WAS surveys are deposited as SN:3290 at the UK Data Archive, as well as being available for free download at website www.was-survey.org (the WAS website is run by the author of this book).

MEASURING GBV IN DHS AND WAS SURVEYS

Some of the early DHS surveys, such as India 1998-9, asked women respondents "Since you completed 15 years of age, have you been beaten or mistreated physically by any person?" and also asked the women respondents "Who has beaten you or mistreated you physically? [..] Anyone else?" (IIPS and ORC Macro, 2000). For this book, I classify GBV as a woman who had been beaten by her husband/partner. Later DHS surveys such as India 2005-6 use more complicated and specific questions (IIPS and Macro International, 2007): "(Does/did) your (last) husband ever do any of the following things to you:

Table 39. Sampling details of WAS surveys

survey	data collection agency	sample size	field work dates	urban or rural	Coverage
Congo-Brazzaville 2011	CIBLE Ltd.	3,150	June-July	both	Five locations
Cameroon 2009	CIBLE Ltd.	3,500	June	both	All 10 provinces
Chad 2008	CIBLE Ltd.	2,587	October	both	5 régions out of 18; fieldwork impossible in eastern Chad, due to conflict in Sudan
Egypt 2005	University of Cairo	5,143	Dec 2005 - Jul 2006	both	5 out of 27 governorates (2 in lower Egypt; Cairo; and 2 in upper Egypt)
India 2002	IMRB Ltd.	1,651	Dec	urban	6 cities: Bombay, Madras, Delhi, Calcutta, Cochin, Patna
India 2007	IMRB Ltd.	2,475	July /August	urban	as 2002, + Ahmedabad, Bhubaneswar, Lucknow, Ludhiana, and Vijayawada
Indonesia 2001 and 2002	University of Indonesia	2,003	Oct2001 and May 2002	urban	Jakarta, Surabaya, Bandung and Palembang
Kenya 2004	SBO Ltd.	4,036	Nov	both	all 8 standard regions
Nigeria 2003	RMS Ltd.	5,048	Nov	both	all 36 states + Abuja
Nigeria 2005	RMS Ltd.	5,011	Feb	both	all 36 states + Abuja
S. Africa 2000	Markinor Pty.	2,000	Sept	urban	11 cities across S. Africa

Source: www.was-survey.org.

a) Slap you?
b) Twist your arm or pull your hair?
c) Push you, shake you, or throw something at you?
d) Punch you with his fist or with something that could hurt you?
e) Kick you, drag you or beat you up?
f) Try to choke you or burn you on purpose?
g) Threaten or attack you with a knife, gun, or any other weapon?
h) Physically force you to have sexual intercourse with him even when you did not want to?
i) Force you to perform any sexual acts you did not want to?"

If comparing early DHS surveys with more recent DHS surveys, it is not obvious which of categories a) to i) above are GBV. For example, g) above refers to a *threat* of violence; but the DHS 1998 India question used the expression "beaten or mistreated physically", which doesn't include threats of violence. To make earlier DHS data comparable with later DHS data, and with other surveys such as WAS, I interpret a respondent who said 'yes' to one or more of categories a) to f) as a victim of physical GBV; other problems such as g), h) and i) are not classified as GBV in this book. More discussion on how GBV should be defined is given in chapter 2.

In eight countries, DHS surveys ask a single GBV question: Colombia 1990; Egypt 1995; Honduras 2005; India 1998-9; Mali 2006; Peru 2000; South Africa 1998; and Zambia 2001. Of these eight countries, five countries also have DHS surveys using the more complex questions like parts a) to i) above: India; Colombia; Egypt; Peru; and Zambia. I investigated them, and found the results in Table 40 below.

Table 40 shows GBV in earlier and the later DHS surveys. The prevalence rates differ from the earlier to the later survey in the same country (in each country except Peru). This change is especially marked in Egypt – I do not know why the prevalence rate changed so much from 1995 to 2005. GBV prevalence rates could have changed due to societal changes between the earliest and latest surveys; or perhaps prevalence rates may differ because of changes in question wording; or there might be a combination of these two factors. It is possible that there was little change in Egypt's GBV prevalence rate from 1995 to 2005, and that the apparent change is due to the different question wording.

Some readers may object to assuming that data from different surveys are comparable, if they use different questions. There are also other problems in comparing GBV prevalence rates: for example, different surveys use different languages; and different surveys use different populations, such as different age ranges of respondents. For many of the surveys discussed in table 41, I cannot find the exact details such as question wording (several DHS reports on the ORC Macro website are in languages other than English, and this applies to other surveys in Table 41).

Data in Table 41 and Figure 2 are based on women respondents, with one exception: Saudi Arabia. The Saudi Arabian survey in Table 41 interviewed women and men, and I cannot identify the prevalence rate reported by only women respondents; but this is the only survey I know of in Saudi Arabia, so I include it in Table 41. My investigation of WAS survey data, not all reported in this book, implies that prevalence rates of violence reported by *men* against their wife is fairly similar to prevalence rates reported by *women* of violence from their husband.

Table 40. GBV prevalence rates in different surveys

Country	GBV prevalence from a single question	GBV prevalence from a set of questions like a) to i) above
Colombia	30% (1990)	32% (2000)
Egypt	16% (1995)	30% (2005)
India	17% (1998)	26% (2005)
Peru	34% (2000)	34% (2004)
Zambia	44% (2001)	40% (2007)

Source: DHS data (year of survey in brackets).

Table 41. GBV prevalence rates, in various surveys

Country	years	coverage	sample size	GBV ever	GBV last year	code
Albania	2002	national	4049	8	5	ab
Albania	2003	Tirana	1039		37	bf
Algeria	2006	national	2043	16	10	c
Angola	2007	Luanda		78		d
Antigua	1990	national	97	30		b
Argentina	2002	Buenos Aires	270	20		bg
Argentina	2004	national		25		ad
Armenia	2003-4	polyclinic in Yerevan	1457	30		e
Australia	1996	national	6300	8	3	ab
Australia	2003		6004	16		bh
Australia	2001		395	29		bh
Australia	2002		2338	23		bh
Australia	2003	South Australia	2884	16		bh
Australia	2002-3	national	6438	25	4	af
Australia	2006		356	27		bh
Azerbaijan	2001	national	5533	20	8	ab
Azerbaijan	2006	national	8444	12		DHS
Bangladesh	1992	national (villages)	1225	47	19	ab
Bangladesh	1993	two rural regions	10368	42		ab
Bangladesh	2003	Dhaka	1373	40	19	ab
Bangladesh	2003	Matlab	1329	42	16	ab
Bangladesh	2006		496	45		bh
Bangladesh	2007	national	10996	50		DHS
Bangladesh	1993-5	Nasimagar Thana	3611	32		b
Barbados	1990	national	264	30		ab
Belarus	2006			29		bi
Belgium	1989	national	956	41		aa
Bolivia	1998	three districts	289		17	b
Bolivia	2003-4	National	17654	46		DHS
Bolivia	2008	National	12429		23	DHS
Bosnia/Hz.	1999	Zenica	540	23		ai
Botswana	2002	National	1495		19	al
Brazil	1999	Embu	86	34		bc

Table 41. (Continued)

Country	years	coverage	sample size	GBV ever	GBV last year	code
Brazil	2001	Sao Paulo	940	27	8	ab
Brazil	2001	Pernambuco	1188	35	13	ab
Brazil	2005	National	815	9		bd
Brazil	2005-6	Recife	1133	12		bj
Burundi	1999	Bujumbura		38		at
Cameroon	2004	National	10656	38	22	DHS
Cameroon	2009	National	1748	25		k
Canada	1993	National	12300	29	3	ab
Canada	1999	National	8356	8	3	ab
Canada	1991-2	Toronto	420	27		b
Canada	2004	Quebec	2120		6	bh
Canada	2004			7	2	as
Cape Verde	2005	national		16	8	au
Centr Afr R	2006	National	11316	35	29	bk
Chad	2008	National	944	26		i
Chile	1993	Santiago province	1000	60		an
Chile	1997	Santiago	310		23	ab
Chile	2004	Santa Rosa	442	25	4	ab
China	1999-0	National	1665	15		ab
China	2004	gynaecology clinic	1665	34		bh
China	2004	gynaecology clinic	600	38	21	bh
China	2005	Fuzhou: gynaecology clinic	685	43	26	bh
Hong Kong	2005			6	1	as
Colombia	1990	National	8642	29		DHS
Colombia	2000	National	11585	40		DHS
Colombia	2004-5	National	41344	38	20	DHS
Congo Braz	2011	national	954	26		WAS
Costa Rica	1990	child welfare clinic	1388	54		aa
Costa Rica	1994	San José	1388	10		ac
Costa Rica	2003		1388	33	7	as
Cote d'Ivoir	2005	national	5183		12	ak
Czech Rep	2003	national		35	8	af
DR Congo	2007	national	9995	56	52	DHS
Denmark	2003	national		20	1	af

Country	years	coverage	sample size	GBV ever	GBV last year	code
DominicnR	1999	national	1286	25	13	DHS
DominicnR	2002	national	23384	18	10	DHS
DominicnR	2007	national	27195	16		DHS
East Timor	2002	Dili and Alieu	288		25	o
East Timor	09-10	national	13137	38	29	be
Ecuador	1992	Quito barrio	200	60		ab
Ecuador	1995	national	11657		12	ab
Ecuador	2004		200	31	10	as
Egypt	2004	El-Sheik Zayed	631	11	11	ab
Egypt	2006		6566	34		bh
Egypt	2005	national	19474	33		DHS
Egypt	1995-6	national	14779	13		DHS
Egypt	2005-6	national	2556	20		bl
El Salvador	2002	national	10689	20	6	ab
Eritrea	2001	central region		40		ba
Eritrea	2001	Asmara		65		av
Ethiopia	1995	Meskanena Woreda	673	45	10	b
Ethiopia	2002	Meskanena Woreda	2261	49	29	ab
Ethiopia	2008	Kofale district		53	30	bm
Finland	1997	national	4955	28	7	ab
Finland	2005	national	7000	20		bn
France	2002	national	5908	9	3	ab
Georgia	1999	national	5694	5	2	ab
Germany	2003	national	10264	23		ab
Ghana	2008	national	4916	21		DHS
Ghana	1997-8	national	2011		23	bo
Guatemala	1990	Sacatepequez	1000	36		aa
Guatemala	2002	national	6595		9	ab
Guinea		7 regions		22		aw
Haiti	2000	national	10159	17	14	DHS
Haiti	2005-6	national	10757	14		DHS
Honduras	2001	national	6827	10	6	ab
Honduras	2005-6	national	19948	5		DHS
Hungary	2003		3615	32		bh
Iceland	1996			14		ah
Iceland	08-10	national	3000	22	2	ai

Table 41. (Continued)

Country	years	coverage	sample size	GBV ever	GBV last year	code
India	1999	six states	9938	40	14	ab
India	2004		500	48	24	bh
India	2004	Lucknow	506	35	25	ab
India	2004	Trivandrum	700	43	20	ab
India	2004	Vellore	716	31	16	ab
India	2005	south India	397	29		bh
India	2007	national: urban only	1238	7		bp
India	1993-4	Tamil Nadu	859	37		b
India	1993-4	Uttar Pradesh	983	45		b
India	1995-6	Uttar Pradesh, 5 dist.	6695	30		b
India	1998-9	national	90303	19		DHS
India	2005-6	national	124385	36		DHS
Indonesia	2000	central Java	765	11	2	ab
Indonesia	2001	Jakarta, Surabaya, Bandung, and Palembang	591	5		h
Indonesia	2002		503	6		h
Iran	2003-4	Tehran	1000	59		bq
Iran	2005	national	386	37		bh
Iran	2005	Sanandaj city	1040	38	15	br
Iran	2005	Babol city	2400	42	15	bs
Iraq	2008	national	1700	12		aj
Ireland	2002	GP practice	2615	39		bh
Ireland	1995	national	679	18	7	ar
Israel	1994	Gaza/W. Bank: Palestinians	2410	69	52	ab
Israel	1997	Arab population	1826		32	ab
Israel	1998	national	849	11	4	f
Israel	2004	national	2996		6	bt
Israel	2000-1	national	2544	13	6	bv
Israel	2005-6	Palestinian population	4212		23	g
Italy	2004	primary care centre	542	14	5	bh
Italy	2005	family practice	444	27	20	bh
Italy	2006	national	25000	12	2	q,as
Japan	2001	Yokohama	1276	13	3	ab
Japan	2001		211	52		bh

Country	years	coverage	sample size	GBV ever	GBV last year	code
Jordan	2005	national	262	43	17	bh
Jordan	2007	national	10876	20		DHS
Cambodia	1996	six regions	1374	16		a
Cambodia	2000	national	2403	18	15	a
Cambodia	2000	national	15351	16	14	DHS
Cambodia	2005-6	national	16823	12	9	DHS
Cambodia	2006			30		bi
Kenya	2003	national	8195	40	26	DHS
Kenya	2004	national	1564	47		bu
Kenya	1984-7	Kisii district	612	42		ab
Kenya	2008-9	national	8444	36		DHS
Kiribati	2008	national		60	32	au
Korea Rep.	1988	Seoul and Suwon	708		14	bw
Korea Rep.	1989	national	707		38	a
Korea Rep.	2004	national	5916	21	13	r
Kyrgyzstan		national	1600	29		t
Lebanon	2004	Palestinian refugees	417	22	9	bt
Lesotho	2002	national	1488		16	al
Liberia	2006-7	national	7092	36		DHS
Lithuania	1999	national	1010	42		l
Lithuania	2000	national	517	33		bx
Macedonia	2000	national		24		bi
Madagascr	2007	Antananarivo	400	65		by
Malawi	2000	national	24918	21	13	DHS
Malawi	2002	national	1683		11	al
Malawi	2005	national	3546	30		r
Malaysia	1992	national	713	39		am
Maldives	2006	national		18		as
Mali	2006	national	14583	2		DHS
Mexico	1996	Guadalajara	650	27		ab
Mexico	1996	Monterrey	1064	17		ab
Mexico	1999		2418		7	bh
Mexico	2001	hospital	1255	14		bh
Mexico	2002	Mexico City: hospital	1780	26	9	bz
Mexico	2003	national	34184		9	ab

Table 41. (Continued)

Country	years	coverage	sample size	GBV ever	GBV last year	code
Mexico	2004		1641	36		bh
Mexico	2006	national	83159	21	10	s
Mexico	1998-9	Cuernavaca and Cuautla	914	12		ca
Moldova	1997	national	4790	15	8	ab
Moldova	2005	national	7440	24	14	DHS
Morocco	2009-0	national		6		
Mozambiq	2002	national	1471		11	al
Mozambiq	2004		1471	36	15	as
Myanmar	2005		286		27	bh
Namibia	2002	Winhoek	1367	31	16	a
Namibia	2002	national	1465		17	al
Nepal	2005	national	587	35		cb
Netherlnds	1986	national	989	21		ab
NewZealnd	2001	national	2526	21	3	m
NewZealnd	2002	Auckland	1309	30	5	ab
NewZealnd	2002	North Waikato	1360	34		ab
NewZealnd	2004		174	44	21	bh
Nicaragua	1995	Leon	360	52	27	ab
Nicaragua	1997	Managua	378	69	33	ab
Nicaragua	1997	national	13634	18	12	DHS
Nicaragua	1998	national	8507	30	13	ab
Niger	2006	national	11629	31		cc
Nigeria	1993		1000	31		b
Nigeria	2000	Imo: Owerri, Orsu, Oru	308	79		cd
Nigeria	2002	primary care centre	300		16	bh
Nigeria	2004	Edo and Delta states	581	34		n
Nigeria	2005	national	431		31	bh
Nigeria	2005	national	2385	9		j
Nigeria	2008	national	33385	18		DHS
Norway	1989	Trondheim	111	18		ab
Norway	2003	national	2143	27	6	ab
Pakistan	2003	obstetric/gynaecolo gy clinic	307	56		bh

Country	years	coverage	sample size	GBV ever	GBV last year	code
Pakistan	1999	Karachi	150	34		ce
PNG	1982	national: rural villages only	628	67		ab
PNG	1984	Port Moresby: low income	298	56		b
PNG	1984	urban: elite	99	62		aa
Paraguay	2004	national	5070	19	7	ab
Paraguay	1995-6	national, except Chaco	5940	10		ab
Peru	1997	metro Lima: low/mid income	359		31	b
Peru	2000	National	27843	41		DHS
Peru	2001	Lima	1019	50	17	ab
Peru	2001	Cusco	1497	62	25	ab
Peru	2004-8	National	20915	39		DHS
Philippines	1993	National	8481	10		ab
Philippines	1998	Cagayan de Oro/Budiknon	1660	26		ab
Philippines	2004	Manila	1000	47	29	bh
Philippines	2004	Paco	1000	21	6	ab
Philippines	2008	national	13594	12		DHS
Poland	2004	national		15	3	af
Portugal	1995			14		ah
Puerto Rico	1995-6	national	4755	13		ab
Qatar	2007	national	1200	14		p
Reunion	2002	national	1200	15	3	u
Romania	1999	national	5322	29	10	ab
Romania	2003	national	1245	11	4	bi
Russia	1999	three provinces	5482	22	7	a
Rwanda	2005	national	11321	34	10	DHS
Rwanda	2008	Kigali and 3 rural areas	1056	26		bb
Samoa	2000	national	1204	41	18	ab
SaoTome/P	2008-9	national	1980	33	21	DHS
Saudi Arab		Jeddah	230	41		cf
Serbia	2003	Belgrade	1189	23	3	ab
Serbia	2002	Kosovo: villages in Peja	332	12	11	ch

Table 41. (Continued)

Country	years	coverage	sample size	GBV ever	GBV last year	code
Seychelles		National		55		ay
Sierra Leon	2009	northern Sierra Leone	605	28		v
Singapore	2009	National	2006	7	2	w
Slovakia	2003	national		29		x
Slovakia	2008	national	827	21		aq
Solomon Is	2008			46		au
S. Africa	1998	E. Cape	396	27	11	ab
S. Africa	1998	Mpumalanga	419	28	12	ab
S. Africa	1998	N. Province	464	19	5	ab
S. Africa	1998	national	10190	13	6	ab
S. Africa	1998	national	11735	11		DHS
S. Africa	2002		1306	25	10	bh
S. Africa	2001-2	Soweto	1395	56	26	cg
Spain	2004	Madrid region	2136		2	ci
Spain	2003		2015		8	bh
Spain	2006	primary care centre	449	23		bh
Spain	2006-7	national	10202	14		cj
Sri Lanka	1990	Colombo: low-income	200	60		aa
Sri Lanka	2001	Kantale	417	30	22	ck
Sri Lanka	2004	Badullla district	1200	18	11	ck
Sudan	2001-2	Omdurman	394	42		cl
Swaziland	2002	national	1122		21	al
Sweden	2000	national	5868	18	4	a
Sweden	2000	gynaecology clinic	207		6	bh
Sweden	2003		1168	36		bh
Sweden	2004	gynaecology clinic	2439	32		bh
Switzerland	2003	national	1882	9	1	af
Switzerland	1994-6	national	1500	13	6	a
Syria	2003		411	23		bt
Syria	2005	national	1891	20		ao
Tajikistan	2000	national	400	50		bi
Tajikistan	2005	Khatlon region	400	36	19	r
Tanzania	1990	Dar es Salaam	300	60		aa
Tanzania	2002	Dar es Salaam	1442	33	15	a

Country	years	coverage	sample size	GBV ever	GBV last year	code
Tanzania	2002	Mbeya	1256	47	19	a
Tanzania	2005	Mohsi	1444	20	16	bh
Togo				41		az
Thailand	1994	Bangkok	619	20		b
Thailand	2002	Bangkok	1048	23	8	ab
Thailand	2002	Nakonsawan	1024	34	13	ab
Trinidad	2010	central Trinidad: Couva		41		cm
Tunisia	2008			20		ae
Turkey	1998	E and SE Anatolia	599	58		a
Turkey	2003		475	65		bt
Turkey	2005		506	59	41	bh
Turkey	2004		116	51	41	bt
Turkey	2005	Bursa: primary care	1427	34		bh
Turkey	2006		583	38		bh
Turkey	2009	national	12795	39	10	ap
Uganda	1991	Kampala	80	46		aa
Uganda	2003	Mbale	457	54	14	cn
Uganda	2006	national	8531	47		DHS
Uganda	1995-6	Lira and Masaka	1660	41		ab
Ukraine	1999	national	5596	19	7	a
Ukraine	2001	national		21	8	bi
Ukraine	2007	national	6841	12		DHS
UK	1993	north London	430	30	12	ab
UK	1999	east London: GP practice	1207	41	17	co
UK	2004	N.England: gynaeclgy clinic	920	21	4	bh
UK	2001	National	12226	19	3	ab
UK	2006	England and Wales		19	3	as
USA	1986	national	2143	28	11	aa
USA	1994	national	2555		6	z
USA	1990-1	Alaska, Maine, Oklahoma, and W. Virginia	12612		6	y
USA	1999	Colorado	409		8	bh
USA	1999	Health Maintenance Org	10599	37	4	bh

Table 41. (Continued)

Country	years	coverage	sample size	GBV ever	GBV last year	code
USA	2000	Washington	2012	24		bh
USA	2000	Montana	1017		3	bh
USA	2000	South Carolina	314	11		bh
USA	2001	hospital: Brooklyn, NY	375	38	16	bh
USA	2001		1821	19		bh
USA	2006	California	1786		27	bh
USA	2000	California	734	45	10	bh
USA	2001	California: Fresno County	1155		11	bh
USA	2001	California	3408		6	bh
USA	2002		6790	13		bh
USA	1998	Georgia	3130	30	6	bh
USA	1996	New Mexico: medic practice	2418		7	cp
USA	2003	Iowa	689		3	bh
USA	2003	Washington	3527		2	bh
USA	2006	New York	112	40		bh
USA	2005		637	16		bh
USA	1995-6	National	8000	22	1	ab
USA	2003-5	Washington and Idaho	3568	44	4	cq
Uruguay	1997	Montivideo and Canelones	545	10	10	ab
Vietnam	2004	Ha Tay province	1090	25	14	ab
Yemen	2000			47		Cf
Zambia	1992	Lusaka and Kafue rural	171	40		Aa
Zambia	2002	National	1605		36	Al
Zambia	2007	National	7146	47		DHS
Zambia	2001-2	National	7658	46		DHS
Zimbabwe	1996	Midlands province	966	17		Ab
Zimbabwe	2002	national	1543		17	Al
Zimbabwe	2005-6	national	8907	30		DHS

Data in table 41 are all the surveys I know of, which I consider suitable for this book (for example, I exclude hospital data, because it may overstate the risk of GBV because many women will be in hospital *due to* GBV). In Table 41, some country names are shortened – for example, PNG is an abbreviation for Papua New Guinea. Codes in the right-hand column of table appendix 1 are sources; they are listed in table 42. The sample size column refers to the number of women who answered the question (for surveys which interviewed men and women, only the number of women is shown in this column).

In table 41, there are two measures of how many women experienced GBV. The column labelled 'ever' means the fraction of (female) respondents who ever experienced GBV; there are different versions, in different surveys – sometimes, it refers to whether she was beaten by her husband since her current marriage began; other surveys refer to current or former marriages; yet other surveys also include violence from former boyfriends and/or cohabiting partners, as well as married partners. The second measure, labelled 'last year', refers to the 12 months period up to the day of the interview. This has the advantage that it is less influenced by the age of respondent – so, for example, we can use it to assess whether women of different age-groups have higher or lower risk of experiencing GBV.

Table 42. Data sources for GBV prevalence rates

code	Data source
a	www.unece.org/stats/gender/publications/Multi-Country/Researching_Violence_against_Women.pdf
b	www.infoforhealth.org/pr/l11/l11tables.shtml#top
c	www.euromedgenderequality.org/image.php?id=143
d	www.state.gov/g/drl/rls/hrrpt/2009/af/135937.htm
e	www.usaid.gov/our_work/global_health/pop/news/responseviolence.html
f	brookdale-en1.pionet.com/default.asp?catid={567204BF-9FEA-4A08-A307-188A304557A8}
g	www.womenwarpeace.org/opt/docs/Domestic_PCBS_opT.pdf
h	www.was-survey.org/id25.html
i	www.was-survey.org/id16.html
j	www.was-survey.org/id30.html
k	www.was-survey.org/2009-cameroon.html
l	www.aifs.gov.au/acssa/statistics.html#internatsurvey
m	www.justice.govt.nz/publications/publications-archived/2003/the-new-zealand-national-survey-of-crime-victims-2001-may-2003/publication
n	uaps2007.princeton.edu/download.aspx?submissionId=70609
o	www.rhrc.org/resources/East%20Timor_gbv_en.pdf
p	webapps01.un.org/vawdatabase/searchDetail.action?measureId=17400
q	www.ettasos.com/download/12.pdf
r	www.alianzaintercambios.org/files/doc/1236282110_Researching%20violence.pdf
s	www.un.org/womenwatch/daw/egm/vaw_indicators_2007/papers/Invited%20Paper%20Mexico%20ENDIREH.pdf

John Simister

Table 42. (Continued)

code	Data source
t	www.un.org.kg/en/publications/document-database/article/86-Document%20Database/4016-crisis-centers-of-kyrgyzstan
u	www.reunion.sante.gouv.fr/services/enveff.pdf
v	www.carl-sl.org/home/index.php?option=com_contentandview=articleandid=436:summary-of-a-report-on-the-prevalence-of-gender-based-violence-in-northern-sierra-leoneandcatid=5:reportsandItemid=20
w	www.ncss.org.sg/vwocorner/research_gateway/Family_abstract_12.pdf
x	webapps01.un.org/vawdatabase/searchDetail.action?measureId=24004
y	www.cdc.gov/mmwr/preview/mmwrhtml/00025182.htm#00000386.htm
z	www.pubmedcentral.nih.gov/picrender.fcgi?artid=1308495andblobtype=pdf
aa	www-wds.worldbank.org/servlet/WDSContentServer/WDSP/IB/1999/04/28/000009265_3970716144635/Rendered/PDF/multi0page.pdf
ab	www.un.org/womenwatch/daw/vaw/publications/English%20Study.pdf
ac	www.bvsde.paho.org/bvsacd/cd66/1073eng.pdf
ad	www.state.gov/g/drl/rls/hrrpt/2005/61713.htm
ae	www.unhcr.org/refworld/publisher,IRBC,,,4b20eff748,0.html
af	www.oecd.org/dataoecd/30/26/45583188.pdf
ag	www.cahrv.uni-osnabrueck.de/reddot/D_20_Comparative_reanalysis_of_prevalence_of_violence_pub.pdf
ah	www.cahrv.uni-osnabrueck.de/conference/SummaryGermanVAWstudy.pdf
ai	webapps01.un.org/vawdatabase/searchDetail.action?measureId=40643
aj	www.oxfam.org/sites/www.oxfam.org/files/oxfam-in-her-own-words-iraqi-women-survey-08mar2009.pdf
ak	www.measuredhs.com/pubs/pdf/AIS5/AIS5.pdf
al	www.ncbi.nlm.nih.gov/pmc/articles/PMC2042491/?tool=pubmed
am	www.icrh.org/projects/developing-strategies-to-combat-violence-against-women-in-developing-countries-health-care-
an	www.prb.org/Articles/2001/DomesticViolenceAnOngoingThreattoWomeninLatinAmericaandtheCaribbean.aspx
ao	webapps01.un.org/vawdatabase/searchDetail.action?measureId=27929
ap	webapps01.un.org/vawdatabase/uploads/Turkey%20-%20National%20Research%20on%20Domestic%20Violence%20Against%20Women%202008.pdf
aq	webapps01.un.org/vawdatabase/uploads/Slovak%20Republic%20-%20Summary%20-%20Representative%20research%20on%20vaw%202008.pdf

code	Data source
ar	ewlcentreonviolence.org/IMG/pdf/Unveiling_the_hidden_data.pdf
as	unstats.un.org/unsd/demographic/products/Worldswomen/Annex%20tables%20by%20chapter%20-%20pdf/Table6Ato6E.pdf
at	www.omct.org/files/2001/01/2174/burundieng2001.pdf
au	unstats.un.org/unsd/demographic/products/Worldswomen/Annex%20tables%20by%20chapter%20-%20pdf/Table6Ato6E.pdf
av	genderindex.org/country/Eritrea
aw	olddoc.ishr.ch/hrm/tmb/treaty/cedaw/reports/cedaw_39/cedaw_39_guinea.pdf
ax	asiapacific.unfpa.org/webdav/site/asiapacific/shared/Publications/2010/Case%20Studies.pdf
ay	www.genderseychelles.gov.sc/pages/programmes/SexDisaggredatedData.aspx
code	Data source
ba	www.omct.org/files/2004/07/2409/eng_2003_05_eritrea.pdf
az	www.ggp.up.ac.za/gender_equality/course_material/2009/bayard%202.doc
bb	www.unifem.org/attachments/products/baseline_survey_on_sexual_and_gender_based_violence_rwanda.pdf
bc	www.bvsde.paho.org/bvsacd/cd64/en_28530.pdf
bd	www.ess.ufrj.br/prevencaoviolenciasexual/download/015datasenado.pdf
be	www.measuredhs.com/pubs/pdf/FR235/FR235.pdf
bf	Burazeri et al (2005)
bg	Pontecorvo et al. (2004)
bh	Alhabib et al (2010)
bi	Rosenberg et al. (2006)
bj	Ludermir et al. (2010)
bk	ICASEES (2009)
bl	Simister and Zaky (2009)
bm	Dibaba (2008)
bn	Piispa et al. (2006)
bo	Ardayfio-Schandorf (2005)
bp	Simister and Mehta (2010)
bq	Nojomi et al. (2007)
br	Ghazizadeh (2005)
bs	Faramarzi et al. (2005)
bt	Boy and Kulczycki (2008)
bu	Simister (2010)
bv	Eisikovits et al. (2004)
bw	Kim and Cho (1992: p. 280)
bx	Schröttle et al. (2006)

Table 42. (Continued)

code	Data source
by	Binet and Bénédicte (2007)
bz	Díaz-Olavarrieta et al (2002)
ca	Castro et al. (2003)
cb	Paudel (2007)
cc	INS (2009)
cd	Odimegwu and Okemgbo (2003)
ce	Fikree and Bhatti (1999)
cf	Almosaed (2004)
cg	Dunkle et al. (2004)
ch	Women's Wellness Center (2006)
ci	Zorrilla et al. (2009)
code	Data source
cj	Vives-Cases et al. (2009)
ck	Jayatilleke et al. (2010)
cm	Nagassar et al. (2010)
cn	Karamagi et al. (2006)
co	Richardson et al. (2002)
cp	Tollestrup et al. (1999)
cq	Thompson et al. (2006)

REFERENCES

Hadi, A. (2005). Women's productive role and marital violence in Bangladesh, *Journal of Family Violence,* 20 (3), 181-9.

Ackerson, Leland K. and Subramanian S. V. (2008), 'Domestic violence and chronic malnutrition among women and children in India', *American Journal of Epidemiology,* 167 (10): 1188-96.

Ahmed, A. M., and Elmardi, A. E. (2005). A study of domestic violence among women attending a medical centre in Sudan. *East Mediterranean Health Journal,* 11 (1-2), 164-74.

Akmatov, M. K., Mikolajczyk, R. T., Labeeb, S., Dhaher, E. and Khan, M. M. (2008). Factors associated with wife beating in Egypt: *Analysis of two surveys* (1995 and 2005). BMC Women's health, 8 (15).

Alhabib, S., Nur,, U. and Jones, R. (2010). Domestic violence against women: systematic review of prevalence studies. *Journal of Family Violence,* 25: 369-82.

Alhabib, S., Nur,, U. and Jones, R. (2010). Domestic violence against women: systematic review of prevalence studies. *Journal of Family Violence,* 25: 369-82.

al-Hadramy, M. S. (1989), Catecholamines in heat stroke, *Military Medicine* 154 (5: May), 263-4.

Amirthalingam, K. (2005). Women's rights, international norms, and domestic violence: Asian perspectives. *Human Rights Quarterly,* 27 (2), 683-708.

Ammar, H. (2006). Beyond the shadows: Domestic spousal violence in a "democratizing" Egypt, *Trauma, Violence and Abuse,* 7 (4), 244-59.

Anderson C. A. (1989), Temperature and aggression: ubiquitous effects of heat on occurrence of human violence, *Psychological Bulletin* 106 (1: Jul), 74-96.

Anderson C. A. and Anderson D. C. (1984), Ambient temperature and violent crime: tests of the linear and curvilinear hypothesis, *Journal of Personality and Social Psychology* 46 (1: Jan), 91-7.

Anderson, W.D. and Summers, C.H. (2007). Neuroendocrine mechanisms, stress coping strategies, and social dominance: comparative lessons about leadership potential. Annals of the *American Academy of Political and Social Science,* 614: 102-30.

Andersson A. M., Carlsen E., Petersen J. H. and Skakkeback N. E. (2003), Variation in levels of serum inhibin B, testosterone, estradiol, luteinizing hormone, follicle-stimulating hormone, and sex hormone-binding globulin in monthly samples from healthy men during a 17-month period: possible effects of seasons, *Journal of clinical endocrinology and metabolism* 88 (2: Feb), 932-7.

Aranda, M.P., Castaneda, I., Lee, P-J and Sobel, E. 2001. 'Stress, social support, and coping as predictors of depressive symptoms: gender differences among *Mexican Americans'*. *Social Work Research*, 25 (11): 37-48.

Astbury, J. (2006). Violence against women and girls: mapping the health consequences. *International Congress Series*, 1287: 49-53.

Atkinson, M. P., Greenstein, T. N. and Lang, M. M. (2005). For women, breadwinning can be dangerous: Gendered Resource Theory and wife abuse. *Journal of Marriage and Family*, 67 (5), 1137-48.

Barnett, O. W. (2000). Why battered women do not leave, part 1: external inhibiting factors within society, *Trauma, Violence, and Abuse*, 1 (4), 343-72.

Barrington, Ernest J. W. (1983), Hormone, *Encyclopaedia Britannica* 8, 1074-88, Chicago, Helen Hemingway Benton.

Bates, L. M., Schuler, S. R., Islam, F. and Islam, M. K. (2004). Socioeconomic factors and processes associated with domestic violence in rural Bangladesh. *International Family Planning Perspectives*, 30 (4), 190-9.

Berk, R. A., Newton, P. J. and Berk, S. F. (1986). What a difference a day makes: an empirical study of the impact of shelters for battered women. *Journal of Marriage and Family*, 48 (3): 481-90.

Bertrand, M. (1997). The United Nations: past, present and future, *The Hague: Kluwer Law International*.

Bhattacharya, M. 2000. '*Iron bangles to iron shackles: a study of women's marriage and subordination within poor households in Calcutta'*, Man in India 80 (1 and 2): 1-29.

Binet, C., and Bénédicte, G. (2007). Etude sur la violence conjugale à Antananarivo. *Bulletin d'information sur la population de Madagascar*, 32, 1-5.

Bird S., Delgado R., Madrigal L., Ochoa J. B. and Tejeda W. (2007), Constructing an alternative masculine identity: the experience of the Centro Bartolomé De Las Casas and Oxfam America in El Salvador. *Gender and Development*, 15 (1): 111-21.

Bittman M., England P., Sayer L., Folbre N., and Matheson G. (2003). When does gender trump money? Bargaining and time in household work. *American Journal of Sociology*, 109 (1), 186-214.

Bott, S., Morrison A. and Ellsberg M. (2005). Preventing and Responding to Gender-based Violence in Middle and Low-income Countries: A Global Review and Analysis. *World Bank Policy Research Working Paper* 3618, www-wds.worldbank.org/external/ default/WDSContentServer/IW3P/IB/2005/06/28/000112742_20050628084339/Rendere d/PDF/wps3618.pdf, accessed 31 October 2007.

Bowden, S. and Offer, A. (1994). Household appliances and the use of time: the United States and Britain since the 1920s. *Economic History Review*, 47 (4), 725-48.

Boy, A., and Kulczycki, A. (2008). What We Know About Intimate Partner Violence in the Middle East and North Africa. *Violence Against Women*, 14, 53-70.

Brownmiller, S. (2000). In our time: memoir of a revolution. New York: Delta.

Brück K. (1989), Thermal balance and the regulation of body temperature, in R. F. Schmidt and G. Thews (eds.), *Human physiology* (2nd edition), Berlin, Springer-Verlag.

Burazeri, G., Roshi, E., Jewkes, R., Jordan, S., Bjegovic, V., and Laaser, U. (2005). Factors associated with spousal physical violence in Albania: cross sectional study. *British medical Journal,* 331, 197-201.

Burton B., Duwury N., Rajan A. and Varia N. (1999), 'Introduction', in ICRC, Domestic violence in India: a summary report of three studies, *International Center for Research on Women,* Washington, www.icrw.org/docs/DomesticViolence3.pdf, downloaded 13th March 2002.

Burton, B., Duvvury, N. and Varia, N. (2000). Justice, change, and human rights: international research and responses to domestic violence. Washington, DC: International Center for Research on Women and the Centre for Development and Population Activities, www.icrw.org/docs/domesticviolencesynthesis.pdf, accessed 31 October 2007.

Callaway, B. (1984). Ambiguous consequences of the socialisation and seclusion of Hausa women. *The Journal of Modern African Studie*s, 22 (33), 429-50.

Campbell I. T., Walker R. F., Riad-Fahmy D., Wilson D. W. and Griffiths K. (1982). Circadian rhythms of testosterone and cortisol in saliva: effects of activity-phase shifts and continuous daylight. *Chronobiologia*, 9(4): 389-96.

Carrillo, R. (2000). Introduction: Planting Seeds of Change. In C. Spindel, E. Levy and M. Connor (eds.), With an end in sight: Strategies from the UNIFEM Trust Fund to Eliminate Violence Against Women, UNIFEM: New York. www.unifem.org/materials/item_detail.php?ProductID=14 (On-line).

Castro, R., Peek-Asa, C., and Ruiz, A. (2003). Violence against women in Mexico: A study of abuse before and during pregnancy. *American Journal of Public Health,* 93 (7), 1110-6.

Cauffman, E. (2008). Understanding the Female Offender. *The Future of Children,* 18 (2), 119-42.

CBS (Central Bureau of Statistics) [Kenya], MOH (Ministry of Health) [Kenya], and ORC Macro (2004). *Kenya Demographic and Health Survey 2003*. Calverton, Maryland: CBS, MOH, and ORC Macro.

CDCP (Centers for Disease Control and Prevention) and ORC Macro. 2003. *Reproductive, maternal and child health in Eastern Europe and Eurasia*: a comparative report. Atlanta, GA (USA) and Calverton, MD (USA).

Clark, C. J., Silverman, J., Khalaf, I. A., Ra'ad, B. A., Al Sha'ar, Z. A., Al Ata, A. A., and Batieha, A. (2008). Intimate Partner Violence and interference with women's efforts to avoid pregnancy in Jordan. *Studies in Family Planning*, 39 (2), 123-32.

Cohen, D. and Vandello, J. (1998). Meanings of violence. The Journal of Legal Studies, 27, (S2), 567-84.

Coomaraswamy, R. (2000). Combating domestic violence: obligations of the state. UNICEF Innocenti Digest 6, 10-1, Innocenti Research Centre: Florence. www.unicef-irc.org/cgi-bin/unicef/Lunga.sql?ProductID=213 downloaded 12th August 2009.

Counts, D. A., Brown, J. K. and Campbell, J. C. (1992). Sanctions and sanctuary: cultural perspectives on the beating of wives. Boulder, Colorado: Westview.

CSO and Macro International (2000). Zimbabwe *Demographic and Health Surve*y 1999. Calverton, Maryland: Central Statistical Office (Zimbabwe) and Macro International.

CSR (Center for Social Research) (2005). A Research study on the use and misuse of Section 498A of the Indian Penal Code: Study summary. Downloaded 26th August 2011 from www.csrindia.org/attachments/Research%20-%20498A.pdf.

Daly, M., Delaney, L., Doran, P. and MacLachlan, M. (2011), 'The role of awakening cortisol and psychological distress in diurnal variations in affect: a day reconstruction study. Emotion, 11 (3): 524-32.

Delsol C., Margolin G. and John R. S. (2003), A typology of maritally violent men and correlates of violence in a community sample, *Journal of Marriage and Family*, 65 (3): 635-51.

Díaz-Olavarrieta.,C., Ellertson, C., Paza, F., Ponce de Leon, S., and Alarcon-Segovia, D. (2002). Prevalence of battering among 1780 outpatients at an internal medicine institution in Mexico. *Social Science and Medicine,* 55 (9), 1589-602.

Dibaba, Y. (2008), Prevalence and correlates of intimate partner physical violence against women in Kofale District, Ethiopia. *Tropical Doctor*, 38, 52-4.

Dolan, C. S. (2001). The 'good wife': struggles over resources in the Kenyan horticultural sector, *Journal of Development Studies, 37*(3), 39-70.

Dunkle, K. L., Jewkes, R. K., Brown, H. C., Yoshihama, M., Gray, G. E., McIntyre, J. A., and Harlow, S. D. (2004). Prevalence and patterns of Gender-Based Violence and revictimization among women attending antenatal clinics in Soweto, South *Africa. American Journal of Epidemiology* 160 (3), 230-9.

Dutt A.K. and Noble A.G. 1982. 'The culture of India in spatial perspective: an introduction', in Noble A.G. and Dutt A.K. (eds.), India: cultural patterns and processes, Boulder, Colorado: Westview.

Eckardt, A. L. and Eckardt, A. R. (1980). The holocaust and the enigma of uniqueness: a philosophical effort at practical clarification. *Annals of the American Academy of Political and Social Science*, 450, 165-78.

Edwards, S., Evans, P., Hucklebridge, F. and Clow, A. (2001). Association between time of awakening and diurnal cortisol secretory activity. *Psychoneuroendocrinology*, 26 (6): 613-22.

Eisikovits Z. et al. (2004). The first Israeli national survey on domestic violence. *Violence against women*, 10 (7), 729-48.

Ellsberg, M. C., Winkvist, A., Peña, R., and Stenlund, H. (2001). Women's strategic responses to violence in Nicaragua. *Journal of Epidemiology and Community Health*, 55, 547-55.

Ellsberg, M., and Heise, L. (2005). *Researching violence against women: A practical guide for researchers and activists*. Washington DC: World Health Organization, PATH.

El-Zanaty F. and Way A. 2006. Egypt Demographic and Health Survey 2005. Cairo, Egypt: Ministry of Health and Population, National Population Council, El-Zanaty and Associates, and ORC Macro.

El-Zanaty F., Hussein E. M., Shawky G. A., Way A. A. and Kishor S. 1996. Egypt Demographic and Health Survey 1995. Calverton, Maryland: National Population Council [Egypt] and Macro International Inc.

Engle, P. L. and Menon, P. (1999), Care and nutrition: concepts and measurement, World Development, 27 (8), 1309-37.

Entwisle, B. and Coles, C. M. (1990), *Demographic surveys and Nigerian women*, Signs 15 (2), 259-84.

Evertsson, M. and Nermo, M. (2004), 'Dependence within Families and the Division of Labor: Comparing Sweden and the United States', *Journal of Marriage and Family*, 66 (5), 1272-86.

Ezeigbo, T. A. (1990). Traditional women's institutions in Igbo society: implications for the Igbo female writer. *African Languages and Cultures* 3 (2), 149-65.

Faramarzi, M., Esmailzadeh, S., and Mosavi, S. (2005). Prevalence and determinants of intimate partner violence in Babol City, Islamic Republic of Iran. *East Mediterranean Health Journal*, 11 (5-6), 870-9.

Fasona, M. J. and Omojola, A. S. (2005). Climate change, human security and communal clashes in Nigeria. *Human security and climate change*: an international workshop, Oslo.

Fearon, J. D. (2003). Ethnic and cultural diversity by country. *Journal of Economic Growth*, 8 (2): 195-222.

FIDA Kenya (2002). *Domestic violence in Kenya: report of a baseline survey among women in Nairobi, Federation of women lawyers.* Downloaded 1st November 2004 from www.fidakenya.org

FIDA Kenya (2006). *Baseline survey on the level of awareness and impact of CEDAW on rural women in Kenya, Federation of women lawyers.* Downloaded 11th October 2009 from www.fidakenya.org/publication/Baseline%20Survey.pdf

FIFCFS (Federal Interagency Forum on Child and Family Statistics) (2001). 'America's children'. USA government, downloaded 7th April 2001 from childstats.gov/ac2000/econ4a.htm

Fikree, F. F., and Bhatti, L. I. (1999). Domestic violence and health of Pakistani women. International Journal of Gynecology and Obstetrics, 65 (2), 195-201.

Fox G. L., Benson M. L., Demaris A. A. and Van Wyk J. (2002), Economic distress and intimate violence: testing family stress and resource theories, *Journal of Marriage and Family*, 64 (3), 793-807.

Frank S. M., Higgins M. S., Fleisher L. A., Sitzmann J. V., Raff H. and Breslow M. J. (1997), Adrenergic, respiratory, and cardiovascular effects of core cooling in humans, *American Journal of physiology* 272 (Feb: 2 Pt 2), R557-62.

Fuller-Rowell, T. E., Doan, S. N. and Eccles, J. S. (forthcoming: 2011). Differential effects of perceived discrimination on the diurnal cortisol rhythm of *African Americans and whites. Psychoneuroendocrinology.*

Ghazizadeh, A. (2005). Domestic violence: a cross-sectional study in an Iranian city. *East Mediterranean Health Journal.* 11 (5-6), 880-7.

Greenstein, T. N. (1996). Husbands' participation in domestic labor: interactive effects of wives' and husbands' gender ideologies. *Journal of Marriage and Family*, 58 (3): 585-95.

GVHC (Gender Violence and Health Centre) (2009). 'Project portfolio 2009-2011', Gender Violence and Health Centre, downloaded 30th August 2011 from genderviolence. lshtm.ac.uk/files/2009/10/GVHC-Project-Portfolio.pdf

Gwagwa, N. (1998). Money as a source of tension, in Larsson A, Mapetla M. and Schlyter A. (eds.), *Changing gender relations in Southern Africa: issues of urban life* (pp. 33 – 55), Lesotho: National University of Lesotho.

Haddad, L. and Reardon, T. (1993), Gender bias in the allocation of resources within households in Burkina Faso: a disaggregated outlay equivalent analysis, *Journal of Development Studies,* 29 (2), 260-76.

Haller, J., Makara, G.B. and Kruk, M.R. (1998), 'Catecholaminergic involvement in the control of aggression: hormones, the peripheral sympathetic, and central noradrenergic systems'. *Neuroscience and Behavioral Reviews*, 22 (1): 85-97.

Halleröd, B. (2005), 'Sharing of housework and money among Swedish couples: do they behave rationally?' *European Sociological Review*, 21 (3), 273-88.

Hamel, J. (2005). Treatment of intimate partner abuse: a comprehensive approach. *Springer*: *New York.*

Hassan F, Refaat, A., and El Defrawi, M. (2000). Domestic violence against women in an urban area: Ismailia, Egypt, *Egyptian Journal of Psychiatry, 22*. www.arabpsynet.com/ Journals/EJP/ejp22.2.htm#and downloaded 12th August 2009.

Heaton, T. B., Huntsman, T. J. and Flake, D. F. (2005). The Effects of Status on Women's Autonomy in Bolivia, Peru, and Nicaragua. *Population Research and Policy Review*, 24 (3), 283-300.

Heise, L. L. with Pitanguy J. and Germain A. (1994). Violence against women: the hidden health burden. World Bank discussion paper 255: *International Bank for Reconstruction and Development.*

Heyzer, N. (1998), 'Working towards a world free from violence against women: UNIFEM's contribution'. *Gender and Development* 6 (3), 17-26.

Hindin, M. J., Kishor S. and Ansara, D. L. (2008). Intimate Partner Violence among couples in 10 DHS countries: predictors and health outcomes. DHS Analytical Studies No. 18. Calverton, Maryland, USA: Macro International Inc.

Hodgson, D. L. (1999). Pastoralism, patriarchy and history: changing gender relations among Maasaai in Tanganyika, 1890-1940. *Journal of African History*, 40 (1), 41-65.

Holden, C. J., Sear R. and Mace R. (2003), Matriliny as daughter-biased investment. *Evolution and human behaviour*, 24: 99-112.

Humphreys, M. A. (1995), Thermal comfort temperatures and the habits of hobbits, in F. Nicol, M. Humphreys, O. Sykes and S. Roaf (eds.), Standards for thermal comfort: indoor air temperatures for the 21st century, London, SPON.

ICASEES (Institut Centrafricain des Statistiques, et des Etudes Economiques et Sociales) (2009). Suivi de la situation des enfants et des femmes -3 résultats de l'enquête nationale à indicateurs multiples couplée avec la sérologie VIH et anémie en RCA 2006. www.childinfo.org/files/MICS3_CAR_FinalReport_2006_Fr.pdf (On-line).

ICRW. 2001. 'Domestic violence in India II: exploring strategies, promoting dialogue', *International Center for Research on Women*, Washington DC. www.icrw.org/docs/ indiainfobulletin.pdf downloaded 15th August 2006.

IIPS (1995). National Family Health Survey (MCH and Family Planning), India 1992-93. *International Institute for Population Sciences: Bombay*, www.measuredhs.com/ pubs/pub_details.cfm?ID=609andctry_id=57andSrchTp=type   downloaded   23rd November 2008.

IIPS (International Institute for Population Sciences) and Macro International (2007). National Family Health Survey (NFHS-3), 2005–06: *India: Volume II. Mumbai:* IIPS. www.measuredhs.com/pubs/pdf/FRIND3/FRIND3-VOL2.pdf downloaded 14th August 2011.

IIPS (International Institute for Population Sciences) and ORC Macro (2000). National Family Health Survey (NFHS-2), 1998-99: *India. Mumbai: IIPS*. www.measuredhs.com/ pubs/pdf/FRIND2/FRIND2.pdf downloaded 24th July 2011.

Inglehart, R. and Welzel, C. (2011). The WVS cultural map of the world. Accessed 9th July 2011, from www.worldvaluessurvey.org/wvs/articles/folder_published/article_base_54

INS (Institut National de la Statistique) (2009). Enquete Demographic et de Sante au Niger en 2006: La documentation de l'etude. Institut National de la Statistique, *Republique du Niger.*

Jayatilleke, A. C., Poudel, K. C., Yasuoka, J., Jayatilleke, A. U., and Jimba, M. (2010). Intimate partner violence in Sri Lanka. *BioScience Trends,* 4 (3), 90-5.

Jeffery, P., R. Jeffery and A. Lyon (1989), *Labour Pains and Labour Power: Women and Childbearing in India,* London: Zed books.

Jeffrey, R. (1989). 'Women and the "Kerala model": four lives, 1870s-1980s', South Asia 12 (2): 13-32.

Jejeebhoy, S. J. (1995). *Women's education, autonomy, and reproductive behaviour*: experience from developing countries, Oxford: OUP.

Jejeebhoy, S. J. and Cook, R. J. (1997). State Accountability for wife-beating: The India challenge', *Lancet,* 349 (March), SI10–2.

Jewkes, R. (2002). Intimate partner violence: causes and prevention, *The Lancet 359,* (April), 1423-9.

Jezova D., Kvetnansky R. and Vigas M. (1994), Sex differences in endocrine response to hyperthermia in sauna, *Acta Physiologica Scandinavica* 150 (3), 293-8.

Johnson, M. P. (2005). Domestic violence: it's not about gender – or is it? Journal of Marriage and Family, 67 (5): 1126-30.

Johnson, M. P., and Ferraro, K. J. (2000). Research on domestic violence in the 1990s: making distinctions, *Journal of Marriage and the Family, 62* (4), 948-63.

Kabeer, Naila (1994), Reversed realities: gender hierarchies in development thought, Verso: New York.

Kalu, A.U., Oboegbulem, S.I. and Uzoukwu, M. (2001). Trypanosomosis in small ruminants maintained by low riverine tsetse population in central Nigeria. Small Ruminant Research 40 (2), 109-15.

Kapoor, S. (2000). *Domestic violence against women and girls,* UNICEF Innocenti Digest 6, 2-27, *Innocenti Research Centre: Florence.* www.unicef-irc.org/cgi-bin/unicef/ Lunga.sql?ProductID=213 downloaded 12th August 2009.

Karamagi, C. A. S., Tumwine, J. K., Tylleskar, T., and Heggenhougen, K. (2006). Intimate partner violence against women in eastern Uganda: implications for HIV prevention. BMC Public Health, 6: 284-95.

Kemper, Theodore D. (1990), *Social structure and testosterone*, New Brunswick: Rutgers University Press.

Kennedy, E. and Haddad, L. (1994). Are pre-schoolers from female-headed households less malnourished? A comparative analysis of results from Ghana and Kenya. *Journal of Development Studies,* 30 (3), 680-95.

Kennedy, E. and Peters, P. (1992), Household food security and child nutrition: the interaction of income and gender of household head, *World Development,* 20 (8), 1077-85.

Kenney, C. T. (2006). The power of the purse: allocative systems and inequality in couple households. *Gender and Society*, 20 (3), 354-81.

Kerr, R. B. (2005), 'Food security in Northern Malawi: gender, kinship relations and entitlements in historical context', *Journal of Southern African Studie*s, 31 (1), 53-74.

Kim, K., and Cho, Y. (1992). Epidemiological survey of spousal abuse in Korea. in E. C. Viano (Ed.), *Intimate Violence: Interdisciplinary Perspectives. Bristol*, PA: Taylor and Francis.

Kintz, D. (1989). Formal men, informal women: how the Fulani support their anthropologists. Anthropology Today, 5 (6), 12-4.

Kishor, S. and Johnson, K. (2004). Profiling domestic violence: a multi-country study. Calverton, Maryland: ORC Macro. Accessed on 31st May 2011, from www.measuredhs. com/pubs/pdf/OD31/OD31.pdf

Kodoth, P. and Eapen, M. (2005). Looking beyond Gender Parity: Gender Inequities of Some Dimensions of Well-Being in Kerala. *Economic and Political Weekly*, 40 (30), 3278-86.

Koenig, M. A., Ahmed, S., Hossain, M. B. and Mozumder, A. B. M. K. A. (2003). Women's Status and Domestic Violence in Rural Bangladesh: Individual- and Community-Level Effects. *Demography*, 40 (2), 269-88.

Koenig, M. A., Stephenson, R., Ahmed, S., Jejeebhoy, S. J. and Campbell, J. (2006). Individual and contextual determinants of domestic violence in North India. *American Journal of Public Health,* 96 (1), 132-8.

Kosambi, M. (ed.), 1993. 'Violence against women: reports from India and the republic of Korea', UNESCO: Bangkok, RUSHSAP series of monographs and occasional papers: 37. Downloaded 27th February 2008, from http://unesdoc.unesco.org/images/ 0009/000966/096629eo.pdf.

Krishnan, S. (2005). Do structural inequalities contribute to marital violence? Ethnographic evidence from rural south India. *Violence Against Women, 11*, 759-75.

Kritz, M. M. and Gurak, D. T. (1989). Women's status, education and family formation in Sub-Saharan Africa. *International Family Planning Perspectives*, 15 (3), 100-5.

Kritz, M. M. and Makinwa-Adebusoye, P. (1999). Determinants of women's decision-making authority in Nigeria: the ethnic dimension. Sociological Forum, 14 (3), 399-424.

Kukkonen-Harjula, K., Oja, P., Laustiola, K., Vuori, I., Jolkkonen, J., Siitonen, S. and Vapaatalo, H. (1989), 'Haemodynamic and hormonal responses to heat exposure in a Finnish sauna bath'. *European Journal of Applied Physiology and occupational Physiology,* 58 (5): 543-50.

Levin C., Ruel M., Morris S., Maxwell D., Armar-Klemesu M. and Ahiadeke C. (1991). Working women in an urban setting: traders, vendors and food security in Accra. *World Development*, 27 (11), 1977-91.

Lewis Wall, L. (1998). Dead mothers and injured wives: the social contest of maternal morbidity and mortality among the Hausa of Northern Nigeria. *Studies in Family Planning,* 29 (4), 341-59.

Lim, In-Sook (1997). 'Korean immigrant women's challenge to gender equality at home: the interplay of economic resources, gender, and family'. *Gender and society*, 11 (1), 31-51.

Lindman, R., von der Pahlen, B., Öst, B. and Eriksson, C. J. P. (1992), Serum testosterone, cortisol, glucose, and ethanol in males arrested for spouse abuse. *Aggressive Behavior*, 18: 393-400.

Lott, D. F. and Hart, B. L. (1977). Aggressive domination of cattle by Fulani herdsmen and its relation to aggression in Fulani culture and personality. *Ethos,* 5 (2), 174-86.

Luard, Evan (1979), *The United Nations: how it works and what it does*, London: MacMillan.

Ludermir, A. B., Lewis, G., Valongueiro S. A., de Araújo, T. V., and Araya, R. (2010). Violence against women by their intimate partner during pregnancy and postnatal depression: a prospective cohort study. *Lancet,* 11, 376 (9744), 903-10.

Lundberg, S. and Pollak, R. A. (1996), Bargaining and distribution in marriage, *Journal of Economic Perspectives*, 10 (4), 139-58.

Lundgren, E., Heimer G., Westerstrand J., and Kalliokoski, A.-M. (2002). *Captured queen: men's violence against women in "equal"* Sweden - a prevalence study. webapps01.un.org/vawdatabase/uploads/Sweden%20-%20Captured%20Queen%20-%20Mens%20violence%20against%20women.pdf (On-line).

Malinda Anthony, C.K.S. (2002), 'Indoor climate of multi-storey hospital buildings in hot humid regions: an attempt to achieve comfortable climatic design in Ampara, Sri Lanka', www.hdm.lth.se/aee/Papers/2002/20_AEE2002.pdf downloaded 2nd August 2007.

Manning, P. (1990), 'The slave trade: the formal demography of a global system', *Social Science History* 14 (2): 255-79.

Martin S.L., Moracco K.E., Garro J., Tsui A.O., Kupper L.L., Chase J.L. and Campbell J.C. 2002. 'Domestic violence across generations: findings from northern India', *International Journal of Epidemiology* 31: 560-72.

Martinelli, C. and Parker, S. W. (2003), 'Should transfers to poor families be conditional on school attendance? A household bargaining perspective', *International Economic Review,* 44 (2), 523-44.

Mason, K. O. (1986). The status of women: conceptual and methodological issues in demographic studies. *Sociological Forum*, 1 (2), 284-300.

Mathur, K. M. (1996). Crime, human rights and national security. New Delhi, *Gyan Publishing House.*

Mazur, A. (2005). Biosociology of dominance and deference. Lanham, Maryland, *Rowman and Littlefield.*

McKenry, P. C., Julian, T. W. and Gavazzi, S. M. (1995). Toward a biopsychosocial model of domestic violence. *Journal of Marriage and Family*, 57 (2), 307-20.

McMillan, L. (2007). Feminists organising against gendered violence. *Basingstoke: Palgrave.*

Mehta, P. H. and Josephs, R. A. (2010). Testosterone and cortisol jointly regulate dominance: evidence for a dual-hormone hypothesis. *Hormones and Behaviour,* 58 (5): 898-906.

Millman, S. R. and DeRose, L. F. (1998), Food deprivation, in DeRose L., Messer E. and Millman S. (eds.), Who's hungry? And how do we know? Food shortage, poverty, and deprivation, Tokyo: *United Nations University Press.*

Mittal, T. (2008). 'Professionals, technocrats, housewives, students … anyone could be a murderer', Tehelka 5 (23), downloaded 21st June 2008 from www.tehelka.com/story_main39.asp?filename=Ne140608anyonecouldbemurdered.asp

Möller, H.-G. (1999). Zhuangzi's "dream of the butterfly": *A Daoist interpretation. Philosophy East and West*, 49 (4): 439-50.

Montaño, S., and Alméras, D. (eds.) (2009). No more! The right of women to live a life free of violence in Latin America and the Caribbean. *ECLAC*, www.eclac.org/publicaciones/xml/4/32194/Nomore.pdf (On-line).

Mumford, K. and Smith, P. N. (2009). What determines the part-time and gender earnings gaps in Britain: evidence from the workplace. *Oxford Economic Papers,* 61 (Supplement: women and wages), i56–i75.

Myres, J. L. (1941). Nomadism. *Journal of the Royal Anthropological Institute of Great Britain and Ireland*, 71 (1/2), 19-42.

Nagassar. R. P., Rawlins, J. M., Sampson, N. R., Zackerali, J., Chankadyal, K., Ramasir, C., and Boodram, R. (2010). The prevalence of domestic violence within different socio-economic classes in Central Trinidad. *West Indian Medical Journal*, 59 (1), 20-5.

NCHS (National Center for Health Statistics) (2001), files 'wtage.txt' and 'wtinf.txt' downloaded from the 'growth figures' section of www.cdc.gov/nchs on 7th April 2001.

NCRB (2001). Crime in India: 1998. Government of India (National Crime Records Bureau), New Delhi, www.ncrbindia.org/bound.htm downloaded 16th November 2001.

NCRB (2006). Crime in India 2005. Government of India (National Crime Records Bureau), New Delhi. Downloaded from ncrb.nic.in/ciiprevious/Data/CD-CII2005/cii-2005/Table%205.2.pdf on 23rd August 2011.

NCRB (2008a). Crime in India: 2006. Government of India (National Crime Records Bureau), New Delhi, http://ncrb.nic.in/cii2006/cii-2006/1953-2006.pdf downloaded 12th January 2008.

NCRB (2008b). Crime in India: 2007. Government of India (National Crime Records Bureau), New Delhi, http://ncrb.nic.in/CII2007/cii-2007/Table%205.2.pdf downloaded 30th November 2008.

Newman, C. (2002), 'Gender, time use, and change: the impact of the cut flower industry in Ecuador'. *World Bank Economic Review* 16 (3): 375-96.

Nicoletti, J., Spencer-Thomas, S. and Bollinger, C. (2010), 'Violence goes to college: *the authoritative guide to prevention and intervention*', Charles C. Thomas Ltd: Springfield, Illinois.

Nojomi, M., Agaee, S., and Eslami, S. (2007). Domestic violence against women attending gynecologic outpatient clinics. *Archives of Iranian Medicine,* 10 (3), 309-15.

NPC (National Population Commission) [Nigeria] and ORC Macro (2004), 'Nigeria Demographic and Health Survey, 2003'. *Calverton,* Maryland: NPC and ORC Macro. Downloaded from www.measuredhs.com/pubs/pdf/FR148/00FrontMatter.pdf 19th February 2011.

Oakley, A. (1982). *Subject women.* Fontana: Glasgow.

Ogunjuyigbe P. O., Akinlo A. and Ebigbola J. A. (2005). Violence against women: an examination of men's attitudes and perceptions about wife beating and contraceptive use. *Journal of Asian and African Studies*, 40 (3): 219-29.

Olmsted, J. (2003). Reexamining the fertility puzzle in MENA. pp. 73-92 in Doumato, E. A. and Posusney, M. P. (Eds.), Women and globalization in the Arab Middle East: Gender, Economy and Society. Boulder: *Lynne Rienner Publishers.*

Ottenheimer, H. J. (2009). The anthropology of language: *An introduction to linguistic anthropology.* Wadsworth: Belmont, California.

Oxaal, Z. (1997). Education and poverty: a gender analysis. Report 53, prepared for the Gender Equality Unit, Swedish International Development Cooperation Agency (SIDA), www.bridge.ids.ac.uk/reports/re53.pdf downloaded 7th May 2011.

Oyediran, K. A. and Isiugo-Abanihe, U. C. (2005). Perceptions of Nigerian women on domestic violence: evidence from 2003 Nigerian Demographic and Health Survey. *African Journal of Reproductive Health*, 9 (2), 38-53.

Pahl, J. (1985). Private violence and public policy – the needs of battered women and the response of the public service. Routledge and Kegan Paul: Boston.

Pahl, J. (1995). His money, her money: recent research on financial organisation in marriage. *Journal of Economic Psychology*, 16 (3), 361-76.

Panter-Brick C., Lunn P. G., Baker R. and Todd A. (2001), Elevated acute-phase protein in stunted Nepali children reporting low morbidity: different rural and urban profiles, *British Journal of Nutrition,* 85 (1), 125-31.

Parish, W. L., Tianfu W., Laumann E.O., Suiming P., and Lo Y. (2004). Intimate Partner Violence in China: national prevalence, risk factors and associated health problems, *International Family Planning Perspectives, 30*(4), 174-81.

Parry, C. D. H., Myers, B. and Thiede, M. (2003). The case for an increased tax on alcohol in South Africa. *South African Journal of Economics* 71 (2), 265-81.

Paudel, G. S. (2007). Domestic Violence against Women in Nepal. *Gender Technology and Development,* 11, 199-233.

Peters, P. (1999). Time allocation in times of structural transformation: A synchronic view on (gender) differences in The Netherlands. *Time and Society*, 8 (2): 329-56.

Phipps, S. and Burton, P. (1992). What's mine is yours? The influence of male and female incomes on patterns of household expenditure. Working paper 92:12, Department of Economics, Dalhousie University.

Piispa, M., Heiskanen, M., Kääriäinen, J., and Sirén, R. (2006). Naisiin kohdistuva väkivalta (violence against women) 2005. *Publications of the National Research Institute of Legal Policy* 225 and HEUNI Publication series No. 51. Helsinki. webapps01.un.org/vawdatabase/searchDetail.action?measureId=25432

Pocock G. and Richards C. D. (1999), *Human physiology: the basis of medicine.* Oxford: OUP.

Pontecorvo, C., Mejia, R., Aleman, M., Vidal, A., Majdalani, M. P., Fayanas, R., Fernandez, A., and Stable, E. J. P. (2004). Violencia domestica contra la mujer: una encuesta en consultorios de atencion primaria. *Medicina* (Buenos Aires), 64, 492-6.

Povey D. (Ed.), Coleman K., Kaiza P., Hoare J. and Jansson K. (2008: 3rd edition). Homicides, firearm offences and intimate violence 2006/07 (supplementary volume 2 to Crime in England and Wales 2006/07). Downloaded 27th October 2011, from webarchive.nationalarchives.gov.uk/20110218135832/http://rds.homeoffice.gov.uk/rds/pdfs08/hosb0308.pdf

Purkayastha, D. (2003), 'From parents to children: intra-household altruism as institutional behavior', *Journal of Economic Issues*, 37 (3), 601-19.

Purnell J. Q., Brandon D. D., Isabelle L. M., Loriaux D. L. and Samuels M. H. (2004). Association of 24-hour cortisol production rates, cortisol-binding globulin, and plasma-free cortisol levels with body composition, leptin levels, and aging in adult men and women. *The Journal of Clinical Endocrinology and Metabolism*, 89 (1), 281-87.

Pyke, K. D. (1994), Women's employment as a gift or burden? Marital power across marriage, divorce, and remarriage, *Gender and Society*, 8 (1), 73-91.

Quicho, I. (2010), 'Mariposa center for change unites with transnational women: *16 days of activism against gender violence*'. Downloaded 25th August 2011 www.mariposacenterforchange.org/Press-Release.php.

Quinn, N. (1977). Anthropological studies of women's status. *Annual Review of Anthropology* 6, 181-225.

Ramírez, E. G. (2007). ENDIREH-2006's achievements and limitations in determining indicators for measuring violence against women in Mexico. www.un.org/womenwatch/

daw/egm/vaw_indicators_2007/papers/Invited%20Paper%20Mexico%20ENDIREH.pdf (On-line).

Ramirez, E. G., Castillejos, L. A., Garcia, G. P., and Islas, I. (2010). *Testing the international questionnaire applied by INEGI, Mexico. General Directorate for Sociodemographic statistics,* downloaded 26th August 2011 from www.eclac.cl/mujer/cepal/documentos/8e.pdf.

Rao V. (1997). Wife-beating in rural south India: a qualitative and econometric analysis, *Social Science and Medicine* 44 (8), 1169-80.

Rao, V. (1998). Domestic violence and intra-household resource allocation in rural India: an exercise in participatory econometrics. In Krishnaraj, M., Sudarshan, R., and Sharif, A. (eds.),*Gender, population, and development*, Oxford and Delhi: OUP.

Rasmussen, S. (2009). 'Do tents and herds still matter? Pastoral nomadism and gender among the Tuareg in Niger and Mali', pp. 162-74 in Brettell C. B. and Sargent C. F. (Eds.), *Gender in cross-cultural perspective* (5th edition), New Jersey: Pearson.

Raynor, P. and Rudolf, M. C. J. (2000), Anthropometric indices of failure to thrive, *Archive of Disease in Childhood,* 82 (5), 364-5.

Richardson, J., Coid, J., Petruckevitch, A., Chung, W. S., Moorey, S., and Feder, G. (2002). Identifying domestic violence: cross sectional study in primary care. *British Medical Journal,* 324 (2), 1-6.

Roberts M. B. V. (1986: 4th edition), *Biology: a functional approach,* Nelson: Walton-on-Thames.

Roden M., Koller M., Pirich K., Vierhapper H. and Waldhauser F. (1993). The circadian melatonin and cortisol secretion pattern in permanent night shift workers. *American Journal of Physiology* 265 (1 Pt 2): R261-7.

Rogers, B. (1980). The domestication of women: discrimination in developing societies, London: Kogan Page.

Rosenberg, R. (2006). Domestic violence in Europe and Eurasia, United States Agency for International Development (USAID). www.usaid.gov/locations/europe_eurasia/dem_gov/docs/domestic_violence_study_final.pdf accessed 31st May 2011.

Rotton J. and Cohn E. G. (2001), Temperature, routine activities, and domestic violence: a reanalysis, *Violence and Victims,* 16 (2), 203-15.

Ruhlen, M. (1987). A Guide to the World's Languages, volume 1: *Classification.* Stanford CA, Stanford University Press.

Satish Kumar C., Gupta S. D. and Abraham, G. (2002). 'Masculinity and violence against women in marriage: an exploratory study in Rajasthan', in 'Men, masculinity and domestic violence in India: summary report of four studies', *International Center for Research on Women.* www.icrw.org/docs/DV_India_Report4_52002.pdf downloaded 12th August 2006.

SBO (2009). *SBO Research,* www.sboresearch.co.ke/ downloaded 5th August 2009.

Schröttle, et al. (2006). Comparative reanalysis of prevalence of violence against women and health impact data in Europe – obstacles and possible solutions: testing a comparative approach on selected studies. Co-ordination Action on Human Rights Violations (CAHRV), www.cahrv.uni-osnabrueck.de/reddot/D_20_Comparative_reanalysis_of_prevalence_of_violence_pub.pdf downloaded 26th August 2011.

Shell-Duncan, B., and Hernlund, Y. (2000). Female "circumcision" in Africa: dimensions of the practices and debates, in Shell-Duncan and Hernlund (Eds.) (2000), *Female*

Circumcision in Africa: Culture, Controversy, and Change, Lynne Rienner: Boulder, Colarado.

Shelton, B. A. and John, D. (1996), 'The Division of Household Labor', Annual Review of Sociology, 22, 299-322.

Shutterstock (2011), 'Arrested', image 273463, copyright Jack Dagley Photography / Shutterstock.com, www.shutterstock.com downloaded 28th November 2011.

Simister, J. (2001), 'Thermal stress and violence in India and Pakistan', *Indian Geographical Journal,* 76 (2): 89-100.

Simister, J. (2010). Domestic Violence and Female Genital Mutilation in Kenya: Effects of ethnicity and education. *Journal of Family Violence,* 25 (3), 247-57.

Simister, J. (2011a), 'Assessing the 'Kerala Model': education is necessary but not sufficient', Journal of South Asian Development, 6 (1).

Simister, J. (2011b), 'Effects of domestic violence on women's health', in Jenitta Mary I. and Chidambaranathan C. (Editors), *Women and health. Pointer Publishers.*

Simister, J. (forthcoming), 'More than a billion women face 'Gender Based Violence'; where are most victims?', *Journal of Family Violence.*

Simister, J. and Cooper, C. (2005), 'Thermal stress in the USA: effects on violence and employee behaviour', *Stress and Health*, 21: 3-15.

Simister, J. and Cooper, C. (2011), 'Extreme temperature as a cause of violence', chapter in Aidan Renshaw and Emelina Suárez (Editors), Violent crime and prisons: Population, health conditions and recidivism: *Nova Science Publishers*, pp. 1-34. ISBN: 978-1-60741-668-5.

Simister, J. and Makowiec, J. (2008). Domestic violence in India: effects of education. Indian *Journal of Gender Studies*, 15 (3), 507-18.

Simister, J. and Mehta, P. S. (2010), Gender-Based Violence in India: long-term trends. *Journal of Interpersonal Violence*, 20 (10), 1-18.

Simister, J. and Van de Vliert, E. (2005), 'Is there more violence in very hot weather? Tests over time in Pakistan and across countries worldwide', *Pakistan Journal of Meteorology* 2 (4), 55-70.

Simister, J., and Zaky, H. (2009). Wife's earnings, child nutrition, and Gender-Based Violence in Egypt. *Middle East Development Journal,* 1 (2), 209-26.

Skinner T., Hester M. and Malos E. (2005). 'Methodology, feminism and gender violence', in Skinner T., Hester M. and Malos E. (eds.), *Researching gender violence: feminist methodology in action,* Willan: Cullompton.

Sramek P., Simeckova M., Jansky L., Savlikova J. and Vybiral S. (2000), Human physiological responses to immersion into water of different temperatures, *European Journal of Applied Physiology* 81 (5), 436-42.

Stamp, P. (1985). 'Research note: balance of financial power in marriage: an exploratory study of breadwinning wives'. *Sociological Review*, 33 (3), 546-57.

Sullivan, O. (2011). An end to gender display through the performance of housework? A review and reassessment of the quantitative literature using insights from the qualitative literature. *Journal of family theory and review*, 3: 1-13.

Svedberg, P. (1990), Undernutrition in Sub-Saharan Africa: is there a gender bias? *Journal of Development Studies*, 26 (3), 469-86.

Tangka, F. K., Jabbar, M. A. and Shapiro, B. I. (2000). Gender roles and child nutrition in livestock production systems in developing countries; a critical review. *Socio-economics and Policy Research*, Working Paper 27. ILRI (International Livestock Research Institute), Nairobi, Kenya.

Terburg, D., Morgan, B. and van Honk, J. (2009). The testosterone-cortisol ratio: A hormonal marker for proneness to social aggression. *International Journal of Law and Psychiatry*, 32 (4): 216-23.

Thompson, R. S., Bonomi, A. E., Anderson, M., Reid, R. J., Dimer, J. A., Carrell, D., and Rivara F. P. (2006). Intimate Partner Violence: prevalence, types, and chronicity in adult women. *American Journal of Preventative Medicine*, 30 (6), 447-57.

Turner, M. D. (2000), Drought, domestic budgeting and wealth distribution in Sahelian households, *Development and Change,* 31 (5), 1009-35.

Umberson, D., Anderson, K. L., Williams, K. and Chen, M. D. (2003). Relationship dynamics, emotion state, and domestic violence: a stress and masculinities perspective, *Journal of Marriage and Family* 65 (1), 233-47.

UN (1948), '*The universal declaration of human rights*', www.un.org/en/documents/udhr/ downloaded 14th December 2010.

UN (2006), '*Ending violence against women: From words to action*', Report of the UN Secretary-General, www.un.org/womenwatch/daw/public/VAW_Study/VAWstudyE.pdf downloaded 5th December 2010.

UN General Assembly (1994), '*Declaration on the Elimination of Violence against Women*', www.un.org/documents/ga/res/48/a48r104.htm downloaded 5th September 2011.

UN Statistics Agency (2011). 'Indicators on education: school life expectancy (in years). Primary to tertiary education'.unstats.un.org/unsd/demographic/products/socind/ education.htm downloaded 11th August 2011.

UN Women (2011). '*Violence against wome*n – facts and figures', Say No: unite to end violence against women. www.saynotoviolence.org/issue/facts-and-figures downloaded 19th August 2011.

UNECE (2010). *Measuring violence against women.* Downloaded 26th August 2011, from www1.unece.org/stat/platform/display/VAW/Measuring+violence+against+women.

van Honk, J., Harmon-Jones, E., Morgan, B. E. and Schutter, D. J. (2010). Socially explosive minds: the triple imbalance hypothesis of reactive aggression. Journal of Personality, 78 (1): 67-94.

VerEecke, C. (1989). From pasture to purdah: the transformation of women's roles and identity among the Adamawa Fulbe. *Ethnology,* 28 (1): 53-73.

Visaria, L. (1999). *Violence against Women in India: Evidence from Rural Gujarat.* In ICRW (Ed.), Domestic violence in India: a summary report of three studies. Washington, DC: ICRW, http://pdf.usaid.gov/pdf_docs/PNACJ903.pdf accessed 31st May 2011.

Vives-Cases, C., Gil-González D., Plazaola-Castaño J., Montero-Piñar M.I., Ruiz-Pérez I., Escribà-Agüir V., Ortiz-Barreda G., Torrubiano-Domínguez J., and G6 para el Estudio de la Violencia de Género en España (2009). Violencia de género en mujeres inmigrantes y españolas: magnitud, respuestas ante el problema y políticas existents. Gaceta Sanitaria, 23 Supplement 1, 100-6.

Voicu M., Voicu B. and Strapcova, K. (2008). Housework and gender inequality in European countries. *European Sociological Review,* 25 (3), 365–77.

Ward, J. and others (2005). *Broken bodies - broken dreams: violence against women exposed.* OCHA/IRIN: Nairobi.

Watts, C. and Zimmerman, C., (2002). Violence against women: global scope and magnitude. *Lancet*, 359, 1232-7.

Weatherbase (2006). www.weatherbase.com/weather/city.php3?c=BRandrefer= downloaded 15th July 2006.

Werthmann, K. (2002). Matan Bariki, 'women of the barracks': *Muslim Hausa women in an urban neighbourhood in northern Nigeri*a. Africa, 72 (1), 112-30.

WHO (World Health Organization)/LSHTM (London School of Hygiene and Tropical Medicine) (2010). Preventing intimate partner and sexual violence against women: taking action and generating evidence. Geneva, *World Health Organization.*

Wilson, F. (2008), 'Gender Based Violence in South African schools', 'International Institute for Educational Planning' Working paper, given at the *'Directions in educational planning' symposium at IIEP.*

Wolf, T. P., Logan C., Owiti J., and Kiage P. (2004). *A new dawn? Popular optimism in Kenya after the transition*, Afrobarometer Working Paper No. 33, http:// afrobarometer.org/papers/AfropaperNo33.pdf downloaded 9th August 2009.

Women Win (2011). 'The international guide to addressing Gender-Based Violence through sport'. Downloaded 25th August 2011 from gbvguide.org/intro

Women's Wellness Center (2006), *'Prevalence of Gender-Based Violence: preliminary findings from a field assessment in nine villages in the Peja Region, Kosovo'.* www.rhrc.org/resources/Kosovo_report__FINAL_RHRC_6-11-08.pdf (On-line).

WVS (2006a), *'World and European Values Surveys four wave integrated data file*, 1981-2004'. The World Values Survey Association (www.worldvaluessurvey.org) and *European Values Study Foundation* (www.europeanvalues.nl), downloaded 15th November 2008 from www.worldvaluessurvey.org/.

WVS (2006b). 'Survey notes', downloaded 30th November 2008 from margaux. grandvinum.se/SebTest/wvs/articles/folder_published/survey_1019

WVS (2009). World Values Survey 1981-2008 official aggregate v.20090901. World Values Survey Association (www.worldvaluessurvey.org). Aggregate File Producer: ASEP/JDS, Madrid.

Yount K. M., Halim N., Hynes M. and Hillman E. R. (2011). Response effects to attitudinal questions about domestic violence against women: a comparative perspective. *Social Science Research* 40 (3): 873-84.

Zimmer-Tamakoshi, L. (2009). "Wild pigs and dog men": rape and domestic violence as "women's issues" in Papua New Guinea. In Brettell C. B. and Sargent C. F. (Eds.), Gender in cross-cultural perspective, Fifth edition, Pearson Education: Upper Saddle River, New Jersey.

Zorrilla, B., Pires, M., Lasheras, L., Morant, C., Seoane, L., Sanchez, L. M., Galán, I., Aguirre, R., Ramírez, R., and Durbán, M. (2009). Intimate partner violence: last year prevalence and association with socio-economic factors among women in Madrid, Spain. *European Journal of Public Health*, 20 (2), 169-75.

Zuo, J. and Bian, Y. (2001), 'Gendered resources, division of housework, and perceived fairness. A case in urban China', *Journal of Marriage and Family*, 63 (4): 1122-33.

INDEX

M

N

O

S